ASSIMILATION VERSUS SEPARATION

ASSIMILATION VERSUS SEPARATION

Joseph the Administrator and the Politics of Religion in Biblical Israel

WITHDRAWN

Aaron Wildavsky

Transaction Publishers
New Brunswick (U.S.A.) and London (U.K.)

Copyright © 1993 by Transaction Publishers, New Brunswick, New Jersey 08903.

Library of Congress Catalog Number: 92-20151
ISBN: 1-56000-081-3
Printed in the United States of America

Library of Congress Cataloging-in-Publication Data
Wildavsky, Aaron B.
Assimilation vs. separation : Joseph the Administrator and the politics of religion in biblical Israel / Aaron Wildavsky.
   p. cm.
Includes bibliographical references.
   ISBN 1-56000-081-3 $32.95
1. Bible. O.T. Genesis XXXVII-L—Criticism, interpretation, etc. 2. Joseph (Son of Jacob) I. Title.
BS1235.2.W458   1993
222'.11092—dc20
                                                      92-20151
                                                          CIP

For David Daube and Helen Smelser Daube

Contents

Acknowledgments

Thus the achievement of these scholars, who established a tradition rooted in the Torah and growing out of it, is a prime example of spontaneity in receptivity. They are leaders because they know themselves to be led. Out of the religious tradition they bring forth something entirely new, something that itself commands religious dignity: commentary. Revelation needs commentary in order to be rightly understood and applied—this is the far from self-evident religious doctrine out of which grew both the phenomenon of biblical exegesis and the Jewish tradition which it created. . . . This leads to the viewpoint expressed daringly in talmudic writings, namely, that the total substance of the Oral Torah, which had in fact been the achievement of the scholars, comes from the same source as the Written Torah, and that it was therefore basically always known. . . . But underneath this fiction . . . there lies a religious attitude . . . . I refer to the distinctive notion of revelation including within itself as sacred tradition the later commentary concerning its own meaning. . . . Commentary thus became the characteristic expression of Jewish thinking about truth . . . . What had originally been believed to be consistent, unified and self-enclosed now becomes diversified, multifold, and full of contradictions. It is precisely the wealth of contradictions, of differing views, which is encompassed and unqualifiedly affirmed by tradition. There were many possibilities of interpreting the Torah and tradition claimed to comprise them all. . . . In Judaism, tradition becomes the reflective impulse that intervenes between the absolutness of the divine word—revelation—and its receiver.[1]

In this book on the Joseph stories, as well as in my earlier volume on *The Nursing Father: Moses as a Political Leader*, my aim is to make "the Midrash," the commentary on the Bible, live in our time as it has in earlier days. I conceive of myself as continuing the tradition as described by Gershom Scholem in the headnote to this section. The belief that every commentary grounded in the text, as this one tries to be, is part of the original revelation, sustains my work. It is a great thing, in my eyes, and something for which I am infinitely grateful, to be able to draw upon and participate in this tradition. Participation in the collective enterprise of biblical interpretation, even or especially with those who disagree, also belongs to those who have enlightened me about the Joseph stories. This is why I seek to include a range of interpretations, not only my own, but all that comprise the tradition.

Translation, which is part of interpretation, also belongs in the tradition. The stories about Jacob's son Joseph are told in sections 37 through 50 of the Book of Genesis. In my experience, most readers no longer know them. Interested readers should begin with any standard version of these stories. My personal favorite is the King James version because, in my hearing, it is still the most beautiful. In the book that follows, however, I use the new translation of The Jewish Publication Society[2] because it is the most accurate. If it sounds less elevated and more colloquial than the King James, that better fits the character of the person whom these stories are about.

I have received more than I have given to the exposition and interpretation of the Joseph stories. Michael Hildenbrand assisted me in locating and interpreting the literature on Joseph within and outside of the tradition of Torah commentary. Though he tells me his knowledge of Ugaritic and related lore does not help in interpreting the Joseph stories, his grounding in biblical language and interpretation was a great resource. Liz Doyle read a variety of contemporary Hebrew accounts that differed from mine. Several people read early versions of the manuscript. Eugene Bardach, Allen Christensen, David Eneloe, Marc Galanter, Stanley Lebergott, Laurence A. Turner, Avraham Wolfensohn and Jacob Milgrom contributed memorable thoughts. Wolfgang Palaver introduced me to the work of René Girard. My editor, Diana Menkes, kept me on the straight and narrow road of exposition to intelligent laymen, my intended audience. Her preference for sparse exposition has strengthened my style. The blessing that follows belongs to all those who have preceded and will come after my midrash on Joseph who was worthy and on the people who chose Moses in his stead:

> Upon Israel and upon the Rabbis, and upon their disciples and upon all the disciples of their disciples, and upon all who engage in the study of the Torah in this place and in every place, unto them and unto you be abundant peace, grace, loving kindness, mercy, long life, ample sustenance and salvation, from their Father who is in Heaven. And say ye Amen.
> —*Kaddish de Rabbanan*, translated by R. Travers Herford

Notes

1. Gershom Scholem, *The Messianic Idea in Judaism and Other Essays On Jewish Spirituality* (New York: Schocken Books, 1971), 287, 288, 289, 290, 292.
2. The Torah: The Five Books of Moses, A new translation of The Holy Scriptures according to the Masoretic text, 1st Sec. (Philadelphia: Jewish Publication Society of America, 1962).

Introduction:
The Political Consequences of a God-Centered Religion

The paradox . . . lies in the fact that only by humbly agreeing to accept God's rule can Israel free itself of control by other nations. The nations . . . rest on one side of the balance, while God rests on the other. Israel must then choose between them. There is no such thing for Israel as freedom from both God and the nations, total autonomy and independence. There is only a choice of masters, a ruler on earth or a ruler in heaven.[1]

There is a great disjunction between the Book of Genesis and the Book of Exodus. The natural progression from the patriarchs—Abraham, Isaac, and Jacob—through the major figure in the last part of Genesis—Jacob's son Joseph, already one of the Egyptian Pharaoh's highest officials—is abruptly broken off in Exodus. With just one connective sentence, though one loaded with meaning, readers are told that there arose a Pharaoh who did not know Joseph; period, end of story. From then on everything is about Moses. Except for learning that Moses carries Joseph's bones from Egypt to the Promised Land, that is basically all we hear about him in the rest of the Torah. Moses, the person who brings God's law to the people and who takes them to the borders of the Promised Land, is not Joseph's successor; Moses is Joseph's permanent replacement as Israel's guide.

If we compare these two outstanding men, we discover that they are, to use anthropologist Claude Lévi-Strauss's evocative term, binary opposites. They are different in every conceivable dimension; their significant characteristics and actions are mirror images. So Moses, born in Egypt, becomes Hebraicized; Joseph, who grows up a Hebrew, becomes Egyptianized. The Joseph who leads his people into Egypt is superseded by the Moses who takes his people out. The opposition between the two is so great and so consistent (see Chapter 8) that it is difficult to believe it is unintended. The question arises, then: What we are to make of this turn from Egypt toward Canaan, from Joseph-the-assimilator to Moses-the-lawgiver? My thesis is that the Torah portrays Joseph and Moses as opposites so as to reveal the fateful choices that exist concerning what

1

form of rule and what type of relationships with foreign peoples are to guide Jewish life.

If we look at the Bible as a whole, thinking of Jewish experience not as confined to the Torah but as embracing subsequent biblical history, we find the Hebrew people living under three political and hence moral conditions: ruling themselves and other people in the land of Israel; being governed by foreign potentates within their own land; and, in the Diaspora, being governed by non-Jews. Exile, whether from their own land or from their own beliefs and practices, is a characteristic Jewish condition.[2]

A religion suitable for ruling and being ruled, for being ruled abroad and being ruled at home, must have special characteristics. The people involved must be able to carry on their practices wherever they are and however long they are in exile. The Torah teaches that Jews must survive to redeem God's promise and that they must survive not merely physically but religiously as Jews who practice Judaism. The crucial questions for exiles are whether and to what degree they will assimilate and how they will relate to the ruling power in order to survive.

The choice of Moses over Joseph tells us what was then decided: that Jews should try to be loyal subjects, bringing good upon whoever rules over them but not at the price of altering their practices. The rejection of Joseph, that is, of assimilation as the price of survival, is a turning point in the development of Judaism. To make that fateful choice effective, to make it themselves, as *The Federalist* says, by choice and reflection, the Israelites must be able to visualize the alternative in all its splendor under Joseph's Pharaoh and face the consequences in all their misery under the Pharaoh who Moses knew. Because the path chosen makes more sense contrasted with the path not taken, we have the lifetime story of Joseph as our guide to what is *not* permissible for Jews to do in order to survive. In order to understand why assimilation is impermissible for the children of Israel, we must understand the special character of Israelite religion.

A God-Centered Religion

Judaism is a God-centered religion. It is God who creates, who breathes life, who chooses a people to whom to make His promises in return for their willingness to try keeping His commandments. Strictly speaking, Jews do not obey values, they obey God. As Rabbi Heschel put it, "Plato lets Socrates ask, what is good? But Moses' question was: What does God require of thee?"[3] That God's will prevails signifies only that Jews try harder to ascertain what that is and work toward it. Though worldly wisdom is not despised, nor military strength, it is never by itself enough. God may be gracious, but He cannot be bought off by what seems to mere humans to be good deeds. "In fact," Allen Ross observes, "there are times when God must cripple the natural strength of His servants so that they may be bold in faith."[4] Hermann Cohen explains that when Moses says he does not go to the land of promises because God was angry with him "on your account" (Deut. 3:26), he means that

> a trespass on Moses' part has to be devised for the sake of the people, in order not to becloud pure monotheism for them by the illusion of a demigod, a superman. Instead of drawing the water from the rock by word, he struck it, "because you did not sanctify Me," because you, Moses and Aaron, through the use of the rod eliminated the spiritual power of the word, you have impaired the holiness of God, which is based on spirituality.[5]

If Judaism is aptly said to be a religion of observance, that is because it is centered on God's commandments, not on man's will.

Joseph keeps saying (to Pharaoh, to his brothers) that everything that happens is due to God's will. But he does not pray nor does God appear to him nor does he eat or dress or (often) behave as if he were a religious person. Moses does.

The principle of separation of man from God, Yahweh from other gods, and the Hebrews from other peoples, is deeply woven into the fabric of Jewish life, not only in temple and synagogue observances but throughout the widest realm of daily life. Bringing Jews together through common practices might well be a unifying factor against the divisiveness of rival kingdoms within ancient Israel and rival attractions between the cultures of a host country in the Diaspora and the commandments of Judaism.

The innumerable prohibitions against mixing—combining wool and linen in the same garment, yoking an ox and an ass together, boiling a kid in its mother's milk—might make mixing peoples repugnant. As Soler explains,

> these words . . . can be translated as: you shall not put a mother and her son into the same pot, any more than into the same bed. Here as elsewhere, it is a matter of upholding the separation between two classes or two types of relationships. To abolish distinction by means of a sexual or culinary act is to subvert the order of the world.

Everyone belongs to one species only, one people, one sex, one category. And in the
same manner, everyone has only one God. . . .[6]

The prohibition against incest, Soler continues, demonstrates the principle of being only one thing at one time: "once a woman is defined as
'mother' in relation to a boy, she cannot also be something else to him.
. . . It thus becomes evident that the sexual and the dietary prohibitions
of the Bible are coordinated."[7] These prohibitions, as Mary Douglas
argues in her classic work on "The Abominations of Leviticus," serve to
separate the Hebrew people from others by weaving monotheism into
their daily practices and their social relations.[8]

We cannot say that Joseph, like Moses, should have "kept kosher,"
given that the rules were laid down and then embellished long after his
time. Suffice it to note that Joseph did not dress or eat or behave like the
Hebrews of his time. Nor did he follow the precept either of being what
he appeared to be or being only one thing at a time (cf. his appearance
as an Egyptian administrator while hiding from his brothers the fact that
he was also their brother).

Fidelity First

Fidelity is the great theme. And it is always in short supply. The Joseph
stories, like the accounts in Genesis that come before, explore fidelity
between the human and the divine, between husband and wife, fathers
and sons, mothers and fathers, sons of different wives, down to grandfa-
thers and grandchildren. The Hebrews are not only contaminated by
foreigners, the Hebrews contaminate themselves by violating their moral
law. The stories are not one-sided. Foreigners who follow the moral law
have something to teach Hebrews who do not. Ultimately, fidelity to God
triumphs over ethnicity. The wisdom of this world is given its due—Joseph could not survive without his share of it—but it is fidelity to God's
laws that matters more.

In Judaism it is the law, not the man, who is transcendent. Greenberg
puts it well:

Here God is not merely the custodian of justice or the dispenser of "truth" to man, he
is the fountainhead of the law, the law is a statement of his will. The very formulation
is God's; frequently laws are couched in the first person, and they are always referred
to as "words of God," never of man. . . . The only legislator the Bible knows of is
God; the only legislation is that mediated by a prophet (Moses and Ezekiel). This
conception accounts for the commingling in the law corpora of religious and civil

law, and—even more distinctively biblical—of legal enactments and moral exhortations. The entire normative realm, whether in law or morality, pertains to God alone.[9]

The God of the Hebrews is personal: the people are to obey "My commandments, My laws, and My teachings" (Gen. 26:5). The promises are doubled by a promise to keep all previous promises (Gen. 46:3). The double construction that forces itself upon us on nearly every page of the Joseph stories is a none-too-subtle reminder that the people of Israel always have the choice of being like the other nations—that is, like Egypt—or obeying their special and onerous code of laws.

Jews may be loyal to their foreign rulers, like Joseph to his Pharaoh; but they must not ape foreign practices any more than worship their gods. The trick is to make loyal service to secular masters compatible with social separation.

What about the patriarchs' (and later, Judah's) fear of their family's dying out, thereby wiping out the possibility of future generations? Such fears are real in that there are surrounding circumstances that reasonably give rise to them (Abraham's age, Joseph's slavery, Judah's loss of two sons). To believe in this premature end, however, would be to disbelieve God's promises. Thus the Joseph stories are about not only sexual but religious fidelity.[10]

To show the Lord's continuous intervention so as to keep His word, the first wife of each of the patriarchs is barren, finding it so difficult to conceive that God must take over for her. "This triple barrenness of the wives," Kikawada and Quinn observe, "strikingly parallels at the familial level the three-fold extinction threat to the species . . . characteristic of the middle three stories of the primeval history."[11] Humanity is threatened with extinction when Adam and Eve violate their Maker's commandments, when Cain murders Abel, and when the world is flooded in Noah's time. The threat to the species is replicated in the Akedah, the test of Abraham in his willingness to kill Isaac; were his blood to flow from a throat his father cut, Isaac's life would ebb away at the same time as God's promise to make a great nation out of Abraham's seed. In a corresponding manner, "The Joseph story tells how God forced one family to give up its nomadic life (and move to a civilized center) in order that His promise to preserve its life and make it flourish be fulfilled."[12] But God manifestly did not tell them to stay there.

What is so bad about Egypt? It teaches obedience to an earthly, not a heavenly, ruler, to a Pharaoh who thinks he is a god. By serving Pharaoh

too well, Joseph diverts Judaism from the practices God commands to
the ways of whoever holds power.

Wisdom or Anti-Wisdom

The stories about Joseph and his family in the desert and in the
Diaspora at Pharaoh's court ask what kind of leader is fit to lead this
people into the land promised them by their God. On the one hand, there
is God's promise that if the descendants of Abraham follow his commandments they will inherit the land. On the other, there is the necessity
of human action to make good the promise, even against adverse conditions. For the would-be leader and his might-be faithful followers, the
great dilemma is what to do when promise and performance conflict.
May God's law be broken, the question is, to fulfill God's promise?

The answer is not given directly but rather illustrated by locating the
rival visions in two extraordinary persons, Joseph and Moses. The choice
the tradition makes is obvious: not for nothing is the Torah popularly
known as The Five Books of Moses. Nevertheless, the implications of
following Joseph's worldly wisdom have to be understood before that
wisdom is rejected or, better put, superseded. That is why the longest
consecutive series of stories in Genesis is devoted to Joseph.

The Joseph stories in the Bible, which stand between family and
nation, the patriarchs (Abraham, Isaac, and Jacob) and Moses, the
law-bringer, are, like the rest of Genesis, instructions in morality. Unlike
the founders or messengers of other religions, however, these Hebrew
patriarchs are not paragons; far from it. Abraham, until the binding of his
son Isaac, lacks faith. Isaac is passive, more acted upon than acting. And
to these qualities of his grandfather and father, Jacob adds deception. If
Joseph is not among the patriarchs, left behind, except for his bones, as
soon as his part is played out, this is not because he is uninteresting or
unimportant or unworthy. On the contrary, his way, as the Book of
Proverbs attests, becomes part of the education of everyone who wishes
to act prudently.

Arguably the cleverest in his clever family, Joseph shows the least
insight into his own failings. He does become acutely aware of his
shortcomings in dealing with other people, but not in his hunger for
power. Chief among his moral lapses is Joseph's too great service to the
wrong master, for Joseph comes close to idolatry, whether this be defined

as self-worship or bowing down to the false god, Pharaoh. For this reason, Joseph is virtually expunged from the rest of the Torah.

There is truth in Joseph, just not all the truth. The laborer is worthy of his hire and the servant (or employee or adviser) owes his master fidelity. The epitome is Abraham's senior servant who follows his master's instructions to the letter in gaining a wife for Isaac (Gen. 24:2). This servant, like Joseph in relation to his Egyptian master, Potiphar, had charge "of all that he [his master] owned" (Gen. 24:7). The difference is that Abraham's servant was justified in his fidelity. Not so Joseph as Pharaoh's administrator.

From beginning to end, the conflict between wisdom (here meaning wise in the ways of man), which Joseph develops in abundance, and holiness (fidelity to God's law), which he possesses only intermittently, is played out. There are advantages to knowledge; Hebrews are urged to use all the intelligence they can muster. Knowing the ways of an often-wicked world is part of prudence. Playing the fool is not recommended. Going along so as to get along is not rejected wholesale. It is better to do well rather than worse.

But wisdom is not all there is. Above wisdom, supposedly controlling its use, is the moral code, based on the separation between God and man. One such difference is that human beings are subject to prohibitions of behavior that in biblical parlance must not be done in Israel. Because the land promised to the people of Israel belongs to God, they are commanded to keep it forever; the loss of one's land, as the story of Tamar and Judah and of Ruth reminds us, is the equivalent of the extinction of personhood. What, then, shall we say about Joseph the administrator to Pharaoh, who first took the land from Egyptian farmers and then forced them to settle elsewhere? Are serfdom and forced deportations morally acceptable because they involve foreigners?

Because of the legendary status occupied by the progenitor of his people and the low esteem in which his father, Jacob-the-trickster, has been held, Joseph-the-provider, as he is known in popular culture, the man who saved the known world of his time from starvation, has often been treated as if he were not a true member of his family. The reader who forgets that Joseph is Jacob's son has lost an important part of the story. Of course, Joseph is different. He faced harder times and he eventually got to operate on a grander scale. But Joseph is also a chip off the old block. Hence we must root his behavior in the life-cum-strife of his troubled family.

An ancient legend, taking up the dual theme of "like father like son" and "measure for measure," cites these unflattering parallels: "Like the father [Jacob with his older brother Esau], the son [Joseph with his older brothers] appropriated his elder brother's birthright. The father was hated by his brother, and the son was hated by his brethren."[13] Continuing this theme, Jacob Milgrom writes:

> For his deception of Esau, Jacob is dogged by misfortune for the rest of his life. . . . As Jacob exploits his father's "darkness" [Isaac's eyesight was failing] to switch sons on him [presenting himself as his brother Esau], so Laban utiliizes the darkness to switch daughters on Jacob. . . . As Jacob dupes and torments his father by his garment [he wears a hairy shirt to imitate his brother's body], he in turn is duped and tormented by his son's garment [when Joseph's brothers falsely claim he was torn apart by a wild beast].[14]

Rabbis speculate, David Daube tells us, that "The Egyptians . . . drowned in the Red Sea because they had drowned the male Israelite babies."[15]

The relations between Joseph and Pharaoh are plainly portrayed: both the foreign Pharaoh and his Hebrew helpers benefit by their cooperation—but not forever. The relationship of dominance between Joseph as a high-level administrator in Pharaoh's hierarchy and his subjects, the Egyptian people, is all too evident: they cease being independent personalities and become serfs. The parallel is there for all to see: as Joseph does to the Egyptian people, so a later Pharaoh in Moses' time will do to the Hebrew people.

There is, then, danger in wisdom: advice, as we would put it, on how to make friends and influence people. Those who aspire to wealth, power, and advancement are encouraged to speak little and learn much, control their sexual urges, choose their friends carefully, speak clearly and briefly, and otherwise act so as to do well. As might be expected from those who follow a naive wisdom approach, young men have been urged to make Joseph their model. Sounding much like Samuel Smiles or Benjamin Franklin's *Poor Richard*, F. R. Myer suggests the following rules extracted from the Joseph stories: "*Make the most of your time*. The biggest fortunes that the world has seen were made by saving what other men fling away; so be miserly over the moments . . . *be punctual . . . be methodical . . . be energetic*."[16]

The Hebrew version of such admonitions (Prov. 1-7) speaks of "the fear of the Lord," meaning, in general, that one should abide by the moral law. Typical advice includes "he becometh poor that dealeth with a slack hand: but the hand of the diligent maketh rich" (Prov. 10:4). And "wealth gotten by vanity shall be diminished: but he that gathereth by labor shall increase" (Prov. 13:11). Perhaps the most apposite comes from Proverbs 29:26: "Many seek the ruler's favor; but every man's judgment cometh from the Lord." The well-known contradictory character of proverbial wisdom—two heads are better than one, but too many cooks spoil the broth—encapsulates Joseph's dilemma: he can do right, as he does in the episode of Potiphar's wife, or he can do well, as he does with Pharaoh, but he has yet to discover how to do both.

Wisdom and folly are closely connected. Joseph's folly, in first humiliating and then trusting his brothers, lands him in the pit; Joseph's wisdom, in telling Pharaoh what he wants to hear and in making himself the obvious person to do what Pharaoh's dreams reveal is necessary, makes him eminent. Yet his worldly folly in resisting the importuning advances of Potiphar's wife prepares the way for his elevation to a high position, and his wisdom in gaining power leads to the enslavement of Egyptians and then to the bondage of his own people.

I think that von Rad and the many interpreters who share his views are right in thinking that the Joseph stories are about what passes for wisdom. I also think, however, that they are wrong in assessing the direction of the lesson. The Joseph stories, in my opinion, are anti-wisdom. While they reveal the advantages of being wise in the ways of the world, their major thrust, as will be shown, is to delineate the limits of wisdom.

The Style Fits the Story

In support of my claim that the Joseph stories epitomize anti-wisdom while recognizing the benefits of prudence, I cite the doubling of every dream and story line in the text. Scholars tend to attribute the doubling, evident since the stories were first read, to the juxtaposition of rival sources, apparently one dream or theme to a source.[17] Because doubling is used throughout the narrative, I argue that one of its purposes is to alert the reader to the possibility that there are two sides to these stories. There is the surface story of the noble youth, cruelly used by his brothers, who rises from the pit of misfortune by a combination of cleverness and godliness to become a glorious ruler, akin to his Pharaoh. Good works and good morals, in this version, go together. Alongside this standard story is another pointing to the moral equivocality, even destructiveness, of Joseph's behavior as chief administrator for Pharaoh.

One could say that the dual perspective evident throughout the stories about Joseph represent victim and victimizer. Perhaps. But then the commentator must be clear about whether Joseph is the victim or victimizer or both.

To become the great work of art everyone agrees the Joseph narrative is, its style has to fit its themes. Two views mean twice-told tales, opening up different perspectives on the same stories. But how?

The stories surrounding Joseph, as commentators throughout the ages have recognized, differ in significant respects from the other tales in Genesis. They are much more closely woven together, forming something like a novella. They are much more secular in that the trappings of religion, except for Joseph's rationalization of his behavior by reference to the Almighty, are entirely absent. The local color is all Egyptian: the account reveals a fascination with Egyptian customs, offices, and practices. Indeed, in a story noteworthy for its economy of words, in which psychological and social complexities are suggested in a few lines, far more is said than is necessary about how Joseph does his duty toward Pharaoh, unless we are expected to look closely into his conception of that duty.

My view is that there are two meanings in the one text. Both are true, the wise and the immoral Joseph, the clever and the too-clever-by-half. Both have their partial justification, the hard-done-by Joseph who triumphs over adversity even when, as with Potiphar's wife, he deserves better, and the *uber chochem* (the higher wise guy) Joseph, so smart he fools himself into believing that he can excuse evil by attributing it to God's will. The dualistic, parallel style in which these stories are written is the product not only of literary skill—a universal opinion—but of a conscious effort to make the meaning and the form coincide.

The Joseph stories illuminate in vivid detail on a large and exotic canvas the dilemmas facing a people who do not wish to assimilate but who cannot live in isolation. Yes, it is good to have friendly relations with foreigners; but no, it is not good to imitate their customs. Yes, it is desirable to be wise in the ways of the world; but no, it is not desirable to emulate them. Yes, serve the powers that be; but no, not too well. Serve their rulers but not their gods; and if their rulers and their gods are but other sides of the same coin of power, both must be rejected. What style is suited for these two-handed morals?

Hebrew is a muscular and lean language. Sentences are short, statements abrupt, verbs (primarily) and nouns (secondarily) carry the action, with adjectives and adverbs seldom prominent. For a text that is intended to teach, allowing each listener/reader to interpret for himself, sparseness is superior. Within this austere framework, various effects can be achieved by the structural device of repetition—of words, phrases, whole incidents—the doubling that I have referred to.

Repetition in the Joseph stories plays both an intellectual and an emotional role, emotional in that the reader is carried along so far, then brought back up with a partial repetition, then carried forward with a nuanced second line, marginally different from the first. You will not easily forget and you will have to pay attention. Swiftly the resolution follows, as action and description intensify. When Joseph tells his brothers about his dreams of domination, he tells them that he is telling them: "Hear this dream which I have dreamed." The pace picks up: "He dreamed another dream . . . saying 'Look, I have had another dream'" (Gen. 37:6). Joseph is rubbing in his capacities to his brothers with an intensity that could hardly be achieved by saying he was intense.

The "parallelism" that Watson asserts "is universally recognized as *the* characteristic feature of biblical Hebrew poetry is also present in its prose."[18] Robert Alter writes that "Biblical poetry has proved so remarkably translatable because self-translation is the generative principle within the text itself." Alter calls the chief method "one of incremental repetition."[19] Thus, after Joseph was taken out of the pit and brought to the home of a high-ranking official named Potiphar, "the Lord was with Joseph, and he was a successful man . . . . And when his master saw that the Lord was with him and that the Lord lent success to everything he undertook, he took a liking to Joseph" (Gen. 39:2-4). Now we know not only that Joseph did well by Potiphar but that Potiphar understood that Joseph's success was due to the Lord's help and that it was this attribute that made Potiphar like him. Note the progression in the next lines:

> He made him his personal attendant and put him in charge of his household, placing in his hands all that he owned. And from the time the Egyptian put him in charge of his household and of all that he owned, the Lord blessed his house for Joseph's sake,

so that the blessing of the Lord was upon everything that he owned, in the house and outside. (Gen. 39:4–5)

To the repetition of the fact that Joseph was in charge not only of Potiphar's household but of all that he owned is added "in the house" as well as outside. We see that adding "inside" to the household takes us to Potiphar's wife, who is urging Joseph to get inside her.

The "impulse to intensification," as Alter terms it,[20] is done in a number of ways. There is the repetition of the same word at the beginning of each parallel clause, known as anaphora, and by other forms of repetition, of sound, sense, context, formula, alliteration, and assonance, all of which are employed in ample measure.[21] Because not every word has a synonym, writers and poets sometimes resort to paronomasia by using the same word to have somewhat different meanings or by invoking similar sounding words to have different meanings.[22] Hyman provides a neat example: When Joseph asks Pharaoh's courtiers, "Why [*maddua*] do you appear downcast today?" (Gen. 40:7), he wants to know the cause of the butler's and baker's sadness. But when Joseph wants his brothers to know he is annoyed at them, he instructs his steward to ask in the accusative, "Why [*lammah*] did you repay good with evil?" (Gen. 44:4). Since the brothers cannot figure out what they have done wrong, they in turn are indignant, asking "Why [lammah] does my lord say such things?" (Gen. 44:7).[23]

By putting the two types of questions together, Joseph, through the speaker, is able to make an argument without being overt, thereby masking to some extent his use of power. Joseph uses this locution when manipulating his brothers, who are not averse to throwing it back at him by questions that express criticisms. The *reductio ad absurdum* goes well with the interrogatory form. Thus the elderly Naomi, long past childbearing age, seeks to dissuade Ruth and Orpah from going with her by asking incredulously, "Are there yet any more sons in my womb, that they may be your husbands?" (Ruth 1:11).[24] Making listeners feel guilty by questions, sharpening questions so they are more pointed than answers, is an ancient Hebrew art.

The artful use of questions, each one ostensibly about the same subject and containing many of the same words yet pointing to quite different contexts and senses, is part of the parallelism that characterizes biblical language.[25] But the meaning one ascribes to this depends on the overall interpretive scheme into which it fits. Parallelism could well be a method for adding to effect by teaching the same lesson in two different but related ways. Far from being a sign of consensus, however, analogous but by no means identical accounts may signify conflict, indeed irresoluble conflict.

Partial reiteration may also serve as a literary-moral device to suggest that each generation repeats the errors of the past, thereby demonstrating, despite surface dissimilarities, a uniformity in human nature. Did Joseph's brothers try to kill him? So, apparently, did Esau try to dispatch Jacob and might have done so had not Jacob's mother spirited him away. Jacob succeeded in winning the rights of the first-born for himself much as Joseph does later.[26] There is no doubt about the parallels, but there is a lot of room for debate about their significance. The parallel that is most prominent is least mentioned: the implications of Joseph's treatment of the Egyptians for the Egyptians' later treatment of the Israelites.

Did the Egyptians Enslave the Hebrews Because Joseph Enslaved the Egyptians?

Does Joseph's behavior toward his family and his ingratiating manner within the Pharaoh's court deserve praise or blame or something in between? The bulk of Jewish commentary is approving—though, as we shall see, not without doubt—while virtually all Christian commentary, seeing in Joseph a precursor of Jesus, is extraordinarily favorable. My view is that Joseph's behavior is a mixture of good and bad, with an accent on the negative largely because his behavior as a high-level administrator and adviser to Pharaoh is arguably immoral. It is not right for Joseph to make Pharaoh into a worse dictator than he already is, or to deprive Egyptians of their land and the power that goes with it, or to move them off their land to strange places. Duty to a benefactor does not extend to enhancing Pharaoh's capacity to behave badly. Duty to one's people does not extend to making foreigners aliens within their own country. Nor should Joseph claim divine guidance for his overbearing behavior toward his brothers. He is unable to deal with them except on a basis of subordination. It is precisely the Hebrew people, for whom Joseph claims all this to have been done at the instigation of the Almighty, who suffer most after he is gone.

Joseph claims that his behavior is justified by divine guidance in saving the Hebrew people for better days. The point of the moral law is that one cannot gain safety, long life, riches, happiness, or anything else desirable by violating its precepts. "He that turneth away his ear from hearing the law," Proverbs 28:9 tells us, "even his prayer shall be abomination." The warning comes still closer in the advice that "to have respect of persons is not good: for for a piece of bread that man will transgress" (Prov. 28:21).

Is my judgment too severe? Perhaps Joseph's harsh treatment is necessary for the survival from famine of both the Egyptians and the Israelites. Perhaps the Hebrew people have to live in Egypt and to be oppressed to appreciate their later liberty. I disagree.

If we turn to the beginnings of the Book of Exodus, viewing it from the standpoint of an ethic of consequences, I contend that Joseph's legacy is not a pretty one. The Pharaoh who did not know Joseph is nothing but an extension of the Pharaoh whom Joseph served so faithfully, except with increased power thanks to Joseph's earlier administrative activities. Joseph's own Pharaoh, as the stories reveal, had sufficient arbitrary power to put those closest to him to death without compunction.

The motif of memory is played out in Exodus, whose Pharaoh cannot seem to remember anything that happened between the plagues and who is described on countless occasions as having his heart hardened by the Lord. This hardening is a consequence of the Pharaoh's narcissism, his belief in his own divinity. Why should a demigod remember anyone if he can make the world any way he wants? Only when leaders are dependent on followers is there reason to be concerned about their views or their welfare, that is, to remember them in political time.[27] Whether and, if so, how Joseph will remember his family after he attains power is a major theme of his life story.

The Torah reports that in later times the Hebrew people were bitterly oppressed by forced labor, with the decisions governing their lives made by Pharaoh and his taskmasters, who tried to kill every newborn male. Worse still, a portion of the Hebrews participated in their own subjugation, describing themselves as Pharaoh's servants when they pleaded with him to lift their burdens (Exod. 5:15–16). Worst of all, decades or centuries later (the account is not precise), the Hebrew people had departed so far from their origins that, according to Moses' remonstrance at the burning bush, they no longer remembered the name of their deity. "When . . . the Israelites . . . ask me 'What is His name?'" Moses asks God, "what shall I say to them?" (Ex. 3:13).

A clue to the significance of this historical sequence, which saw the Hebrew people transformed from a vibrant extended family headed by Jacob and his twelve sons into a fatalistic mass who believed they could do nothing to affect their own fortunes, comes from an early commentary apparently directed at Joseph's brothers: "Because ye have sold Joseph to be a slave, therefore ye say year after year, slaves were we unto Pharaoh in Egypt."[28] Apparently the commentator saw a connection between what Jacob's family did in Egypt and what happened to their successors afterward. Joseph's brothers were obviously wrong first to consider killing him and then to abandon him in the pit of misery. May we not ask, however, with equal conviction, when we know better the story of Joseph the administrator, whether the Egyptians were better able to enslave the Hebrews because Joseph helped so mightily to enslave the Egyptians to Pharaoh?

That this copying of customs leading to aping of behavior is impermissible is the theme of some of the most enigmatic portions of the Torah, known as the wife-sister stories. Their peculiarity is matched only by the insistence with which these stories are told and retold as if they contain a most important message. In my view, the wife-sister stories contain the indispensable moral prologue to the Joseph stories. Though political allegiance to foreigners is allowed, separation, not assimilation, is required.

Notes

1. Jacob Neusner, *Death and Birth of Judaism: The Impact of Christianity, Secularism, and the Holocaust on Jewish Faith* (New York: Basic Books, 1987), 64.
2. See Jacob Neusner, *Self-Fulfilling Prophecy: Exile and Return in the History of Judaism* (Boston: Beacon Press, 1987).
3. Abraham Joshua Heschel, *Between God and Man: An Interpretation of Judaism* (New York: Farrar, Straus and Cudahy, 1959), 96.
4. Allen P. Ross, "Jacob at the Jabbok, Israel at Peniel," *Bibliotheca Sacra* 142 (October–December 1985): 338–54, quote on p. 351.
5. Hermann Cohen, *Religion of Reason: Out of the Sources of Judaism* (New York: Frederick Ungar Publishing, 1972), 76. See also the analysis in Aaron Wildavsky, *The Nursing Father: Moses as a Political Leader* (University of Alabama Press, 1985), Chapter 5, "The Leader Disappears into the Book: Why Moses Does Not Get to the Promised Land," 152–81.
6. Jean Soler, "The Dietary Prohibitions of the Hebrews," trans. by Elbort Forster, *New York Review of Books*, 26/10 (June 14, 1979): 24–30.
7. Ibid.

8. Mary Douglas, "The Abominations of Leviticus," in *Natural Symbols: Explorations in Cosmology* (London: Barrie and Rockliff, 1970); and Mary Douglas, "Deciphering a Meal," in *Implicit Meanings: Essays in Anthropology*, ed., Mary Douglas, (London: Routledge and Kegan Paul, 1975): 249-75.
9. Moshe Greenberg, "Some Postulates of Biblical Criminal Law," *The Jewish Expression*, Judah Giddin, ed. (New Haven: Yale University Press, 1976): 22.
10. Cassuto shows the many similarities in wording between these parallel passages concerning Abraham and Issac and Moses, the Hebrew people, and Pharaoh. After all, Pharaoh also threatens to destroy the people by killing their male children. Umberto Cassuto, *A Commentary on the Book of Genesis*, Part II From Noah to Abraham, Genesis VI9-XI32 (Jerusalem: Magnes Press, 1974): 334-361.
11. Isaac M. Kikawada and Arthur Quinn, *Before Abraham Was the Unity of Genesis 1-11* (Nashville, Tenn.: Abingdon Press, 1985), 119.
12. Ibid., 121.
13. Louis Ginzberg, *The Legends of the Jews*, vol. 2, trans. Henrietta Szold (Philadelphia: Jewish Publication Society, 1977), 4.
14. Jacob Milgrom, Review of E. A. Speiser, *Genesis*, translated with an introduction and commentary, in *Conservative Judaism* 20, no. 3 (1966): 73-79.
15. David Daube, "Fraud on Law For Fraud on Law," *Oxford Journal of Legal Studies* 1 (1981): 51-60; quote on p. 52.
16. F. R. Meyer, *Joseph: Beloved-Hated-Exalted* (New York: Fleming H Revell Co., n.d.), 121.
17. Hermann Gunkel, *The Folktale in the Old Testament*, trans. by Michael D. Rutter (Almond Press, 1987); Hermann Gunkel, *The Legends of Genesis: The Biblical Saga and History* (New York: Schocken, 1964); John Skinner, *A Critical and Exegetical Commentary on Genesis*, 2nd ed. (Edinburgh: T. & T. Clark, 1956); Lothar Ruppert, *Die Josepherzahlung der Genesis* (Munchen: Kosel-Verlag, 1965).
18. See also James L. Kugel, *The Idea of Biblical Poetry* (New Haven, Conn.: Yale University Press, 1981), 69.
19. Robert Alter, *The Art of Biblical Poetry* (New York: Basic Books, 1985), 23.
20. Ibid., 11.
21. Nahum M. Sarna, *The JPS Torah Commentary: Genesis* (Philadephia: Jewish Publication Society, 1989), 332; Wilfred G. E. Watson, *Classical Hebrew Poetry*, Journal for the Study of the Old Testament Supplement Series 26 (Sheffield: Sheffield Academic Press, 1984), 275.
22. Watson, *Classical Hebrew Poetry*, 279; James Muilenburg, "Poetry," *Encyclopedia Judaica* 13 (Jerusalem: Keter Publishing House, 1972), 679-80.
23. Ronald Hyman, "Questions in the Joseph Story: The Effects and Their Implications for Teaching," *Religious Education* 79 (1984): 440.
24. See Ronald Hyman's outstanding discussion in "Questions and the Book of Ruth," *Hebrew Studies* 24 (1983): 21-25; and Hyman, "Questions in the Joseph Story," 438.
25. Muilenburg, "Poetry," 673.
26. By the 12th century, when Rashi wrote his superb commentaries, the parallels between the lives of Jacob and Joseph, Joseph perhaps making explicit what was only implicit in his father, were well known. (*"Rashi" on the Pentateuch: Genesis*, trans. and annotated by James H. Lowe (London: Hebrew Compendium Publishing), 1928, 392-93.)
27. See Wildavsky, *The Nursing Father*.
28. Ginzberg, *The Legends of the Jews*, 17.

1

No Foreigner Can Control Israel: The Wife-Sister Motif Prefigures the Joseph Stories

The Torah can be a teaching for anyone who chooses to seek counsel from it. Asking "Why should a Christian seek political guidance" from the Old Testament, Dale Patrick answers because it is "the 'political' Testament." It tells the story of what happens in a dynamic political process as a people try and often fail to implement God's laws.[1] The reasons for their failure often have to do with human weakness.

What is the temptation of a clever people? To be too clever. By confusing cleverness with morality, they bring misfortune upon themselves.

What is the temptation of a religious people? To take the name of the Lord in vain. By pretending to speak in the name of God, they confuse the history of their errors with His direction.

What is the temptation of high-level administrators? To confuse their patron with their God; to mistake serving their patron with helping their people. The Joseph stories make an excellent text from which to discuss the attributes of the good administrator.

Should Joseph have risen to as high a position as possible, even if that meant adopting foreign ways, so as to help his people to the utmost? Or should Joseph have acted as Daniel and Mordecai did, willing to serve a foreign government but not at the cost of violating God's commandments? There are temptations that come from alignment with the sources of power. "Joseph may remember his roots . . .," Walter Brueggemann observes, "But Egyptian power seduces, overwhelms, commandeers and besides all of that, one can do a lot of good with power. One can indeed feed the world."[2] But, in a God-centered religion, is that enough?

Once analysis of the text disabuses us of the notion that Joseph is meant to be an exemplar, we are in a position to appreciate the dilemmas faced by a people who wish to be loyal to the earthly polity but socially separate in their relationship with foreigners. This dilemma between assimilation and separation is foreshadowed in the remarkable wife-sister stories whose abruptness (they seemingly come out of nowhere), strangeness (why deny the matrimonial tie by calling wives "sisters"?), and repetition (they occur three times) alert us to their immense importance.[3] The wife-sister motif carries coincidence too far. That the episodes are duplicates of each other is indicated by the fact that Isaac and Abraham both deal with a king named Abimelech, who has a high-ranking assistant called Phicol (Gen. 21:22; 26:26).[4] Much is shrouded in mystery; but of one thing there is no doubt: these wife-sister stories are meant to prefigure the Hebrew people's entry into and exodus out of Egypt. Because these myths encapsulate the wisdom the Hebrew people are to learn about their Egyptian experience, they form the indispensable guide to the significance of the stories about Joseph, the son of Jacob, who became administrator to Pharaoh and whose life's meaning is bound up with the experience of the Israelites in Egypt.

The Wife-Sister Stories

Each of the patriarchs, not only Jacob but Abraham and Isaac, go literally and symbolically either to Egypt or to a foreign country called Gerar where they are faced with conquest or assimilation. Their encounters are remarkably similar, one might say doubled to preview the special style of the Joseph stories, as if to insist that thrice-told tales come true.

Because of Sarah and Rachel

The first biblical account follows:

There was a famine in the land, and Abram went down to Egypt to sojourn there, for the famine was severe in the land. As he was about to enter Egypt, he said to his wife Sarai, "I know what a beautiful woman you are. If the Egyptians see you, and think, 'She is his wife,' they will kill me and let you live. Please say that you are my sister, that it may go well with me because of you, and that I may remain alive thanks to you." When Abram entered Egypt, the Egyptians saw how very beautiful the woman was. Pharaoh's courtiers saw her and praised her to Pharaoh, and the woman was taken into Pharaoh's place. And because of her it went well with Abram, he acquired sheep, oxen, asses, male and female slaves, she-asses, and camels. But the Lord afflicted Pharaoh and his household with mighty plagues on account of Sarai, the wife of Abram. (Gen. 12:10-17)

Is "sister" just a convenient subterfuge—an important family member but not a wife—or is there more to the use of this term? Why is there all this emphasis on Sarai as the causal factor—"because of you," "because of her"? And why does Abram prosper materially for turning his wife over to the Egyptians on false pretenses?

The story is repeated in regard to another king, Abimelech of Gerar (the main characters now renamed Abraham and Sarah by the Lord):

> While he was sojourning in Gerar, Abraham said of Sarah his wife, "She is my sister." So Abimelech king of Gerar had Sarah brought to him. But God came to Abimelech in a dream by night and said to him, "You are to die because of the woman that you have taken, for she is a married woman." Now Abimelech had not approached her. He said, "O Lord, will You slay people even though innocent? He himself said to me, 'She is my sister!' And she also said, 'He is my brother.' When I did this, my heart was blameless and my hands were clean." And God said to him in the dream, "I knew that you did this with a blameless heart, and so I kept you from sinning against Me. That was why I did not let you touch her. Therefore, restore the man's wife—since he is a prophet, he will intercede for you—to save your life." (Gen. 20:1-7)

Why must Abimelech be the one to take Sarah back to her husband? Why, like Pharaoh before him, being blameless, must he send Abraham away much richer? Why is harm threatened because of Sarah and Rachel?

After receiving material recompense, as if there was no fault in his behavior, Abraham prays to God in the king's behalf: "and God healed Abimelech and his wife and his slave girls, so that they bore children; for the Lord had closed fast every womb of the household of Abimelech because of Sarah, the wife of Abraham" (Gen. 20:17-18). Why is not only Abimelech but his extended family harmed and then saved if he did Sarah no harm?

A similarly strange story is told about Abraham's son Isaac when he stayed in a place called Gerar because the Lord warned him against going to Egypt:

> When the men of the place asked him about his wife, he said, "She is my sister," for he was afraid to say "my wife," thinking, "The men of the place might kill me on account of Rebekah, for she is beautiful." When some time had passed, Abimelech king of the Philistines, looking out of the window, saw Isaac fondling his wife Rebekah. Abimelech sent for Isaac and said, "So she is your wife! Why then did you say: She is my sister?" Isaac said to him, "Because I thought I might lose my life on account of her." (Gen 26:7-9)

Wives, especially wives engaged in fondling their husbands, are not usually causes of their husband's death. Why would the patriarch of his people fear being killed "on account of" his wife, Rebekah?

These stories are the same in that the moral is identical: Israel is the beautiful woman who is taken by a foreign king until he discovers that she belongs to another and more powerful potentate, the God of the Hebrews. No foreign deity is to take God's place as father of His people.[5] Sarah is the eternal mother of the Hebrew people and no one but God's duly appointed husband can have her. Heaven will harm those who seek to seduce or force the people who are promised to God. "Because of Sarah," there is the message: foreigners who attempt to impregnate Israel, mixing their seed in its womb, even inadvertently, will find themselves unable to procreate. But why, if Abraham places his wife in danger, does he prosper?

The Exodus Foretold

That the three wife-sister stories prefigure the Exodus there can be no doubt. Thinking the Jewish people were like any other, Pharaoh sought to bring them into his domain, intermixing them with the Egyptian people by taking their mother, Sarai, into his harem. Plagues come because the Hebrews are the people of a jealous God who will not allow them to merge into another people. Had Pharaoh known that Hebrews were betrothed to God, he would not have had (or attempted to have, the text does not make this clear) intercourse with her. Now he has learned that a force higher than himself will not allow him to impregnate Israel with Egyptian seed.

The parallel is exact: a later Pharaoh tries to destroy the Hebrew people by killing off all their male children; then only Egyptian men will be able to impregnate Hebrew women. So, too, if Pharaoh impregnates the wife of father Abraham, Pharaoh will be the father of the people and they will be Egyptian, not Hebrew. "Sister" signifies Sarah and Rachel as part of the family of Israel. Not only no wife but no woman of Israel, nay, Israel itself, may be touched by a foreign force.

The wives in these stories, Sarah and Rebekah, are self-sacrificing. They evidently agree to call themselves sisters to protect their husbands, taking what comes, so far as we know, without protest. Yet it must be said that it is the men, the Hebrew patriarchs and the foreign kings, who initiate and carry on the action, while it is their women, including servant girls, who bear the brunt of the danger, whether that is being taken into a foreign king's harem with Lord only knows what consequences or being unable to conceive.

Does this signify that the women in the stories about Joseph are bound to be passive? Not at all. Potiphar's wife and Tamar, the wife of Er, the women we meet in the first two chapters (Gen. 37 and 38) are demanding, action-forcing individuals who violate law and custom, the former to dishonor and the latter to honor their husbands. Tamar is spared her sacrifice by persuading her father-in-law, Judah, that he himself is the guilty party. Later, her example stands as precedent when Judah offers to stand as surety for Benjamin. So do the Egyptian midwives refuse their Pharaoh's command to kill the Hebrew male children.

Good for them. But apparently not so good for Abraham, who left his wife as a sister prey to foreign invasion.

Is Abraham at Fault?

Abraham is in bad odor. He pretends, half-truthfully but essentially falsely (he had married his father's brother's daughter), that she was his sister. He has subjected his wife to gross indignity, perhaps worse, in Pharaoh's harem. The Zohar suspects that Sarai's picture hung in Pharaoh's bedroom.[6] To add insult to injury, Abraham (and later Isaac) gets rich off his wife's presence (to use a neutral term) in another man's harem. There is no need to sidestep the obvious question: Is Abraham pimping? Worse, Abraham, who has just received God's promise to found a people on his family, procures the services of his wife for a foreign king who can negate God's promise by mixing his seed with the patriarch's in the womb of the mother of the Hebrew people. And, if it is possible to make things still worse, Abraham repeats his sacrifice of Sarah's virtue and dignity, as if he benefited from the exchange the first time, with King Abimelech. The question of the prosperity of the patriarchs is certainly open to this mercenary, wife-selling interpretation.

A Dead Sea Scroll found in the first Qumran cave seeks to rationalize Abram's behavior. In this account, Abram dreamt that

> he saw two trees, a cedar and a palm, and a group of people coming to cut down the cedar and planning to leave the palm untouched. The palm bursts out crying and warns

the men that they will be cursed if they cut down the cedar. Thus the cedar is saved for the sake of the palm.

Abram wakes, tells Sarai about the dream that frightened him and interprets its meaning to her; when they reach Egypt, there will be an attempt to kill him, but Sarai will be able to save him.[7]

The palm tree in Hebrew is Tamar who, by playing prostitute to Judah (Gen. 38), acts to maintain the continuity of her husband's name. The threat in this dream is the same as in the wife-sister stories themselves: the destruction of a community via the elimination of its male members.

One commentary, the Babba Kamina, praises Abraham for going to Egypt to save his people.[8] The opposite view is taken by the Zohar— Abraham erred by going to Egypt instead of Israel; for that reason, the Zohar inferred Israel was punished by hard labor in Egypt.[9]

Abraham's sin, according to Nahmanides, was that he lacked trust in God. Otherwise, in possession of God's promise, Abraham should have acknowledged Sarah as his wife.[10] Not to acknowledge the wife of the progenitor of the Hebrew people is not to acknowledge all future generations.

Lack of trust in God is also Umberto Cassuto's theme:

In order to escape the danger, Abram had relied on his shrewdness, and did not put his trust in the paternal providence of the Lord. Now the very ruse that he had relied upon became a source of evil to him. The only peril that he had envisaged was that which might emanate from the commoners of Egypt (v. 12: "And it shall come to pass when the Egyptians see you"), and he thought it would be easy for him, as Sarai's brother, to put them off with words. It never dawned on him that possibly Sarai might be desired by one who could take her without her brother's consent. Thus not what he had anticipated, but something that he had never envisaged, happened. The peril actually arose as a result of his craftiness, from the statement that he was her brother and not her husband. This was Abram's retribution, the punishment fitting the crime. From this we learn that the Torah considered his sin to consist in the fact that he put his trust in cunning and not in God's help.[11]

This criticism, I shall argue, is misplaced.

One clue is the repetition not only of these wife-sister stories but also of certain key phrases. The emphasis is not on the sister role but rather on the women's position as wives of the patriarchs. Five times in this episode Sarai is called "his wife" (Gen. 12:11, 12, 17, 18, 20). Once Pharaoh says that "I took her as my wife" (Gen. 12:19). In the Abram-Abimelech episode, the locution "his wife" or, once, "the man's wife" occurs seven times (Gen. 20:2, 7, 11, 12, 14, 17, 18). "My wife" is repeated five times in the Isaac-Abimelech episode, a repetition the more remarkable because the entire story occupies but a single short paragraph (Gen. 26:7-11).

Foreign kings may have reason to believe that these females are sisters—indeed, they are specifically told that this is so—but this factual circumstance does not matter. Pharaoh is plagued for placing Sarah in his harem whether or not he has intercourse with her. No one tells him his relationship to Sarah is the cause of his and his people's problems. He assumes correctly that he has violated a taboo by crossing a boundary defended by a higher power. He has Abraham and Sarah forcibly removed under military escort because it is the fact of transgression against the Divine, not the motivation, that matters.

Abraham is neither the villain nor the hero of the wife-sister episodes; he is the setting. The function he performs, or that is performed through him, is to preview the great dilemma of the Hebrew people: whether they must assimilate in order to survive, literally give their wives to foreign men, meaning their wives' children would no longer be Hebrews, or whether they can retain their distinctive character as a God-directed people and still survive.

The message of the wife-sister stories, as well as the exodus from Egypt, is unmistakable: survival and prosperity can be joined through following the dictates of the one God. God's will be done. If not, He will bring plague upon those who would force His wife—figuratively, the Hebrew people—to leave Him. If plague is not enough, He will kill the king. Abraham is the vehicle for demonstrating something of such surpassing importance to the people of Israel that it is repeated three times. To improve our understanding, it is necessary to pay attention to the protestations of innocence by these foreign kings.

Unnecessary Acts

Abimelech does not have carnal relations with Sarah and is quick to declare his innocence. Indeed, the Lord appears in a dream to tell Abimelech that He has deliberately kept him from having sex with Sarah. Nevertheless, God still performs what might otherwise be considered not one but two unnecessary acts. In the first, neither King Abimelech nor his servants are able to have children. Note the equivalence: the effort to place the king's seed into Sarah, that is, Israel's womb, is met by rendering ineffective the wombs of the king's family, womb, so to speak, for womb.

The Lord's second act is to tell Abimelech he will be killed, and his people along with him, unless he returns Sarah to her husband ("If you fail to restore her, know that you shall die, you and all that are yours" Gen. 20:7). Is this warning superfluous? For one thing, Abimelech has already shown great wariness in his relationship with Sarah. For another, he is already deathly fearful, as are his retainers, of incurring guilt via Sarah. Like Pharaoh before him, Abimelech is only too glad to get rid of Sarah and, thereby, the danger she represents. But if Abimelech and Sarah stand for precepts important to God—Sarah, the mother of the future Hebrew people, its life-giving source, must not be taken by a foreign ruler, her progeny to mix with his—this "superfluous" admonition emphasizes a vital, one might even say life-and-death, proposition.

The mortal danger in which the introduction of pagan objects into God's chosen people places these perpetrators explains another constant refrain: Pharaoh attributes the plagues he and his people suffer to his relations with Sarai, asking indignantly, "Why did you not tell me that she was your wife?" (Gen. 12:18). Abimelech exclaims to Isaac, "What have you done to us! One of the people might have lain with your wife, and you would have brought guilt [penalty or punishment might better convey the sense of the passage] upon us" (Gen. 26:10). More poignantly still, the first Abimelech asks/accuses Abraham, "What have you done to us? What wrong have I done you that you should bring so great a guilt upon me and my kingdom?" (Gen. 20:9). The double transgression is violating the marriage not only of Abraham and Sarah but of God and His people.[12]

Would not a single story do? Why are there three wife-sister stories? And why do two of them involve Abraham and two Abimelech?

Why Three Wife-Sister Episodes?

Now we are perhaps better able to appreciate E. A. Speiser's heartfelt comment that "this recurrent wife-sister theme in Genesis has been the subject of innumerable comments and speculations. Interpreters through the ages have found the material both puzzling and disturbing."[13] Were not the narrators aware that they were repeating themselves? Why are there two episodes involving the king of Gerar and two different patriarchs? Taken literally as well, the accounts strain credulity. As Speiser puts it, we would have to believe that "Abraham learned nothing from his experience in Egypt" and that "Abimelech would have to be either a fool or a knave to accept Issac's subsequent pretense at face value; yet this passage depicts him as both wise and sincere." Moreover, by this time, the king of Gerar would have been much too old to be sexually interested in Rebekah and, as many other commentators have observed, Sarah, then in her nineties, could hardly have been an object of carnal desire.[14] Subsequently, Speiser hits upon source criticism and claims that all is resolved because the three accounts belong to three different sources from which the Torah was finally compiled.

Even if this explanation were literally true, it would not explain enough. Having the episode belong to different sources does not explain its significance; multiple authorship only heightens the mystery. Why would all three authors feel bound to tell the same tall tale? Why would later editors leave in place three such similar episodes when one would have been enough? It is not only the great importance of their theme but the fact that there are important differences among them, I contend, that justifies the inclusion of three versions.

After God accepts Abimelech's explanation that he "had not approached" (Gen. 20:4) Sarah, that is, had sexual relations with her, He makes a statement to Abimelech that is, so far as I know, without precedent in the rest of the Torah: "If you fail to restore her, know that you shall die, you and all that are yours" (Gen. 20:7). Moses may tell Pharaoh that bad things will happen to him and his people, but God does not threaten him directly. God may prevent a pagan prophet, Balaam, from cursing the Israelites and send an angel to kill him, but He does not directly threaten Balaam with destruction. When the Lord refers to "The outrage of Sodom and Gomorrah" (Gen. 18:20), where Abraham pleads with God not to destroy the entire city, only by implication do we know what He had in mind. Why so severe and so personal a penalty?

Abimelech not only restored Sarah to Abraham, he also said to Sarah, "I herewith give your brother a thousand pieces of silver; this will serve you as vindication [literally, as translators tell us, "a covering of the eyes"] before all who are with you and you are cleared before everyone" (Gen. 20:16). When Abraham insisted on buying the cave of Machpelah in order to bury Sarah, he paid 400 shekels of silver (Gen. 23:1–10), the clear implication being that this was an outrageously high price. The

1,000 shekels was then two and one half times outrageous. The "covering of the eyes" for 1,000 shekels signifies that Sarah had not been shamed in the eyes of the community, that Abimelech had not taken advantage of her. Speiser is undoubtedly right in calling this "a method for diverting or for stalling suspicion."[15] What suspicion? Suspicion that there is a natural cause of Sarah's pregnancy from intercourse with a foreign king, if not Abimelech then more likely Pharaoh before him. That would cast into doubt the legitimacy of the entire line of the Hebrew people. Both the extraordinary threat to which Abimelech is subjected by God Himself and the extraordinary amount he pays to defend Sarah's honor make more sense if her ultimate alliance is with a higher power.

The wife-sister stories concern only two of the three patriarchs of the Hebrew people. Why is Jacob left out? He is not. He does go down to Egypt where his people, starting with his son Joseph, have to decide what kind of relationship they will have with their Pharaoh.

There are three wife-sister stories so that all three patriarchs (Abraham and Isaac as well as Jacob) have to experience the dilemma of assimilation versus separation. Metaphorically speaking, all Jews go to Egypt. The trouble is that Jacob does not need a myth to make it to Egypt; his way there is part of the main narrative. What remains is to explain another puzzle, namely, why, if there are three patriarchs, and each experiences the Diaspora, there are two wife-sister stories about Abraham? There is a second story about Abraham so that the second king, Abimelech, can act as the ideal foreign ruler for the Hebrew people. Now the cycle is complete: the real is juxtaposed to the ideal so the people can choose not only in the light of what is but of what might be.

The Good King in the Diaspora

Observe the peremptory tone of Pharaoh's leave-taking: "Now, here is your wife; take her and begone!" (Gen. 12:19). Note further that while Pharaoh recognizes he must separate himself from this people, he still thinks himself in command: "And Pharaoh put men in charge of him [Abram], and they sent him off with his wife and all that he possessed" (Gen. 12:20). Let us pay attention to how the other two wife-sister episodes end.

King "Abimelech [of Gerar] took sheep and oxen, and male and female slaves, and gave them to Abraham" (Gen. 20:14). In this second episode as in the first (Gen. 12:16), the Hebrew patriarchs go laden with gifts, as they do in the exodus from Egypt. As in Egypt, foreigners must follow the law of the Israelites requiring slaves to be sent away well-provisioned. Even when the harm is inadvertent, even when there is no harm because there is no sex, the Hebrews go laden with gifts.

There is more. Abimelech makes the offer that every Hebrew in the Diaspora hoped for: "Here, my land is before you; settle wherever you please" (Gen. 20:15). The Hebrew people could follow their customs and practices and their religion while remaining separate from a foreign government.

The very name Abimelech combines two words in Hebrew, *Aba* for father and *Melech* for king. Who is the father-king and what does his name signify? Possibly, this is a generic title, signifying "head of family" or beneficent ruler of a tribe or city. Possibly it has a more kindly aspect. The *Jewish Encyclopedia* translates the name either as "the [Divine] father is king" or "the [Divine] king is father."[16] Abimelech's name refers to a patriarchal ruler who cares for all within his purview, even those outside of his family, even, more importantly for Abraham's people, those outside of his tribe.

Abimelech is the ultimate righteous foreigner who maintains separation between the Hebrew people and his own. Here the Hebrew people have the cake of separation and eat the rewards of good political relations with their host people as well.

Observe what has happened: the wife-sister stories have traversed a long distance from the progenitors of the Hebrew people being escorted under armed guard to their being handsomely rewarded to their getting the greatest reward of all—their right to be different guaranteed by their foreign host.

This foreign king behaves honorably, so honorably that he is able to presage Abraham's own challenge to the Almighty before the destruction of Sodom and Gomorrah. Will God "bring death upon the innocent as well as the guilty" (Gen. 18:25)?

A good case in point occurs when one of King David's retainers, accompanying the Ark of the Covenant to its resting place in Jerusalem, steadies it with his hand in order to protect it. At once the retainer is killed by the Almighty. David is greatly displeased because there was no fault in the man (2 Sam. 6:6-8). He does not understand, I think, that the most important boundary of all, the line between the human and the Divine, is so vital that it must be defended against an accidental as well as an intentional breach. If it were possible for the boundary to be violated with good intentions (and who but God knows the truth about human intentions), untold mischief might enter the world. Perhaps the genocidal retribution for the rape of Dinah at Shechem (Gen. 34) evokes a similar theme. Whereas the rest of the Bible seeks to individuate guilt, so that the innocent are not punished with the guilty, (viz. the debates Abraham and Moses have with God), the most important distinction of all—between God and man—is enforced against the innocent.

A Double-Hinged Gate

Joseph is a double-hinged gate: push one way and he brings Israel to Egypt, push another and he brings Egypt to Israel. Standing at the crossroads between worship of a man, the Pharaoh, and of a God whom no man controls, standing between equality (no man should rule over his brothers) and hierarchy, the Joseph stories negotiate between different ways of life.

Just as every interpretation of the Torah that is well-grounded is considered part of the original revelation, so every future event may be read to cast light on its historical antecedents. In that border land where past and future are joined, each shaping the other in the Torah, stands Joseph the administrator to Pharaoh, sold by his brothers into slavery, his adopted Egyptian king beckoning him to a life of lording it over others, his present assured but the future of his people perpetually in peril.

Notes

1. Dale Patrick, "Political Exegesis," in *Encounter With the Text: Form and History in the Hebrew Bible*, Martin J. Buss, ed. (Philadelphia: Fortress Press, 1979), 139–152, quote on 141.
2. Walter Brueggemann, "Dreaming, Being Home, Finding Strangers; And the Seminaries," *Mid-Stream* 26 (1987): 62–76; quote on p. 67.
3. T. D. Alexander has noted "The complete absence of such incidents elsewhere in the Old Testament . . ." ("Are the Wife/Sister Incidents of Genesis Literary Compositional Variants?" *Vetus Testamentum* 42, no. 1 (1992): 145–153; quote on 145). He concludes that "It is now possible to view all three episodes as deriving from a single author, who, in drawing upon earlier traditions, composed the later wife/sister pericopes with a clear knowledge of what he had already written earlier" (152). Many others he cites disagree.

4. S. R. Driver, *The Book of Genesis* (London: Methuen & Co., 1904), 253–254. Also see Daniel H. Gordis, "Lies, Wives and Sisters: The Wife-sister Motif Revisited," *Judaism* 34 (1985): 344–359.
5. See David Daube, "Sin, Ignorance and Forgiveness in the Bible," Claude Montefiore Lecture, 1960 (London: Liberal Jewish Synagogue, printed by Richard Madley Ltd.).
6. Zohar II, 30a.
7. Nahman Avigad and Yigael Yadin, *A Genesis Apocryphon: A Scroll From the Wilderness of Judaea*, Description and Contents of the Scroll Facsimiles, Transcription and Translation of Columns II, XIX–XXII (Jerusalem: Magnes Press, 1956), 23.
8. Babba Kamina, 606.
9. Zohar I, 816.
10. Cited in Louis Ginzberg, *Legends of the Jews* 5, 220.
11. Umberto Cassuto, *A Commentary on the Book of Genesis*, trans. from the Hebrew by Israel Abrahams (Jerusalem: Magnes Press, 1964), 353.
12. For a quite different but most interesting comparative view of these episodes, see Gordis, "Lies, Wives and Sisters," 343–359.
13. E. A. Speiser, *Genesis*, The Anchor Bible (Garden City, NY: Doubleday, 1964), 91.
14. Ibid., 151. Sarna tells us that "according to rabbinic fancy, her flesh was rejuvenated, her wrinkles smoothed out, and her original beauty was restored" (Nahum M. Sarna, *The JPS Torah Commentary: Genesis* (Philadelphia: Jewish Publication Society, 1989), 141). See also Driver, *The Book of Genesis*.
15. Speiser, *Genesis*, 150.
16. *Jewish Encyclopedia* 2, 75.

2

Survival Must Not Be Gained through Sin: The Moral of the Joseph Stories Prefigured through Judah and Tamar, Ruth and Naomi, Joseph and Mrs. Potiphar

Just as the fable of Balaam's ass is meant to teach Moses (and, through him, all would-be leaders) that they must share the fate of their people, even though all they can expect in return is abuse,[1] so the story of Judah and Tamar is a preview of the lesson of the Joseph stories, which is that leaders cannot save their people by violating the moral law. The merit of this interpretation is that it explains why this apparently unconnected story is placed after Joseph's boyhood adventures but before the travails and triumphs of his adult life. If, as I claim, the great question pervading the Joseph stories is what may be done for the survival of one's people, Tamar's triumph over Judah, Ruth's union with Boaz, and Joseph's upholding his master Potiphar's honor give unequivocal answers to that question.

The weight of scholarly opinion, however, does not see any correspondence between these two narratives. "Every attentive reader," according to Gerhard von Rad, the leading interpreter of the Joseph stories in our time, "can see that the story of Judah and Tamar has no connection at all with the strictly organized Joseph stories, in whose beginning it is now inserted."[2] Westermann asserts that the story of Judah and Tamar "has nothing to do" with the Joseph stories,[3] and Speiser's Genesis commentary refers to the Judah and Tamar tale as "a completely independent unit."[4] "It has always been something of a puzzle," Davidson informs us, "as to why this incident was inserted into the Joseph story, and why at this particular point."[5] Others have questioned why the story "should be presented in so scandalous a form" where "the only person in the story who emerges with credit is the Canaanite woman Tamar."[6] A favorite

31

suggestion has been that this presumably irrelevant tale has been inserted just as the story of Joseph captures our attention in order to heighten suspense.[7] Whybray sums up the trend of interpretation by writing that

> although no other explanation of the present position of Genesis 38 has yet commanded general acceptance (source-criticism certainly does not offer such an explanation), the hypothesis that it is an integral part of a unified narrative seems the least likely.[8]

Without following his specific reasoning, I agree with Greenberg's view that "all parts of the story of Judah and Tamar are significant."[9]

Dissatisfied with this pale effort, Benno Jacob observes that twins are born to Tamar, one of whom, Perez, is later counted as an ancestor of David. Thus Jacob concludes, "Before bondage begins, the redeemer is born. Joseph's coming to Egypt begins Israel's bondage. On the other hand, Perez is the ancestor of the Messianic king. The hero of the following story is Joseph, but salvation will come from Judah."[10] I think not; if anything, Joseph is more of an antihero, demonstrating for all to see the path the Hebrew people ought not to take. If my antihero thesis is acceptable, the usual objections to the irrelevance of the Tamar and Judah story fall away. For then the stories about Joseph's decisions as Pharaoh's administrator are preceded by a model of the right way for the Hebrew people to take action.

The stories about the selling of Joseph, of Judah and Tamar, and Joseph's political success in Chapters 37–39 of Genesis are analogous to the connection between Chapters 15–17 of 1 Samuel, the stories of the rejection of Saul, Samuel anointing David, and David's political success. In both occurrences, there are similar hints about the quarrel over the political power between the sons of Leah (Judah and David of the Judah tribe) and the sons of Rachel (Israel and Saul of the Benjamin tribe). The political interpretation is given in the Bible itself, in 1 Chronicles 5:1-2: "Now the sons of Reuben the firstborn of Israel . . . but forasmuch as he defiled his father's bed, his birthright was given unto the sons of Joseph . . . For Judah prevailed above his brethren, and of him came the chief ruler; but the birthright was Joseph's." The story of Judah and Tamar explains why Joseph gets the birthright in his time but his values are not allowed to rule in the future.

The story, though unusual, is simple to tell.[11] Living among the Canaanites, Judah married a Canaanite woman and had three sons, Er, Onan, and Shelah.[12] His oldest son, Er, married a Canaanite woman,

Tamar, but left her without child when he died, apparently in punishment for an action contrary to God's law, though it was common then to attribute any death short of its time to violation of some commandment.[13] Under the then-existing custom of levirate marriage it was the father-in-law's duty to see that a surviving son gave the wife of his deceased brother a son to carry on the family name and to inherit the father's portion, and Judah appointed his second son to fulfill this responsibility. "But Onan, knowing that the seed would not count as his, let it go to waste . . . so as not to provide offspring for his brother" (Gen. 38:9). (From this episode—Onan spilling his seed on the ground—came the term onanism, referring to masturbation as well as coitus interruptus.[14]) Onan did not want to share his father's inheritance with a son credited to his deceased brother.

There has been a small controversy over why God then killed Onan. Catholic scholars especially have not taken kindly to the view that it was Onan's disregard of his obligation to carry on his deceased brother's name, rather than the sin of sex without procreation, for which the Almighty did him in. DeVine tries to settle the matter by arguing that "A. Onan was punished by God *principally* because of his crime against the natural law, and B. *secondarily* because he failed to fulfill the levirate duty." His reason is that intentional failure to procreate involves the violation of a divine commandment, whereas raising up a child to a dead brother is an important but lesser human good.[15] I take Anthony Phillips' view that "it is not sexual ethics but paternity which is uppermost in the legislator's mind."[16] In a society in which a personality is not immortalized in an afterlife but rather is perpetuated through his children, paternity—indeed, clarity in paternity—is uppermost.

Onan's secret wasting of his semen is especially odious because it gave Tamar no opportunity to openly complain that she had been wronged and thus to seek redress in a public manner that would maintain her reputation. Westbrook's interpretation of Onan's motive is just right:

> had Onan refused outright, he would have gained nothing, since either his father or younger brother could perform the levirate instead and provide an heir for the deceased's share. Onan, therefore, thought of a trick. He ostensibly undertook the responsibility given to him, but took care that no heir could possibly result from the union. By performing the duty in form but not in fact he hoped to gain for himself his dead brother's inheritance.[17]

When the should-be levir refused to do his duty under Hebraic law, Carmichael reminds us,

the drawing off of the sandal (as in the Arab divorce ceremony the sandal symbolizes a woman's genitals) from the man's foot (in Hebrew the foot can allude to the male sexual organ) signifies, by a process of transference, the man's withholding conception. Moreover, when after removing a sandal she spits in his face this action is a symbolic reminder of Onan's spilling of the semen on the ground.[18]

As Mary Douglas tells us in her seminal *Purity and Danger*, the body, to Hebrews, stands for the community: inside the body (the community), whatever the body produces is clean, that is, acceptable; but when it leaves the body, whether it is spit or semen, it becomes unacceptable or unclean.[19] The semen is clean both when within the male body and when deposited in the womb of a wife, treated, for this purpose, as part of the man's body. Spilled on the ground, however, as Onan's was, semen pollutes because it is discharged outside the proper boundaries of that community. Semen defiles because it is misplaced, not because it is inherently polluting.

"Onan's crime," Leonard Mars proposes, "was . . . in fact murder." In effect, Onan exterminated Er. By "destroying a major part of his father [the belief at the time was that the first born had more 'of the father in him'" than the sons who came after], Onan "in effect . . . was committing a form of parricide."[20]

Seeming to do his duty, Judah told Tamar that when his youngest son, Shelah, grew up he would give him to her so that she might have a son to carry on her husband's name. In his heart, however, Judah thought otherwise, for he feared that Shelah too "might die like his brothers."[21] Evidently, Judah worried that there was a curse on Tamar. Since Judah's wife had recently died, his family would be extinguished if Shelah, his last surviving son, were to die. Hence he decided to deceive Tamar by not fulfilling his promise. Like son, like father; just as Onan violated God's commandment to increase and multiply, Judah lacked faith in God's promise to the patriarchs, including his father, Jacob, that his family would grow large.

Like Joseph in other respects, Judah is reliving the life of his father. For the same reason that Jacob will fear to send Benjamin to Egypt with his brothers—namely, that he would be killed, as he thought Joseph had been—Judah refused to give Tamar his youngest son. Indeed, the same phrase, *ki amar pen* ("might die," Gen. 38:11, or "meet with disaster," Gen. 42:4), is employed in both texts.[22]

With Judah's false assurance, Tamar returned to her father's house to live as a widow. She kept wearing her widow's weeds to accent her determination to remain Er's widow. But when time passed and she saw that Shelah was full grown and had not been sent to impregnate her as promised, she hit upon a desperate expedient: disguising herself as a temple prostitute,[23] Tamar lay in wait for Judah, who was on his way with a foreign friend, Hirah, to observe the shearing of his sheep. Only he will be shorn instead. The text tells us that Judah turned aside from the path to the sheep shearing to proposition Tamar. "The word used for 'turned aside' (*wayyet*)," Jeansonne rightly remarks, "may also be used figuratively to indicate deviating from what is right or to indicate disloyalty."[24]

> When Judah saw her [Tamar], he took her for a harlot; for she had covered her face. So he turned aside to her by the road and said, "Here, let me sleep with you"—for he did not know that she was his daughter-in-law. "What," she asked, "will you pay for sleeping with me?" He replied, "I will send a kid from my flock." But she said, "You must leave a pledge until you have sent it." And he said, "What pledge shall I give you?" She replied, "Your seal and cord, and the staff which you carry." So he gave them to her and slept with her, and she conceived by him. (Gen. 38:15–18)

Here clothes, the outer garments, conceal the intentions underneath, as they do in the Joseph stories. Judah does not know he is impregnating his daughter-in-law.[25] She asks for a kid, a young goat, which we will find becoming the symbol of deception in Jacob's contentious family. That Judah will be the goat of the story is not yet evident to him.

Seeing that he has no suitable means of payment, Tamar asks Judah to leave a surety[26]: his seal worn on a cord,[27] and his staff, the signs of his identity and his manhood.[28] When Potiphar's wife, in her efforts to take Joseph to bed, holds his garment in her hands, the Hebrew phrase "in my hands" can also be read as "in my power."[29] Similarly, by giving Tamar the staff he carries, Judah puts power over him in her hand. Indeed, she will use his staff as evidence against him.[30] The conjunction of the Hebrew *matteh* for "staff" with the root *regel* for "legs" often serves, as Good tells us, as "the euphemism for the sexual organ."[31]

The next day, however, when Judah sends his friend with the required payment, Tamar is nowhere to be found. (Again, Judah lets someone else do his dirty work.) More truthfully than he knows, the friend is told that no prostitute nad been around there. Upon hearing this, "Judah said, 'Let her keep them,'" referring to his sureties, which might be called his vital signs, "'lest we become a laughingstock!'" (Gen. 38:23). He did not perceive that he had already played the fool.

Three months later word reaches Judah, as head of his family, that Tamar is pregnant. Angry at this violation of morality, Judah harshly calls for Tamar to be burned, a more severe penalty than the usual stoning. Twice he is told of her wrongful act: "Your daughter-in-law Tamar has played the harlot; in fact, she is with child by harlotry" (Gen. 38:24). The repetition, which can denote certainty, is here given an ironic cast. Judah, whose sensitivity to public opinion has been made evident, is egged on by community values to punish his own misdeed. To Judah's deceit has been added hypocrisy—Has he not also engaged in a forbidden sexual act?—and self-deception.

At the hearing held before pronouncing the sentence, Tamar keeps her peace, accusing no one, saying only at the end that her pregnancy was caused by the person whose seal and staff she was then showing. At that point "Judah recognized them, and said, 'She is more in the right than I, inasmuch as I did not give her to my son Shelah.' And he was not intimate with her again" (Gen. 38:26). By her request to "examine these" (Gen. 38:25), she forces him to look inside himself and see his failings. Against his will, Judah has by deceit performed his proper function as the last levir for his family. So he abstains from sex with Tamar to show he recognizes that they have, thanks to her, both fulfilled their duty. Because it is forbidden for a father-in-law to have intercourse with his daughter-in-law, outside of this single circumstance, the point is made that Judah did what was necessary to fulfill his duty as levir and no more.

Fritsch surmises that the Tamar and Judah story is placed right after the beginning of the Joseph narrative in order to contrast her behavior as the ideal Hebrew wife, who would do anything to further family honor, with the behavior of Potiphar's wife, the all too brazen would-be adulteress.[32] I cannot rule this out, but then the moral would be about Egyptian women, that is, referring just to Mrs. Potiphar, and not about Jewish men, and that would be inappropriate.

Among recent commentators, only Robert Alter has offered a sustained interpretation of the Tamar and Judah episode, and that only of the first part. He is undoubtedly right in finding that there are many verbal connections between the Judah and Tamar story and the rest of the text that suggest strongly that they are meant to be read together. Alter thinks "the whole Joseph story, and indeed like the entire book of Genesis, is about the reversal of the iron law of primogeniture, about the election through some devious twist of destiny of a younger son to carry on the line." In support, he observes that it is the line of Judah, the fourth-born son, that will give rise to the kings of Israel.[33] Why should it matter, then, that the future belongs to Judah? Both Judah and Joseph are younger sons.

The same verbs, alternatively suggesting failure to recognize and being recognized or unmasked, Alter carefully notes, connect the later story about Joseph's brothers failing to recognize him as the important official in Egypt with the earlier deceiving of Judah by Tamar and her unmasking of him as the father of her child. After all, it was Judah who proposed deceiving their father with Joseph's blood-stained robe, just as he himself is later deceived by Tamar's veil.[34]

Vawter's literal translation makes the equivalence unmistakable. In regard to Joseph's coat: "then they sent . . . and they said . . . Please examine . . . and he [Jacob] recognized it and said . . . (37:32–33)." In regard to Tamar's proposed execution: "She sent . . . and she said . . . Please examine . . . and he recognized and said. (38:25–26)."[35] We will hear a lot more about who does and does not recognize whom before we are through.

Students of literary style must admire the multiple ways in which the verb "to discern" is used. In addition to repetition of the shock of recognition, referring back so neatly to numerous deceits—made more galling by the brothers asking their father Jacob to discern whether the cloak of favoritism belonged to his most beloved son, Joseph—it also has important legal meaning, making a claim about a fact on the basis of which the claim is denied. When a jury finds that the person is guilty of a theft, that finding, Daube contends, like the Hebrew word for "discerning," closes the case. Whether we are referring to Jacob's half-query, half-enticement to Laban, asking-telling him to discern what belongs to him and what belongs to Jacob, or Tamar's velvet-steely request that Judah discern who owns Judah's staff and signet, the word suggests "a submission of formal evidence with a request to acknowledge it."[36]

I believe the whole should be put into the larger framework of how God's promise to the patriarchs may be fulfilled without violating His laws. The point of the violation of primogeniture is that God works contrary to custom; it shows who has ultimate power. But the stories as a whole are about what is permissible—Joseph's behavior, I contend, is not—when the Jewish family-people are threatened with extinction.

The story of Tamar and Judah, in particular, would make no sense as a violation of the rights of the eldest son, as it is about Tamar's heroic efforts to vindicate these very rights. One could as easily say that Genesis is mainly about deceit. True, Joseph is a younger son (though not the youngest) and he does get to rule over his brothers. Before we equate power with right, however, it is necessary to ask, as I will in Chapter 5, whether what Joseph did to continue the line of the Hebrew people is as morally justified as what Tamar did to keep the memory of her husband alive. At this point it is sufficient to note the parallel between meeting two of the basic human needs—Joseph's storage of food surplus in Egypt for physical survival and Tamar's risk-taking to perpetuate the soul of her husband and the continuity of his people.

Judah is guilty of far more than fornication. By having sexual relations with a woman he believes to be a pagan temple whore, he is also guilty of idolatry or, at the least, disrespect for his God. When he refers to Tamar as "the woman," indicating he did not ask or remember her name, he so depersonalizes what ought to be a loving relationship that his guilt grows greater.

An ancient midrash, a learned interpretation, reads, "The angel said, 'Where are you going, Judah? From whence will kings arise? From whence will redeemers arise?'" guiding him to Tamar. Unfortunately, the text mentions no such being. In accepting this passive view of personal responsibility, which Neusner satirizes as "an angel made him do it,"[37] we would also accept Joseph's excuses to the same effect. If Judah is saved, it is not because what he did can be excused but because he recognized the error of his ways. Tamar, by her dramatic and dangerous action, convinced Judah that he had the levir's duty and thus was considered not guilty.[38] Though a father might not be directly liable for a son's sin, Daube argues, citing Eli's dereliction of duty in failing to discipline his sons, the father as head of family is obligated to try to alter his son's behavior.[39]

What better evidence could there be of rabbinical approval of the preservationist method in Tamar's action than one to which Susan Niditch calls attention: in the Sabbath service certain passages in the Bible may be translated but not read aloud because of their immoral content, including the rape of David's daughter Tamar by her half-brother

Amnon and the incestuous relationship of Jacob's son Reuben with Bilhah, his father's concubine; but the story of Tamar and Judah may be read aloud in the synagogue.[40] Here the sexual act strengthens the community so that it emerges united in fulfilling God's commandment.

Among the passages that may not be read aloud is the famous one about King David committing adultery with another man's wife, Bathsheba. We know from the genealogies that Tamar's twin sons are part of the line of inheritance leading to King David. Thus the staff and the scepter that Judah apparently gave to Tamar she returned to him through her sons.

There are further correspondences: Judah and David are both shepherds and heads of family. Judah being tricked by Tamar is paralleled by Nathan's parable pointing out the immorality of King David's sending Uriah the Hittite to his death in order to have Bathsheba for himself, an immorality so gross that, like Judah, David confesses he is in the wrong: "I have sinned against the Lord" (2 Sam. 12:13).[41] As far as the two Tamars, one is the daughter-in-law of Judah, the other the daughter of David. One is mistreated by a brother-in-law, the other by a half-brother. Judah commands Onan to make love to Tamar in Genesis 38:8 and David sends Tamar to visit the feigning Amnon in 2 Samuel 13:7.[42]

Another phrase in the Torah similar to Judah's statement about Tamar's being in the right comes from God after Moses brings to him the case of the daughters of Zelophehad, whose father had died and who had no sons, arguing, "Let not our father's name be lost to his clan just because he had no son! Give us a holding among our father's kinsmen!" (Num. 27:4). God responds, "The plea of Zelophehad's daughters is just" (Num. 27:7). (One could as well translate as Daube does: "Right speak the daughters of Zelophehad.")[43] After the heads of families in the tribe of Manasseh (a son of Joseph) deplored the fact that if a woman married out of the tribe, the land would be lost to Israel forever, even after the jubilee year when all land was to return to its original owners, the Lord told Moses to reply, "The plea of the Josephite tribe is just" (Num. 36:5). The law was changed to read that "Every daughter among the Israelite tribes who inherits a share must marry someone from a clan of her father's tribe, in order that every Israelite may keep his ancestral share" (Num. 36:8). What the right consists of becomes abundantly clear. The word used, *ken*, means "straight, honest, erect." The greater good is to maintain the continuity of the generations by keeping the offspring of Israel within its own tribes.

There are a host of biblical women who act in opposition to custom and law in order to assert their rights. There is Hagar, who ran away from ill treatment by Abraham's wife, Sarah; Lot's daughters, who took the seed of procreation from their father when they could find none other; Jacob's wife, Rachel, who deceived her father by sitting on the idols that were his gods; Ruth, who climbed out of poverty by enticing Boaz. Women, it is implied, cannot prevail by might but only by pleading the greater justice of their cause. Tamar is chosen to reemphasize the importance of fidelity to God's purposes. She is right, even though in a patriarchal society women are subordinate to men and among an exclusive people she is a stranger. Doubly disadvantaged, she overcomes—we might say trumps—her disadvantages. Tamar is not absolved, nor is she condemned; her case is decided by Judah, who rules in favor of an overarching conception of morality.

When Tamar gave birth to twins, Perez was born first and had a ribbon tied on his hand by the midwife, but then he drew his hand back and his brother preceded him into the world. I take this to signify that who will come out first in life is not something that can be decided by human observation. As the Lord told Samuel when seeking a replacement for Saul (Samuel looked at the big brawny brothers instead of the little David), only the Lord sees into men's souls.

There is one more parallel that is even more striking and that, so far as I am concerned, settles the matter. When Judah, identified by Tamar as the father of her forthcoming children, says "She is more in the right than I," the message is clear: Judah, standing here for Joseph as well, must not place the survival of his family above the moral law. Judah (and hence Joseph) is not entirely wrong—survival does matter—and one may take prudent actions toward that end. Nevertheless, Tamar is "more in the right" than Judah (and hence Joseph) because she fulfills her obligation under the law while he lacks the fear of God, that is, faith in God's promise that His moral law will triumph in the end. God shows it is His purpose by using an unlikely vehicle.[44] This point seems to be quite the opposite of my position that Tamar—and Lot's daughters—flagrantly defied the law in order to perpetuate their family. Which moral law has precedence? For what is right for Tamar—to perpetuate her family by fooling her father-in-law by taking on that responsibility—is wrong for

Judah. His responsibility is to perpetuate his family by following, not rejecting, God's law.

If irony has meaning, the story of Judah and Tamar is a study in that subject. He identifies the woman with whom he had sexual relations as a prostitute. The same root and locution is used to condemn his daughter-in-law for having deserted her marriage vows by becoming an adulteress. One irony is that the two women, the one he embraces and the other he condemns, are the same person. The act of life—he impregnates Tamar, as she desires—and the act of death—he orders her execution—compact birth and death in swift sequence. It is ironic that an act for which Judah pays, he orders Tamar to pay for. A further irony is that the same act, as Bird observes, "is construed differently . . . according to the socio-legal status of the woman involved."[45] Judah's wife is dead, so it is not criminal for him to have relations with a harlot; and though Tamar's husband is dead, it is improper, indeed criminal, for her to have sexual relations with another man. Those contradictions are papered over by Judah's last-minute understanding that Tamar is right in getting him at long last to perform his duty as levir.

The Levir of Last Resort

I have argued that the story of Judah and Tamar is placed immediately after the introduction of the Joseph stories because it prefigures the main question to be asked and the main answer given, namely, that Israel must seek its survival in abiding by the moral law, not in abandoning it. That goes deeper, I think, than has been gone before, but not yet deep enough. If all these stories are about what may be done legitimately to assure the continuity of the Hebrew people, our analysis must reach back to their ultimate guarantor, their God. God's ultimate pledge is that His promises to the patriarchs will be kept, no matter what. Let us review the Judah and Tamar story in this spirit.

If levirate marriage, whatever its variation and form, is about assuring the continuity of the community, the Creator becomes the Preserver as well. The difficulty is that while God wishes His commandments kept, He does not wish to substitute Himself for His people. They must remain free to disobey if their allegiance is to be meaningful. Given human fallibility and temptation to evil, the most the Almighty can do is show the way. And what better way than through reactions to an institution such as the levirate, whose earthly purpose corresponds to His Divine Will.

The beginning of understanding is that the levirate runs counter to material self-interest. While the child does not belong to the brother who plays the part of the levir, he inherits equally, thus reducing the levir's portion. There is a cost to the individual but a benefit only to the name of the deceased or to the persistence of the community.[46] In order to avoid this onus, rabbis in succeeding centuries claimed that the levir himself was the heir to the property involved, thus bringing obligation and reward into concord.[47] Observe that the requirement in Deuteronomy differs:

> When brothers dwell together and one of them dies and leaves no son, the wife of the deceased shall not be married to a stranger, outside the family. Her husband's brother shall unite with her: take her as his wife and perform the levir's duty. The first son that she bears shall be accounted to the dead brother, that his name may not be blotted out in Israel. But if the man does not want to marry his brother's widow, his brother's widow shall appear before the elders in the gate and declare, "My husband's brother refuses to establish a name in Israel for his brother; he will not perform the duty of a levir." The elders of his town shall then summon him and talk to him. If he insists, saying, "I do not want to marry her," his brother's widow shall go up to him in the presence of the elders, pull the sandal off his foot, spit in his face, and make this declaration: Thus shall be done to the man who will not build up his brother's house! And he shall go in Israel by the name of "the family of the unsandaled one." (Deut. 25:5–10)

The terms vary in Tamar's case, as she does not marry Onan or Judah but seeks only to have a son credited to her husband, Er.[48] The difference matters much less, however, than the parallel in that the importance to the community of maintaining the name of the husband is reemphasized through the effort to ridicule the brother who refuses to be the levir. By the same token, a commandment would not be coupled with ridicule were it not difficult to enforce.

In the end, if the deceased's brothers cannot or will not act as levir, it is up to the father. In the story we are analyzing, the role of Judah as paterfamilias is evident. It is he who found a wife for his first son, Er, and upon his death told Onan to "join with your brother's wife and do your duty by her as a brother-in-law, and provide offspring for your brother" (Gen. 38:8).[49] Onan refused and received the death the law pronounces upon the disobedient son.

That is why this story is about Judah. In a morality tale about the perpetuation of a people, the person whose tribe has most nearly sustained itself into the future, the tribe for whom Jews are named, provides the occasion. Judah is the youngest of Leah's sons; if his seed is not carried on, there will be no more after him.[50] In pleading for the life of her son, the woman of Tekoa cried that his death would leave her husband without a name or sons to remember it (2 Sam. 14:7),[51] thereby demonstrating the importance of continuity to a family-centered people. More to my point, if Joseph illustrates the road not to be taken, and if he has already upset the rule of primogeniture, the most moral and the most competent of the remaining sons, the one chosen by God, must carry on the community.

Judah's tale follows after a number of violations of trust in the Jacob family. Reuben violates his father's trust by a wrongful sexual encounter with his father's concubine; Simeon and Levi violate the contract they made with the Shechemites in order, ostensibly, to arrange a peaceful resolution of the violation of their sister Dinah; Judah and his brothers violate their father's trust in regard to their brother's disappearance; and now Judah violates Tamar's trust by making a promise that he knows he will not fulfill. Once he decided not to offer his surviving son, Shelah, to Tamar, thinking that too dangerous, Judah had another alternative—to offer himself—but he does not take that, either. This indirectly provides the occasion for Tamar's intervention to get him to do what he ought to have done in the first place. Brueggemann concludes:

> What is asked of him is that he risk his son for the sake of the community, that he make his son, even his last son, available for the solidarity and future of the community now focused in the person of this defenseless widow. The offense of Judah is like that of Achan (cf. Josh. 7:1; 1 Chron. 2:7) who in fact is Judah's great-great-grandson. It is the sin of looking after private interests at the expense of the community.[52]

"The Judah story is placed here," Judah Goldin declares, "because it was by Judah's counsel that Joseph was sold into slavery and thus Jacob lost a son; hence we are now to be informed how Judah lost two of his own sons."[53] Even if Judah is being paid back son for son, his loss adds poignancy to his hesitation. Unclear about where his duty lies, Judah plays the part of a schemer who is taken in by a superior schemer, Tamar, who schemed more righteously than he.

When Judah says literally that Tamar "is righteous from me," Ramban (Nachmanides, Rabbi Moshe ben Nachman, 1194–1270), observing that Saul said the same to David, acknowledging that he had returned evil for good, writes "the purport of the statement is that Shelah was the brother-in-law, and if he did not wish to take her as his wife, his father is next in line to act as the redeemer."[54] That Judah eventually accepts this understanding will become apparent. When Chronicles reveals that Shelah, Judah's third son, had many children and grandchildren, we know that Judah was able to form his own community.

Judah cannot be said to be a constant man. He gains his Canaanite wife by impetuously turning aside from his brothers, and he meets a disguised Tamar by turning aside without premeditation. He changes his mind often. When Tamar, disguised as a prostitute, speaks to him as a hard-headed businesswoman, Judah takes no offense but agrees on a fee. When Tamar asks for the signs of his authority as a pledge, he gives them to her. Having once condemned Tamar to death, he then takes back the sentence. "In short," O'Callaghan observes, "Judah is presented as a man not in control of his destiny . . . . Tamar could not be more different. . . . She acts decisively and quickly . . . always one move ahead of Judah."[55] It is not only the fact that Tamar wins in the end that captures our attention but the fact that she is the prime mover of the story, making events correspond to her will.[56] There is a clear contrast between Judah's cautious withholding of Shelah and Tamar's courage, since she could expect the penalty for prostitution, let alone incest, to be quite high.[57]

Tamar is forthright. "He denies her a man; she makes him her man."[58] At the time, a young woman either produced children for her husband while remaining faithful to him or was a virgin in her father's house, with no place between.[59] By sending Tamar to her father, Judah makes her an anomaly, a married woman in her parent's home. Should a man rape a woman, he must make restitution by making her his wife, a wife whom, because he has forced her, he can never divorce. This law prevents the occurrence of the nonmarried nonvirgin, just as the practice of the levirate marriage prevents the appearance of another anomaly, the widow without children. Niditch has it exactly right: "The social fabric as a whole is weakened by her [Tamar's] problem and extremely unusual means are allowed to rectify the situation."[60]

Yet Tamar emerges in an advantageous position from a situation fraught with danger. The two sons she bears for her dead husband, Er, are the replacement of the two sons that Judah has lost. Named after the date palm tree, the tree of life in the desert, Tamar is saved because she acts to achieve an honorable purpose, albeit through dishonorable means. To Seybold, "The message seems quite clear. Preservation of the family and propagation of the tribe are natural, and wasting the human seed or failing to impregnate the woman is unnatural. Incest is paradoxically natural under such a compelling natural law."[61] The greater good of propagation in accord with God's will overcomes Tamar's transgression. From a woman originally ordered to be burned, Tamar emerges, through Judah's recognition of the merit of her position, as the mother of kings.[62]

A question remains: Why was a foreign female chosen to play this decisive part in which honor wins out over convention? One possible explanation is that the account was written or edited during Solomon's time, when relations with foreign nations and marriage to foreign women was considered desirable, at least by court writers. More compelling, at least to me, because it speaks with an older and more persistent spirit, is that Tamar is chosen for the same reason as younger sons are, namely, to show God's power by running counter to expectation. Even in Ezra and Nehemiah's time, therefore, when Israelites were forced to give up their foreign wives, locating heroic virtue in a foreign woman would serve to reinforce the view that carrying out God's promise was more important than violation of what ordinarily were strictly enforced commandments.

There are, of course, other spirited women in the Bible, but none meet all the requirements of being counterconventional, being foreign, and saving a Hebrew man by reminding him of the necessity for fidelity to God's commandments. The closest we can come is Moses' wife Zipporah, who intervenes to prevent him from being killed by God's messenger because Moses professes to be going to Egypt to carry out the Lord's will but does not really mean it. Seeing the danger, Zipporah uses a flint to cut off the foreskin of her two sons, thus effectively circumcising them and thereby reminding both God and her man of this major sign of the covenant between them. As a result, God's hand is stayed and Moses identifies his fate with that of his people.[63] A more compressed but equally powerful version of Tamar, Zipporah institutes the substitute sacrifice of circumcision in order to save her husband and, through him, the Hebrew people by reuniting them with God's promise. Like Zipporah, Tamar may also have been the daughter of a priest, which would account for Judah's ordering her to be burned.[64] Were Tamar a priest's daughter, her violation and hence her daring would be even greater.[65]

If Joseph is to be faulted for putting his and his family's survival ahead of the moral law, why, the reader may well ask, is Tamar praised, even admired, for violating that law by deceiving Judah into having intercourse with her? It will help disentangle motives if we inquire more closely into the means and ends entailed in their actions. Tamar plays the prostitute and the deceiver in order to get Judah to fulfill not one but three moral obligations: (1) to give her his son Shelah when his older son Onan refused to act as levir, (2) to fulfill his promise to Tamar that he would do so, and (3) to act as levir if Shelah was not available. Judah sought the survival of his line by violation of the practices designed to secure it, whereas Tamar's violations were incurred in order to secure the survival of the families that make up the community.

Both Joseph's and Tamar's behavior enhance the survival of their family-community, at least in the short run. Joseph's violations, however, are different from Tamar's, for Joseph secures his and his family's survival by assimilation to Egyptian ways so that, in the associative logic of the Bible, he ends up using their oppressive political means in Pharaoh's behalf. Over time, surely enough, the means become the ends as a later Pharaoh makes slaves of Joseph's descendants.

This is where the ends (or objectives) come in: survival, of course. How could God's promises to the patriarchs to make of their family a great people otherwise come to pass? But that is not the only promise. This people is to become God's people. In order for that promise to be fulfilled, the people of Israel must maintain fidelity to their own customs and laws, the customs in their case being part of their laws. Judah violates a custom that is part and parcel of the survival of Hebrew families. Failure to provide a proper levir, therefore, is a sin against the community. Tamar, by contrast, commits an individual, not a communal, sin aimed at securing the survival of the community by exemplifying fidelity to its practices.

Though the institution of the levirate has fallen into disuse, its spirit still lives. What better way to make evident the necessity to sacrifice the parts for the whole in order that the collective may live? And what better way to demonstrate God's commitment to His people than by imagining Him as the grand levir? Looked at in this light, God's promise to the patriarchs is that if all else fails He will act for his people as the Levir of Last Resort.

Following the tradition of doubling, we shall reconsider once more the story of Tamar and Judah. Following precedent, we shall choose stories in which Tamar is confirmed (the story of Ruth) and in which Judah is denied, as he himself agrees (the story of Potiphar's wife, in which Joseph acts as Judah should have done, that is, to save his family by upholding God's law).

"Ruth Speaks That Which Tamar Thought"[66]

Chaim Chertok demonstrates the close relationship between the stories of Judah and Tamar and of Ruth and Naomi:

> The very first line of *Ruth* invokes Judah: Elimelekh, Naomi's husband, "went from Bethlehem of Judah" to Moab. A host of subsequent details, reversals, and echoes argue that the connection between the two . . . is more than genetic, more than thematic. Judah's two older sons die; Naomi's two sons die. Childless Tamar is sent to her father's house; childless Ruth is (mis)directed to her mother's. Judah and Boaz are a generation older than Tamar and Ruth. In her first meeting with Boaz, Ruth is amazed that Boaz should "recognize" her (2:10); "recognize" is the operational keyword which is employed repeatedly in *Genesis* 38 to define the drifting relations between Tamar and Judah. The widow's device in the former is to cover her face; in the latter it is to uncover Boaz. . . . Both stories close with Davidic genealogy.[67]

Since we are interested in Ruth insofar as her story illuminates that of Tamar, I begin by going back to the time when Onan, instead of refusing his obligation, sought to hide his default (though, of course, it could not be hidden from God). Had Onan been honest about his refusal, Tamar could have shamed him by loosening his shoe, according to the Deuteronomic provision, thus putting herself in a position to appeal either to the next son in line or to Judah.[68] Thus Tamar could gain her rightful place only by strong and independent action. What about Ruth?

The story begins by relating how Naomi (a Hebrew living in a foreign country due to famine in Israel) and her two daughters-in-law were widowed (colorfully, their Hebrew husbands have names that could be called "weakly" and "sickly").[69] Naomi advises them to act in their self-interest by returning to homes where they would be supported and have better opportunities to find new husbands. Naomi says she is too old to have a husband and it would take too long, even if she had one and could conceive, for her son to grow up and marry her daughters-in-law. Then Ruth, in her famous language, refuses, "for whither thou goest, I will go; and . . . thy people shall be my people, and thy God my God," ending that only "death part thee and me" (Ruth 1:16–17). This statement, Chertok observes, is an affirmation more powerfully redolent of marriage vows than those issuing from a daughter-in-law.[70] Ruth is a Moabitess.

Lacking support, that is, not having a husband or son, Ruth goes into the fields of Boaz, a relative of Naomi, to subsist by picking up the leftovers from the grain harvest. Impressed by her behavior, Boaz, her rich but fairly remote relative, keeps his young men from troubling her and arranges for her to have a better harvest. Taking Boaz's hint, Naomi advises Ruth to make herself attractive and seduce Boaz after he has finished work. Naomi does not go herself because she no longer wishes to be a wife or bear children even if she could. But she does wish to see her devoted daughter-in-law properly settled. So she devises a stratagem more subtle than it first appears: Naomi signals Boaz that he can do his duty by her by marrying Ruth.

Here is the story:

> And when Boaz had eaten and drunk, and his heart was merry, he went to lie down at the end of the heap of corn: and she [Ruth, as Naomi had prearranged] came softly, and uncovered his feet, and laid her down. And it came to pass at midnight, that the man was afraid, and turned himself: and, behold, a woman lay at his feet. And he said, Who art thou? And she answered, I am Ruth thine handmaid: spread therefore thy skirt over thine handmaid; for thou art a near kinsman. And he said, Blessed be thou of the Lord, my daughter: for thou has shewed more kindness in the latter end than at the beginning, inasmuch as thou followedst not young men, whether poor or rich. (Ruth 3:7-10)

Uncovering the feet, again, is an unmistakable reference to the genitals. When compared with the roughness and crudity of Tamar, not to say Potiphar's wife, Ruth is relatively discreet in asking Boaz to drape their bodies. Compare also Judah's confession to Boaz's declaration that Ruth is essentially right because she chose him to perform his duty for her dead husband rather than going outside the family to a younger man. The implication is that she can have his child. He understands Naomi's plan to substitute her daughter-in-law for her, and he falls in with it.[71]

Four times we are told that Ruth, upon Naomi's instruction, lay down at Boaz's feet in their tryst on the threshing floor. The text is deliberately salacious, and it can be argued that it is even more salacious than it sounds.[72] Carmichael is fully justified in arguing that Ruth's behavior suggests "sexual symbolism similar to that of the sandal and foot in the Deuteronomic levirate ceremony. She is to be his 'sandal,' symbolically indicating to him that he should put it on, at the place of his 'feet,' that is, the genital region."[73]

Opinion is split over whether spreading the skirt is indicative of a desire for intercourse only or for marriage as well. To continue with

Carmichael, "Just as Ruth uncovers Boaz's 'feet' so he can put on his 'sandal(s),' she now indirectly requests him to uncover his loins by removing her skirt and directly asks him to put it over her (nakedness). In neither case will the sandal or skirt be put on in the literal sense." When it is said in Deuteronomy, for instance, that a son ought not to uncover his father's skirt, the plain meaning is that he is not to have intercourse with his father's wife, she constituting the skirt-cum-cover of their sexual relations.[74]

Boaz's moral awakening, like Judah's, is preceded by sexual seduction. As in the earlier model, suggestive phrases—"get thee down to the floor," "laid her down," "blessed be he that did take knowledge of thee," "go in," "uncover" (Ruth 2-3 inter alia)—ends with the suggestion, as Carmichael has it, that Boaz "will put her on as his new footwear."[75] But there is a fly, a nearer relative, in the ointment.

A little vocabulary is in order. Strictly speaking, the levir is the brother of the deceased who gives his widow a son to carry on his name. A goel is a close relation who buys property to keep it within the family.[76] The story of Ruth and Naomi mixes up the two roles, quite possibly deliberately.

Promising to do "the part of a kinsman to thee, as the Lord liveth" (Ruth 3:13), Boaz informs her that there exists a nearer relative who could perform this duty but, if not, he surely will. Immediately we learn that while Naomi is apparently poor, she is about to sell family property to an outsider. The next day Boaz finds the relative and asks him to redeem the land. This the nearer relative agrees to do. But when he hears that Boaz wants him to redeem the inheritance of Naomi's husband by acting as the redeemer, the kinsman declines, saying that his inheritance would be impaired, that is, diluted.[77] Boaz then steps in as a goel and buys the land, stating that he has taken Ruth the Moabitess (her foreign lineage stressed) as his wife "to raise up the name of the dead upon his inheritance, that the name of the dead be not cut off from among his brethren" (Ruth 4:10). Assuming that the same rules apply to Boaz as to his kinsmen, he was making a considerable sacrifice.[78] But his enthusiasm suggests he receives something valuable as well.

Boaz tells the unnamed kinsman, "What day thou buyest the field of the hand of Naomi, thou must buy it also of Ruth the Moabitess, the wife of the dead, to raise up the name of the dead upon his inheritance" (Ruth 4:5). Is it Naomi, the seductive younger woman or Naomi, the smart lady long past her prime, who the nameless relative would have to marry? David Daube thinks Boaz made it deliberately vague so he would end up with Ruth. Boaz makes it appear that the nearer kinsman would have to marry the elderly Naomi while only playing the part of the levir with Ruth. The pleasure of her youthful company would last only until she conceives a child, but, as a consequence, the inheritance of his own sons would have to be shared with the newcomer. The nearer relative figures he is getting the worst of both worlds, marrying the elderly Naomi while paying for land that would belong to Ruth's child. Only after the other relative has refused does Boaz say it is Ruth he will marry. Yet Naomi is the far closer blood relation.

André Lacocque offers a related interpretation. In his view, the nearer relative is willing to buy the property from Naomi as her levir because she is too old to marry him and to have a child. "But now, Naomi is replaced by a young woman, so that serving as *go'el* of Naomi's property—not too bad a business—means also serving as *levir* to Ruth—potentially a disastrous affair [as her child would be heir]."[79]

The relative remains unnamed and unknown because he has chosen not to participate in the family line leading to King David.[80] I propose that the author of Ruth had in mind Deuteronomy 25:10, which sets out the consequences for one who does not do his duty as a levir: his name is to be forgotten! This ties in with Judah, for he was trying to preserve his family line, but by the way he did it (refusing the levir to Tamar), he actually endangered his line. Tamar is the heroine, for she is the one who, by forcing Judah to act as levir, preserves Judah's line.

There were, as usual, competing schools of thought and practice in Israel regarding the ownership of land. There was the one that has preoccupied us about God being the owner who gave the land to the people with its implied moral gloss against the sale of this divine resource; and there was also commercial law about buying and selling land accompanied by customary practices. No doubt, as Horst declares, "The two principles were impossible to reconcile."[81]

The institution of the goel, a levir of property, so to speak, was designed to move ordinary commercial considerations into a path that would uphold continuity of land possession: "If your brother is in straits and has to sell part of his holding, his nearest redeemer shall come and redeem what his brother has sold" (Lev. 25:25). The term *goel*, as Daube demonstrates, ". . . primarily suggests the return of men or things into their own legitimate place . . . . The word simply denotes the rightful getting back of a person or object that had once belonged to one or one's family but had been lost."[82]

The meaning of the goel's purpose and action is to restore property to its original owner.[83] The difficulty with the standard interpretation, as Gordis argues, is that neither Naomi nor Ruth has any land to sell whatsoever. "There is not the slightest indication that Naomi possesses any land . . .," Gordis observes, "or that she has acquired any before or since her return . . . ."[84] Part of the difficulty in interpretation, as Millar Burrows observes, lies in the fact that we have in Ruth a combination of three institutions that are not found together elsewhere: levirate marriage, redemption, and inheritance are all familiar to the reader of the Old Testament, but only here are all three combined.[85] In the levirate marriage the first-born son of the union is the heir to the deceased husband. In redemption, the redeemer (the goel) buys the property, which therefore becomes a part of his own estate. Further difficulties are caused by the fact that Boaz buys Elimelech's land from Naomi, who thus appears as her husband's heir, though ancient Hebrew law did not recognize widows as heirs of their husband's property.[86] Ingenious excuses have been offered; perhaps Naomi's husband, Elimelech, had given her a life contract to the property or she had inherited property from her family. Such a circumstance would have convicted Naomi of gross callousness in sending poor, presumably travel-weary Ruth out to perform the lowliest of work, the gleaning of wheat left behind by others, when she was rich.[87] For a kinsman to purchase land from a kinswoman, moreover, would not imply the levirate relationship.[88] Ruth is definitely not inherited as a part of the estate, as is supposed by those who regard her marriage as an extension of levirate marriage and consider the latter a form of inheritance. Boaz does not inherit Ruth; he acquires her along with the field, which he purchases as redeemer.[89] Something quite different is going on.

There are, in fact, two transactions, not one. The transactions completed, Boaz, who should know better than anyone what he has done, urges the people to witness "that I have bought all that was Elimelech's, and all that was [his sons'] Chilion's and Mahlon's, of the hand of Naomi. Moreover Ruth the Moabitess, the wife of Mahlon, have I purchased to be my wife, to raise up the name of the dead upon his inheritance" (Ruth 4:9-10). At one and the same time, therefore, Boaz signifies that he wishes to be both levir and goel,[90] that he bought the land that belonged to Elimelech and his sons to keep it within the family, and separately, but concurrently, that he is marrying Ruth, Mahlon's wife, in order that her dead husband's name be preserved.

A clue comes as usual from a prior episode in which a woman treats a child of another woman as essentially her own. As Rachel, then unable to conceive, said to Jacob, "Here is my maid Bilhah. Consort with her, that she may bear on my knees and that through her I too may have children" (Gen. 30:3). When the child of Boaz and Ruth was born, the Bible says that "Naomi took the child, and laid it in her bosom, and became nurse unto it" (Ruth 4:16). Indeed, Naomi's female neighbors specifically state that "There is a son born to Naomi" (Ruth 4:17), not only or even primarily a son born to Ruth. The book closes with the birth of their son, Obed, the grandfather of David.

How extraordinarily clever! How determined and single-minded! As soon as Naomi heard that Boaz had reacted favorably to Ruth, Naomi conceived not exactly a child but the next best thing, namely, kindling a passion in an older man for a younger woman so that all their needs, Ruth's for a husband and children, Naomi's for a protector, and Boaz's to marry a young woman, are served.

The outcome of the story follows:

> And all the people that were in the gate, and the elders, said, We are witnesses. The Lord make the woman that is come into thine house like Rachel and like Leah, which two did build the house of Israel: . . . and be famous in Bethlehem: And let thy house be like the house of Pharez, whom Tamar bare unto Judah, of the seed which the Lord shall give thee of this young woman. So Boaz took Ruth, and she was his wife: and when he went in unto her, the Lord gave her conception, and she bare a son. And the women said unto Naomi, Blessed be the Lord, which hath not left thee this day without a kinsman, that his name may be famous in Israel. And he shall be unto thee a restorer of thy life, and a nourisher of thine old age: for thy daughter in law, which loveth thee, which is better to thee than seven sons, hath born him. And Naomi took the child, and laid it in her bosom, and became nurse unto it. And the women her neighbours gave it a name, saying, There is a son born to Naomi; and they called his name Obed: he is the father of Jesse, the father of David. (Ruth 4:11-17)

Ruth the Moabitess is compared to Rachel and Leah, mothers of Israel, and as a reward is linked to King David so as to "be famous in Bethlehem," as the grandmother of David.

Part of the short story of Ruth lies on the surface and part is buried. The surface part is full of symmetries. The book begins and ends on the theme of the continuity of the people and the threats to it. Famine in the land and the deaths of Naomi's husband and her sons at the outset are counterpoised against Ruth's joy of a child, whom Naomi miraculously suckles in the end. In the middle there are parallel harvest scenes in which seeds of grain are intended to be compared to human seeds, the grain harvest to procreation. The fact that Boaz arranges for Ruth to glean more grain than a person in whom he is less interested might do, and that, after Ruth sets her snares for him, Boaz gives her six measures of barley, placing it in her apron—surely an allusion to her coming impregnation through marriage—is plain enough. When Naomi at first tells the women of the community not to call her by her name, which means pleasant, but instead to call her Mara for bitter "for the Almighty hath dealt very bitterly with me" (Ruth 1:20), and when she later blesses the Lord for having been good to her and to Ruth, the profound change is evident. Naomi describes herself as "empty" (1:21) (presumably with neither husband nor child) upon returning to the land of Israel, and both by God's hand. Boaz tells Ruth when he gives her barley, "Go not empty unto thy mother in law" (3:17). And when Ruth gives birth, Naomi's "empty" condition is rectified.[91]

Imbuing sexual attraction with a moral purpose, joining lust to virtue, requires some explanation. As short a story as Ruth is, there are six repetitions of the fact that she was a Moabitess. The overall moral of the story is evident: the perpetuation of the land in the possession of its original owners, the families of Israel, is so desirable that foreign women, including, as in the Judah and Tamar episode, their outrageous sexual behavior, which was otherwise subject to severe sanction, may even be praised.

Joseph has no such alternative; in his relations with Mrs. Potiphar, the wife of his Egyptian master, Joseph must choose between an unlawful liaison or imprisonment or worse. Where Tamar and Naomi choose to use sex to maintain their communities, Joseph refuses sex to maintain his obedience to God's law. Though he could not have known Mosaic law, he is evidently aware of what the God of the Hebrews requires.

Mrs. Potiphar

The telling of a story from different perspectives, the Rashomon of our times, is a biblical specialty. Like the multiple dreams Joseph interpreted, his experiences of subjugation are essentially the same. After

Joseph's brothers sell him to nomadic traders, who in turn sell him to Potiphar, a high Egyptian official (he is twice sold, a neat instance of doubling), he gets ahead as a young man as he did as a boy through the favor of older men: first Potiphar, then the nameless jailer, then the royal cupbearer, and finally Pharaoh, the hierarch of hierarchs. Whether at home or a slave or the honcho of the prison keeper or, indeed, Pharaoh's chief administrator, Joseph is the favorite of whoever is in charge of however small or large a household. Whether he is supervising Potiphar's staff or reporting on his brother's misdeeds, he acts for the head man. At the same time, Joseph's sterling performance for his patrons exemplifies a continuously consistent theme of biblical life: the rulers and nations who help Hebrews in the Diaspora are enriched because they receive God's blessing.

The paradox for Joseph is that he keeps going down in order to get up in the world. His progress is not conventional: "It is better to be the favored son than the favored slave," Seybold points out, "Better to be the favored slave than the favored prisoner."[92] With each step down, however, Joseph moves closer to high office, the pit bringing him to Potiphar and Potiphar's prison bringing him to Pharaoh.

As always, outside the family context Joseph is successful. Seeing that everything he did prospered, Potiphar took this as a sign of divine favor. So, the Torah tells us, "he took a liking to Joseph. He made him his personal attendant and put him in charge of his household, placing in his hands all that he owned" (Gen. 39:4), and "with him there, he paid attention to nothing save the food that he ate" (Gen. 39:6). Standing for nurturance, this food is a euphemism for Potiphar's wife. At the same time, the passage alludes to the familiar situation in which the hands we consider most trustworthy are in a position to deprive us of our most precious objects.[93]

Aside from the abundant marks of success that lead Potiphar, then the jailer, then the Pharaoh to leave their day-to-day operations in Joseph's able hands, two quite different episodes punctuate the life of Jospeh as slave and then as prisoner. Being bought by Potiphar explains how Joseph came to Egypt and what happened to him once he got there. In the second story, Joseph's ingenuity in interpreting the dreams of two high officials gets him out of prison, into Pharaoh's entourage, and thence in charge of famine operations.

But what is the purpose of the little drama we are about to discuss: the attempted seduction of Joseph by his patron's wife, the importunate person who, though never named, I shall call Mrs. Potiphar? Some of the time spent in wondering why the account of the relationship between Tamar and Judah appears in the midst of the Joseph stories might more profitably be devoted to asking what the appearance of Mrs. Potiphar contributes to our understanding of the Joseph stories. How, in particular, does the story of Mrs. Potiphar relate to what has gone on immediately before the tale of Judah and Tamar, Joseph's near killing by his brothers and his sale into slavery, and what will come after, Joseph's ascension to power in Pharaoh's regime?

"Now Joseph was well built and handsome" (Gen. 39:6). This statement, undoubtedly meant to explain Potiphar's wife's attraction to Joseph, is extraordinary on several counts. No man in the Bible, with the possible exception of David, is so described. Indeed, such adjectives are usually applied to women. Joseph's mother, Rachel, is described in identical terms to explain why Jacob preferred her to Leah, her less lovely sister: "Rachel was shapely and beautiful" (Gen. 29:17). The Torah does not physically describe its major characters except where it is absolutely necessary, for example, to differentiate David from his brothers or from Goliath by his size and age, to show the superiority of the Lord's vision. Jeansonne gives new meaning to the statement that Joseph was attractive by reminding his readers "that Abraham's assessment of Sarah's beauty led to her endangerment and that Jacob's immediate love for Rachel was complicated by her father and sister. By recalling these incidents, the narrator encourages us to surmise that Joseph is in danger."[94]

In the Bible, individuals are judged not by how they look but by how they behave, not in contemplation but in action. In short, describing Joseph this way is not necessarily a compliment. Nor is it a final judgment on whether the beauty of his countenance will be paralleled by the loveliness of his deeds.

The following sentence has few parallels in the Bible: "After a time, his master's wife cast her eyes upon Joseph and said, 'Lie with me'" (Gen. 39:7). For sheer brazenness, this is hard to beat,[95] though Judah's request to Tamar and Jacob's demand to Laban that he marry Rachel after working seven years for her—"Give me my wife . . . that I may consort with [literally "go into"] her" (Gen. 29:21)—come close. Mrs. Potiphar's phrase is a combination of the urgency of her desire and Joseph's position as a slave. That a high-ranking woman should give herself to a slave is awkward. Her feelings are mixed, combining lust with loss of status. She does not feel right, evidently, in treating Joseph either as lover or as slave. Consequently, to hide her loss of honor, she commands a love that cannot be commanded. The Hebrew words suggest as well a certain softening of her commands, while they can also be interpreted as requests for intimacy apart from the sexual.[96]

Joseph refuses. Since Potiphar had withheld nothing from him except his wife, Joseph asks rhetorically, "How then could I do this most wicked thing, and sin before God?" (Gen. 39:9). The Torah is ingenious, using words suggesting that despite her continuous coaxing, Joseph "did not yield to her request to lie beside her, to be with her" (Gen. 39:10).

One day when Joseph enters the house to do his work he finds only Mrs. Potiphar there, and she again asks him to lie with her, but he flees, leaving her holding onto his cloak (the double entendre is not in the Hebrew). Immediately she calls to all who can hear that Joseph has tried to rape her but that she has resisted his advances, pulling off his garment in the process. She holds on to that garment all day, whether to remind herself of what she has lost or to show her husband the evidence of attempted rape. Twice she says that "the Hebrew slave whom you brought into our house came to me to dally with me"(Gen. 39:17). Anti-Semitism, perhaps just xenophobia, is used against Joseph despite his devotion to duty. Moral passivity, blaming an outside force, is no more a successful defense for Mrs. Potiphar than it would be for Pharaoh's administrator.

Twice Potiphar's wife accuses Joseph. The first time she speaks in words similar to those Judah used when soliciting Tamar: "This one came to lie with me; but I screamed loud" (Gen. 39:14). The second time, keeping Joseph's coat beside her, as if she could not bear to let even that much go, she states, "when I screamed at the top of my voice, he left his coat with me and fled outside" (Gen. 39:18). The cloak of her passion and of her deceit makes credible the screams she must utter if, according to Hebraic law, a woman is to escape blame for adultery.[97] Her ambiguity in referring to what happened—"Does she mean to say the Hebrew servant, whom he [Potiphar] brought to them came to insult her? Or does she say that he brought the Hebrew servant to them to insult her?"[98]—allows her alternatively to blame her husband and Joseph. The difference is that in Judaism adultery with a married woman is a sin against God, and therefore the husband cannot waive the penalty, whereas under the law of other nations adultery is a sin against the husband, who can therefore alter the penalty as Potiphar does by keeping Joseph alive, so there will be other stories to tell.[99] Indeed, Mrs. Potiphar was not under Hebraic law; she was an Egyptian.

Whatever the reasons Potiphar's wife had for her behavior (some commentators believe that the word for courtier in Hebrew also means eunuch, which would certainly make the wife needy[100]), Joseph's behavior is morally impeccable. He argues not only that adultery is bad in itself but that God's moral law is binding even when He appears not to be present. The primary sin is not against the husband but against God. In order to leave the wife a way out, Joseph, harking back to the emphasis on the marriage relationship in the wife-sister stories, always refers to her as his master's wife. "The fear of God," Benno Jacob comments, "consists in respecting that which another man has reserved for himself."[101] Nothing could be more delicate in view of the circumstances, or daring in view of the risk, or moral in view of the pressure.

Yet "delicacy" does not at all describe Joseph's relationship with his brothers. Nor does his heightened consciousness of the duty he owes to his master correspond with his sense of duty he owes his father. In the episode of Potiphar's wife we have, it is true, evidence of Joseph the moral exemplar; but we also have a criticism by comparison of Joseph's quite different behavior toward the members of his family. His "company manners" should not hide from us the chasm that separates his behavior toward those he left behind from those who are present.

Some see Joseph as especially virtuous because he resists continuous importuning from a figure who could amply reward him. The dialogue in the sayings of *The Fathers According to Rabbi Nathan* is scintillating:

> When that wicked woman came along she kept outraging him by her words. She said to him: "I shall shut thee up in prison!" He answered: "The Lord looseth the prisoners" (Ps. 146:7). She said to him: "I shall put out thine eyes!" He answered: "The lord openeth the eyes of the blind" (Ps. 146:8). "I shall make thee to stoop!" she said. "The Lord raiseth them that are bowed down" (ibid.), he retorted. "I shall fill thee with wickedness!" she said. "The Lord loveth the righteous" (ibid.), he retorted.[102]

Joseph is almost too good.

Is Mrs. Potiphar a deliberate contrast with Mrs. Tamar Er, the wife of Judah's deceased son? The disparities are striking. One is of high status, the other a widow who is being deceived sexually in that the proper levir is being withheld from her. Mrs. Potiphar is deceiving her husband by seeking intercourse with Joseph. In both instances, there is a blunt demand for sex, but Mrs. Potiphar says the words herself while Tamar waits for Judah to utter them. Most striking is the difference in motive between Mrs. Potiphar, who seeks her personal pleasure, and Mrs. Er, who seeks to preserve her husband's soul and, with it, the continuity of his community. Even when threatened with a horrible death by burning, Tamar neither lies nor implicates her father-in-law and soon-to-be-father of her child, Judah, but rather informs him discreetly that he is the guilty party. Mrs. Potiphar admits of no wrongdoing, compounding her sin by lying and subjecting the man she wanted to make love to her to imprisonment or worse.

Are we regaled with Mrs. Potiphar's antics in order to disparage Judah, who deceived Tamar, had sex with a woman he believed to be a prostitute, and almost had her killed for his own misdeed; are we to compare him with noble Joseph whose refusal to engage in illicit sex, at least against a man who had helped him, landed him in a dungeon? It seems so; yet it is out of character for the Torah to portray a human being as wholly good.

Perhaps a more subtle point is being made. Just as Tamar is in a much weaker position than Mrs. Potiphar, before his elevation to power Joseph is in a lot weaker position than Tamar. Weaker in position and wealth as they are, Joseph and Tamar are higher in moral status. Both seek to carry out God's will, Tamar positively by heeding the commandment to be fruitful and Joseph negatively by refusing to sin against God by taking another man's wife. What will happen, the implied question is, when Joseph has power? Whom will he emulate?

Joseph's encounter with Mrs. Potiphar is joined to the story that precedes it by tangible signs. Man's sexual temptation and womanly deception are central to both stories. An item of clothing figures large in both stories. Joseph's blood-stained coat signified his father's favoritism and his brothers' deception; the inner cloak that Potiphar's wife holds onto as evidence that Joseph tried to rape her is similarly misleading.[103] The goat into whose blood Joseph's garment was dipped, the goat that Tamar asks for in return for her sexual services, and Joseph's becoming the sacrificial goat for his master's wife's intrigues, keep the parallel going.[104] An eye for an eye, deceit for deceit, a coat that humiliated his brothers is metaphorically replaced by a coat in Mrs. Potiphar's hands that humiliates Joseph. "And as the brothers used his coat as circumstantial evidence for his death," Lowenthal notices, "so the woman is about to use it to 'prove' his crime."[105] As always, however, the most important connection is moral: How far should Joseph go in order to secure his own preservation?

One could ask exactly how did Joseph end up in this dangerous situation? Being the head man, he would have known where each servant would be at all times and therefore would have known when his master's wife would be alone in the house. Why did he still enter? When Potiphar's wife charges that Joseph "came in" to her, Jeansonne observes, "the phrase can also mean sexual penetration."[106] Did he trust himself so much? Or does Joseph's entry into a house empty except for his temptress reveal an inner struggle?

In a narrative there is more than one way to indicate feelings. A writer might describe Joseph as decisive or as vacillating in rejecting Mrs. Potiphar's advances. Actually neither fits; instead, the word for "he refused," *wayema'en*, "has a rare Masoretic [the official Hebrew version of the Torah] cantillation mark which indicates sustained deliberation (cf. 19:6; 24:12; etc.)."[107] Her ambivalence is illustrated by having her lie down with Joseph's clothes in her hands.[108]

Strangely enough, commentators in the *Midrash* blamed Joseph for leading on his master's wife:

Free from anxieties, he turned his attention to his external appearance. He painted his eyes, dressed his hair and aimed to be elegant in his walk. But God spoke to him saying, "Thy father is mourning in sackcloth and anxious, while thou doest eat, drink and dress thy hair. Therefore I will stir up thy mistress against thee."[109]

As is often the case, the twelfth-century French interpreter Rashi, who is still much read and used today, put it more pungently; he has the Almighty saying "I will enrage the bear, Potiphar, against thee!" The root of this evil, Rashi writes, referring to Joseph's boyhood dreams, began "as soon as Joseph recognized himself as ruler."[110]

Perhaps the most interesting effort to defend Joseph against the view that he was merely cloaking his ambitions comes from the account of this story in the Koran:

At this a member of her own family gave the circumstantial evidence, saying "If the shirt of Joseph is rent from the front, the woman speaks the truth and he is a liar. And if his shirt is rent from the back, she speaks a lie and he is truthful." When the husband saw that the shirt was rent from the back, he said, "This is one of your cunning devices . . . for you were indeed the wrongdoer."[111]

Put this side by side with the account of Aaron and the golden calf: "They [the Hebrew people] gave it [their gold] to me and I hurled it into the fire and out came this calf!" (Exod. 32:24); they have the same tone of shifting the blame. Observe also the use of family language in which husbands and wives speak of "your son" or "your daughter" when the behavior they remark upon is undesirable.

The special term *beged* is employed six times as clothing, perhaps because it has a similar sound to the Hebrew root, *b-g-d*, that is used in cases of marital infidelity.[112] The repetition five times over of words using the Hebrew root for talk, *d-b-r* (Gen. 39:17, 19) suggests that all Mrs. Potiphar's palaver may have been protesting too much.[113]

Joseph the *tzaddik*, the saint, the moral exemplar, the person who is willing to sacrifice himself for devotion to God's law, is the Joseph who, for the right reasons, is willing to face imprisonment or death. In this story he is the opposite of Judah in the preceding Tamar episode, who sought to keep his family going by violating God's law. The next question to be taken up is whether Joseph will remain so faithful when he assumes power.

While Joseph pondered the justice of being thrown into jail because his master's wife subjected him to what today would be called sexual harassment, the chief jailer became favorably disposed toward him. As Joseph's relations with the Potiphar family, husband and wife, came to an end, his prison life continued on much as before. The narrator says that the Lord was with Joseph. Consequently, Joseph was put in charge of all the prisoners and of implementing whatever policy was carried out. The chief jailer did not exercise minute supervision but, on the contrary, gave Joseph the widest possible latitude, as had Potiphar.

Before our eyes a pattern is forming: treated unjustly and harshly, Joseph wins the favor of his master, Potiphar, and then the chief jailer. With each defeat, Joseph meets a higher-ranking patron and advances further. Whether this is desirable is what his stories are about. There can be no doubt that it is informative. Now the interest in dreams that has harmed Joseph is about to help raise him from the living death that is imprisonment.

The story of Joseph's dream interpretations, the subject of the following chapter, will display an interesting correspondence to the episode of Potiphar's wife. Joseph's valuable services for Potiphar—helping his house thrive—and for the butler—preparing him for restitution to his former position by correctly interpreting his dream—are met with imprisonment, in the first instance by Mrs. Potiphar's false accusations and in the second by the butler's forgetfulness as soon as he no longer needed Joseph. The falsification and the negation of memory teach Joseph a valuable lesson about the importance of self-interest in human affairs. From that point on, he knows that good intentions, indeed good deeds, are not enough unless they are perceived by the recipient as being in his own interest.

Notes

1. For my analysis, see Aaron Wildavsky, *The Nursing Father: Moses As a Political Leader* (University of Alabama Press, 1985).
2. Gerhard von Rad, *Genesis: A Commentary* (Philadelphia: Westminster, 1972), 356. Nor is von Rad by any means alone in his conclusions. His great predecessor, Hermann Gunkel, said the same.
3. Claus Westermann, *Genesis 37–50* (Minneapolis, Minn.: Augsburg Publishing House, 1986), 49.
4. Cited in Robert Alter, *The Art of Biblical Narrative* (New York: Basic Books, 1982), 3–4.
5. Robert Davidson, *Genesis 12–50* (Cambridge: Cambridge University Press, 1979), 224.
6. A. S. Herbert, *Introduction and Commentary, Genesis 12–50* (London: SCM Press, 1962), 126.
7. See Robert E. Longacre, *Joseph: A Story of Divine Providence: A Text Theoretical and Textlinguistic Analysis of Genesis 37 and 39–48* (Winona Lake: Eisenbrauns, 1989), 26.
8. R. N. Whybray, "On Robert Alter's *The Art of Biblical Narrative*," *Journal for the Study of the Old Testament* 27 (1983): 75–86; quote on 79.
9. Martin Greenberg, "Judah and Tamar," *Dor le Dor* 16 (1987): 123–25; quote on 124.
10. Benno Jacob, *The First Book of the Bible: Genesis*, His Commentary abridged, ed. and trans. by Ernest I. Jacob and Walter Jacob (New York: KTAV Publishing, 1974), 263.
11. In her "Women's Monumental Mark on Ancient Egypt," Barbara Lesko tells us about an archeological finding that reveals a real Egyptian occurrence that resembles the story of Judah and Tamar, that is, of a father (king of Egypt) who gives his seed to give children to his daughter-in-law, whose husband (his son) cannot (according to medical experts) have children of his own. (Barbara S. Lesko, "Women's Monumental Mark on Ancient Egypt," *Biblical Archeologist* 54, no. 1 (March 1991): 13.)
12. "The death of Judah's wife is probably mentioned as an extenuating circumstance to account for his consorting with a harlot." Nahum M. Sarna, *The JPS Torah Commentary: Genesis* (Philadelphia: Jewish Publication Society, 1989), 267.
13. The commentators reasoned that Er was deemed wicked because "he would 'plough on the roof' [having sexual relations anally and so avoiding conception]" (Jacob Neusner, *Genesis Rabbah: The Judaic Commentary to the Book of Genesis: A New*

American Translation, vol. 3, Parashiyyot Sixty-Eight through One Hundred on Genesis 28:10 to 50:26 (Atlanta, Georgia: Scholars Press, 1985), 209). This interpretation shows that they also understood the story to be about fulfilling God's command to procreate. Er is said to be "evil in the eyes of the LORD," fulfilling the reverse of his name in Hebrew "ra'" which means "evil" (Fokkelien van Dijk-Hemmes, "Tamar and the Limits of Patriarchy Between Rape and Seduction (2 Samuel 13 and Genesis 38)," in *Anti-Covenant: Counter-Reading Women's Lives in the Hebrew Bible*, Mieke Bal, ed. (Sheffield: Almond Press, 1989), 147.

14. Driver has pointed out that the particular construction used here should be understood as a frequentative use of the perfect and translated "whenever he went in" instead of "when he went in." S. R. Driver, *The Book of Genesis* (New York: Edwin S. Gorham, 1905), 328; Ronald J. Williams, *Hebrew Syntax: An Outline*, 2nd ed. (Toronto: University of Toronto Press, 1976), 85; E. Kautzsch, ed., *Gesenius' Hebrew Grammar*, rev. ed., A. E. Cowley (Oxford: Clarendon Press, 1910), 336.

15. C.F. DeVine, "The Sin of Onan Gen. 38:8-10," *Catholic Bibilical Quarterly* 4 (1942): 336-37.

16. Anthony Phillips, "Another Look at Adultery," *Journal for the Study of the Old Testament* 20 (1981): 7.

17. Raymond Westbrook, *Property and the Family in Biblical Law* (Sheffield, England: Journal for the Study of the Old Testament Press, 1991), 76.

18. Calum M. Carmichael, "A Ceremonial Crux: Removing a Man's Sandal as a Female Gesture of Contempt," *Journal of Biblical Literature* 96 (1977): 329.

19. Mary Douglas, *Purity and Danger* (London, Routledge & Kegan Paul, 1966), 118-123.

20. Mars cites Johannes Pederson's magisterial, *Israel: Its Life and Culture* (London: Oxford University Press, 1926), 436.

21. Rashi reasonably construes Judah's comment to mean he feared that any man Tamar married would die. (*"Rashi" on the Pentateuch: Genesis*, trans. and annotated by James H. Lowe (London: Hebrew Compendium Publishing Co, 1928), 406). Thus, Judah's fear was not only for a particular son but for the survival of his family, which required male heirs.

22. See the interesting discussion in Sarah Ben-Reuven, "I will be the Pledge and you may require him of my hand," *Beth Mikra* 33 (1987/88): 337.

23. There is no certain evidence about whether Tamar is dressed as a temple prostitute or whether there actually was such a position.

24. Sharon Pace Jeansonne, *The Women of Genesis: From Sarah to Potiphar's Wife* (Minneapolis, Minn.: Fortress Press, 1990), 100.

25. For this reason, the rabbis advocated getting to recognize the female members of your own family.

26. "The fact that Judah carried nothing at that moment with which to pay for the woman's services proves that he acted on impulse in 'turning aside to her by the road'—another example of the biblical motif of God using human frailty for His own purposes" (Sarna, *Genesis*, 268).

27. A cylindrical shaped object, "When rolled across the soft surface of a clay tablet it served as a man's signature; hence it was usually worn suspended from the neck as a handy form of identification" (Bruce Vawter, *A Path Through Genesis* (New York: Sheed and Ward, 1956), 250).

28. "Philo . . . contrasts Judah's pledges to Tamar with the gold 'collar' and 'royal ring' which Pharaoh gave to Joseph" [*On Dreams*, 244 (Judah Goldin, "The Youngest

Son or Where Does Genesis 38 Belong," *Journal of Biblical Literature*, 96 (1977): 27-44; quote on 28.)

29. Westermann, *Genesis 37-50*, 66.
30. Gary A. Rendsburg, *The Redaction of Genesis* (Winona Lake, Indiana: Eisenbrauns, 1986), 84.
31. Edwin M. Good, "The 'Blessing' on Judah, Gen. 49, 8-12," *Journal of Biblical Literature* 82 (1963): 427-32; at 429-30. Good cites passages in 2 Kings 18-27; Isaiah 36:17-20; and Ezekiel 16:25. Staff or scepter is treated as a sign of leadership or royalty. See Isaiah 14:5 and Ezekiel 19:11-14. For extensive discussion of Moses' staff as a sign of leadership and a snare to those who might think they are divine, see my *The Nursing Father*.
32. Charles T. Fritsch, "God Was With Him: A Theological Study of the Joseph Narrative," *Interpretation* 9 (1955): 21-34; at 23. Umberto Cassuto ("The Story of Tamar and Judah," *Biblical and Oriental Studies* (Jerusalem: Magnes Press, 1973), 30) points out that "the Talmudic sages already noted that the parallel provided by the word hakar-na' [discern]; see *B. Sota* 10b, and *Gen. Rabba*, secs. lxxxiv, lxxxv. Possibly other parallels may be added: se'ir 'iziym ['he-goat'] in xxvii 31 and gedy 'iziym ['a kid of the goats'] in xxvii 17-20 (*Gen. Rab.* sec. lxxxvii): waym'an lhitnchom ['and he refused to be comforted'] in xxvi 35 and vaynchom yhudah ['and Judah was comforted'] in xxvii 12 (*Gen. Raba.* sec. lxxiv), and similar analogies."
33. Alter, *Art of Biblical Narrative*, 5-9. This is too literal. In my opinion, the reversal is in the story because, running counter to custom, it shows the glory of God, who alone can prevail against nature.
34. Ibid., 9-10. Or, to quote a commentary over 1500 years old: "The Holy One Praise be He, said to Judah, 'You deceived your father with a kid. By your life, Tamar will deceive you with a kid.' . . . The Holy One Praise Be said to Judah, 'You said to your father, *Hakar-na*, by your life, Tamar will say to you, *Hakar-Na*'" (*Bereshit Rabba*, 84:11-12).
35. Bruce Vawter, *On Genesis: A New Reading* (Garden City, N.Y.: Doubleday, 1977), 400.
36. David Daube, *Studies in Biblical Law* (Cambridge: Cambridge University Press, 1947), 5-6.
37. Neusner, *Genesis Rabbah*, 212.
38. H. H. Rowley, "The Marriage of Ruth," in *The Servant of the Lord and Other Essays on the Old Testament*, 2nd ed. (Oxford: Basil Blackwell, 1965), 176.
39. David Daube, *Sons and Strangers*, the presidential address delivered at the Second International Conference of the Jewish Law Association, New York, 1983. (The Institute of Jewish Law, Boston University School of Law, 1984), 12.
40. Susan Niditch, "The Wronged Woman Righted: An Analysis of Genesis 38," *Harvard Theological Review* 72 (1979): 143-149, at 149.
41. By contrast, Saul tries to put the blame on other people: "*They* have brought them from the Amalekites . . . . to sacrifice unto the Lord *thy* God; and the rest *we* have utterly destroyed" (1 Samuel 15:15) and "Saul said unto Samuel: Yea *I have obeyed the voice of the Lord, and have gone the way which the Lord sent me*" (1 Samuel 15:20), and continues Saul, "*But the people took of the spoil*" (1 Samuel 15:21, emphasis supplied). There are, no doubt deliberately, many parallels between David and Judah. Rendsburg observes that as the King of Tyre, Hiram, was David's mainstay, Judah's friend, Hirah, has a similar name. And there is also only a small difference between the name of Judah's wife, Bat-sua, and David's notorious

Bath-sheba. Gary A. Rendsburg, "David and His Circle in Genesis XXXVIII," *Vetus Testamentum* 36 (1986): 438–446; quote on 442–43.

42. Rendsburg, "David and his Circle in Genesis XXXVIII," see 444.

43. David Daube, "Unjust Enrichment: A Might-Have-Been," *Rechts historisches Journal* 9 (1990): 291–300, quote on 295.

44. Steven D. Mathewson, "An Exegetical Study of Genesis 38," *Bibliotheca Sacra* 146 (October-December 1989): 373–392, at 386.

45. Phyllis Bird, "'To Play the Harlot': An Inquiry into an Old Testament Metaphor," in *Gender and Difference in Ancient Israel*, Peggy L. Day, ed. (Minneapolis, Minn.: Fortress Press, 1989), 75–94, quote on 77.

46. Eryl W. Davies, "Inheritance Rights and the Hebrew Levirate Marriage Part 2," *Vetus Testamentum* 31 (1981): 257–68.

47. Ibid., 258.

48. Westermann, *Genesis 37–50*, 52.

49. David Daube, "Consortium in Roman and Hebrew Law," *The Juridical Review*, 62 (1950): 71–91, see 73.

50. Louis Katzoff, "What's In a Biblical Name?" *Dor le Dor* 9 (1981): 148–49.

51. Isaac Schapera, "The Sin of Cain," in *Anthropological Approaches to the Old Testament, Issues in Relilgion and Theology*, Bernhard Lang, ed. (Philadelphia: Fortress Press, 1985), 26–42; see 40.

52. Walter Brueggemann, *Genesis: A Bible Commentary for Teaching and Preaching*, *Interpretation* series (Atlanta: John Knox Press, 1982), 310.

53. Goldin, "The Youngest Son or Where Does Genesis 38 Belong," 27.

54. Ramban (Nachmanides), *Commentary on the Torah: Genesis*, trans. and annotated by Rabbi Dr. Charles B. Chavel (New York: Shilo Publishing, 1971), 476.

55. Martin O'Callaghan, "The Structure and Meaning of Gen. 38—Judah and Tamar," *Proceedings of the Irish Biblical Association* 5 (1981): 72–97; quote on 77.

56. Johanna W. H. Bos, "Out of the Shadows Genesis 38; Judges 4:17–22; Ruth 3," *Semeia* 42 (1988): 37–67.

57. See Richard Elliott Friedman, "Deception for Deception," *Bible Review* 2 (1986): 22–31; at 30.

58. Ibid.

59. Niditch, "The Wronged Woman Righted: An Analysis of Genesis 38," 145–46.

60. Ibid., 146.

61. Donald A. Seybold, "Paradox and Symmetry in the Joseph Narrative," in *Literary Interpretations of Biblical Narrative*, Kenneth R. R. Gros Louis, ed. (Nashville, Tenn.: Labingdon, 1974), 59–73; quote on 67.

62. Westermann, *Genesis 37–50*, 55.

63. See my *The Nursing Father*, 41–44.

64. Sarna, *Genesis*, 269–70. According to Leviticus 20:14, "If a man marries a woman and her mother, it is depravity; both he and they shall be put to the fire, that there be no depravity among you." The only other violation for which the people involved are to be burned is mentioned in Leviticus 21:9: "When the daughter of a priest degrades herself through harlotry, it is her father whom she degrades; she shall be put to the fire."

65. M. Zipor, "Restrictions On Marriage for Priests (Lev. 21,13–14)," *Biblica* 68 (1987): 259–67; quote on 261.

66. Quoted in Stuart A. West, "Judah and Tamar—A Scriptural Enigma," *Dor le Dor* 12 (1984): 246–52; at 250–51.

67. Chaim Chertock, "The Book of Ruth—Complexities Within Simplicity," *Judaism* 34 (1985): 293-94.
68. Thomas and Dorothy Thompson, "Some Legal Problems in the Book of Ruth," *Vetus Testamentum* 18 (1968): 79-99
69. David Daube, *Ancient Jewish Law: Three Inaugural Lectures* (Leiden: E.J. Brill, 1981), 33.
70. Chertok, "Book of Ruth," 292.
71. Daube, *Ancient Jewish Law*, 39.
72. See, for instance, my discussion of the Zipporah episode in *The Nursing Father*, 42-43.
73. Carmichael, "A Ceremonial Crux," 332-33.
74. Ibid. Suggestions that uncovering the skirt implies marriage may be found in Ezekiel 16:8, where the Lord tells him "behold, thy time *was* the time of love; and I spread my skirt over thee, and covered thy nakedness: yea, I sware unto thee, and entered into a covenant with thee . . . and thou becamest mine." Robertson Smith, in his *Kinship and Marriage in Early Arabia*, states that when a woman became a widow, the heir of the dead man, if he wanted to marry her, could throw his garment over her, thereby securing her dowry unless she got away first to her own people. (Quoted in F. Buhl, "Some Observations on the Social Institutions of the Israelites," *The American Journal of Theology* 1 (1897): 728-740, quote on 734-35.
75. See Calum M. Carmichael, "'Treading' In the Book of Ruth," *Zeitschriftur die Alttestamentliche Wissenschaft* 92 (1980): 248-266; quote on 248. See also Carmichael, "A Ceremonial Crux," 321-336.
76. "Levirate Marriage and Halizah," *Encyclopedia Judaica*, M.E., 11: 11.
77. Davies, "Inheritance Rights," 258-59; Samuel Belkin, "Levirate and Agnate Marriage in Rabbinic and Cognate Literature," *Jewish Quarterly Review* 60 (1970):273-329 at 285.
78. Davies, "Inheritance Rights," 259.
79. André Lacocque, *The Feminine Unconventional: Four Subversive Figures in Israel's Tradition* (Minneapolis, Minn.: Fortress Press, 1990), 98.
80. Edward F. Campbell, Jr., *Ruth, The Anchor Bible* (New York: Doubleday, 1985), 141-43.
81. Quoted in Donald A. Leggett, *The Levirate and Goel Institutions in the Old Testament With Special Attention to the Book of Ruth* (New Jersey: Mack Publishing Co., 1974), 85, from F. Horst, "Das Eigentum nach dem Alten Testament," in Gottes Recht, 1961, 205. See also K. H. Henrey, "Land Tenure in the Old Testament," *Palestine Exploration Quarterly* 86 (1954): 5-15, at 5.
82. David Daube, *Studies in Biblical Law*, 39-40. See also N. H. Snaith, "The Hebrew Root of G'l (one)," *Aluos* 3 (1961/62): 60. There are also distinctions among three different ways that a widow can marry a surviving heir—by redemption, by succession, or by the levirate law. The story of Ruth demonstrates features of redemption marriage but also those of the levirate.
83. Leggett, *Levirate and Goel Institutions*, 2; Snaith, "Hebrew Root."
84. Robert Gordis, "Love, Marriage, and Business in the Book of Ruth: A Chapter in Hebrew Customary Law," in *A Light Unto My Path, Old Testament Studies in Honor of Jacob M. Myers*, Howard N. Bream, Ralph D. Heim, and Carey A. Moore, eds. (Philadelphia: Temple Press, 1974), 254.
85. Millar Burrows, "The Marriage of Boaz and Ruth," *Journal of Biblical Literature* 59 (1940): 445.
86. Ibid., 446.

87. The shocking climax of Irving Louis Horowitz's powerful childhood autobiography comes when, after a lifetime of enforced privation, his mother discovers that her husband had lots of money in various banks. She never spoke to him again. Irving Louis Horowitz, *Daydreams and Nightmares: Reflections on a Harlem Childhood* (Jackson and London : University Press of Mississippi, 1990).

88. Gordis, "Love, Marriage, and Business," 255.

89. Burrows, "Marriage of Boaz and Ruth," 449.

90. The most useful analysis comes from Daube, *Ancient Jewish Law*, 34-47. I have expanded Daube's interpretation. I have also made use of Samuel Belkin, "Levirate and Agnate Marriage," 273-329; Leggett, *Levirate and Goel Institutions*; and Buhl, "Some Observations," 735; from all of whom I have learned something valuable and none of whose interpretations I have adopted entirely. To Buhl, for instance, Naomi, as a woman, cannot be heir to the land as the text at various places suggests. The only possible heir was the next male relative to Naomi's husband, presumably the nameless one. Buhl notes that in the David stories, the wife of the rich but nasty Nabal, Abigail, left the place she lived to go with David, one reason being that however rich her husband, she did not inherit (Buhl, "Some Observations," 735).

91. See the discussion in Chertok, "Book of Ruth," 295.

92. Seybold, "Paradox and Symmetry," 62-63.

93. For such speculations, see Sarna, *Genesis*, 272; and the various traditional interpretations in the *Soncino Chumash: The Five Books of Moses with Haphtaroth*, ed. by the Rev. Dr. A. Cohen (London: Soncino Press, 1966), 242.

94. Jeansonne, *The Women of Genesis*, 110.

95. Sarna, *Genesis*, 273.

96. Note that the phrase "to be with her" in Samuel 13:20 (referring to the rape of Tamar, Absalom's sister, by another of King David's sons, Amnon) is a cover term for intercourse.

97. Howard Jacobson, "A Legal Note on Potiphar's Wife," *Harvard Theological Review* 69 (1976): 177.

98. W. Lee Humphreys, *Joseph and His Family, A Literary Study* (Columbia: University of South Carolina Press, 1988), 72.

99. Nahum M. Sarna, *Understanding Genesis* (New York: McGraw Hill, 1966), 217.

100. Ramban, *Genesis*, 483, 486.

101. Jacob, *Genesis*, 266.

102. *The Fathers According to Rabbi Nathan*, trans. from Hebrew by Judah Goldin (New Haven: Yale University Press, 1955), 83.

103. Seybold, "Paradox and Symmetry," 63.

104. See Sarna, *Genesis*, 263-64, for further connections. An unknown but gifted commentator, aib, Wa-Yesheb, 22a, observes that as Joseph was the cause of two separate tearings of garments—his father's and his brother's (Gen. 34 and 37)—he was punished by having his own garment rendered by Potiphar's wife. Ingenious, but the first cause is at least controversial.

105. Eric I. Lowenthal, *The Joseph Narrative in Genesis* (New York: KTAV Publishing House, 1973), 38.

106. Jeansonne, *The Women of Genesis*, 112.

107. Seybold, "Paradox and Symmetry," 35.

108. John Holbert, "Joseph and the Surprising Choice of God," *Perkins Journal* 38 (1985): 37.

109. Lowenthal, *Joseph Narrative in Genesis*, 75.

110. *"Rashi" on the Pentateuch: Genesis,* trans. and annotated by James H. Lowe (London: Hebrew Compendium Publishing, 1928), 413.
111. S. Abul Maududi, *The Meaning of the Quran,* vol. 5 (Lahore Pakistan: Islamic Publications, 1973), 133.
112. Sarna, *Genesis,* 274.
113. Ibid., 275–76.

3

The Dreamer Is the Dream

In all the stories about Joseph there are six dreams, two by Joseph himself, one each by the butler and the baker, and two by Pharaoh. Each pair is repeated by the person who dreamed it. In each pair, one dream repeats the message of the other, albeit in slightly different form. Thus these are dreams squared, four times told tales whose meaning reveals the character of the dreamer. Each one gets what is coming to him, though not without his wondering if it was what he deserved. Each pair of dreams is more complex than the one that preceded it, in accord, Westermann writes, "with the three forms of society in which the dreams take place—in the family, among the Pharaoh's servants, at the royal court."[1] Clearly, the progression of the dreams as well as their content holds meaning.

Joseph's boyhood dreams are about the younger and weaker brother dominating his older and stronger brothers and parents. For the one who desires power that is denied both by convention and by might, dreams are especially appropriate because things can be imagined that might later occur in the mundane world.[2] "But insofar as a dream is recognized to be inseparable from personality," Sarna interprets, "it meant also that the dreamer . . . bore a measure of responsibility for his dreams. Joseph's visions of lordship, therefore, betrayed his true aspirations and contained, at the same time, the potentiality of fulfillment. That is why they could arouse hostilities so intense as to culminate in a conspiracy to murder."[3] Had Joseph the ability to make his dreams come true, moreover, he might be making himself a god, standing revealed as an idolater.[4] That is one reason why it is important for Joseph to deny that he has this ability, saying that it belongs only to God.

There is ample evidence of Egyptian efforts during ancient times to make dream interpretation a science. In those days it was widely believed that dreams foretold the future. As an extension of the personality of the dreamer, therefore, dreams gave insight into matters, whether hopes or fears, hidden from the direct perception of the dreamer. Not to be able to interpret a dream, especially one that repeated itself, was considered dangerous.[5]

No one has done better than Johannes Pederson to connect the Hebrew concept of the soul or spirit of the dreamer to the content of his dream:

> When Joseph has the power to dream as he did, then this implies a claim. He has had king's dreams, but this can only happen to a king's soul. The fact of being the ruler, before whom the others throw themselves, has passed into his soul and makes it the soul of a ruler, with the demand of the ruler for the subjection of the others. That which happens at a later period, when Joseph stands as the vizier of Egypt, and the brothers lie in the dust before the powerful ruler, is no new situation. It means that the dream of Joseph persisted, was real. His soul was really the soul of a ruler; it must have that kind of dream. Thence the hatred of his brothers. Through his dreams Joseph has become a potential ruler, and some day this potentiality will be fulfilled, unless it be extirpated. Therefore they want to kill him or, at least, to get him out of the way; thus they prevent the persistence of his dream or, what comes to the same thing, they prevent his soul from carrying through its claim, to unfold itself according to its nature.[6]

The Torah knows two kinds of dreams. In one, God speaks to individuals directly, especially to the patriarchs. These are what Benno Jacob calls "divine speeches."[7] The second type belongs to the dreamer and predicts future events. They vary from the two dreams that Joseph recounts to his brothers and father, dreams so self-evident in their desire for domination that they require no further interpretation (as we may gather from the hostility and dismay they cause), to dreams reflecting the character of the dreamer, so that to know him was to know the meaning of his dreams. "Each one," Rashi informs us, "dreamt a dream suggesting the real thing that was to happen to them."[8] Their character was to be their fate.

In Genesis, God comes to people in dreams—Abimelech (20:3) and Laban (31:24)—and speaks to people in dreams—Abimelech (20:6-7) and Jacob (31:11-13). But only in the Joseph narratives do we find the cognate accusative to "dream a dream." This Hebrew mode of expression is common enough in the Bible; in fact, later in discussing parallels between Joseph and Daniel we will find Nebuchadnezzar saying that he had "dreamed a dream" (Dan. 2:3). But in Genesis the idiom is used for dreams only for Joseph (37:5, 6, 9, 10), the Egyptian butler and baker (40:5,8), and Pharaoh (41:15). Later, after Joseph reveals himself to his brothers, he remembers the "dreams he dreamed." In the rest of Genesis dreams are explicitly said to come from God; He is the mover in the dream and its giver. Only with Joseph and the Egyptians do we see the self-centered "I dreamed a dream," as if they had worked it up themselves. Only with them do we find the possessive "his dream" (37:8, 20; 40:5, 9) and "my dream" (40:9, 16; 41:8, 11, 12, 17, 22).

I submit that the dreams of Joseph are deliberately expressed like pagan Egyptian dreams to create doubt about their origin. Thus from the first chapters of the narratives we see Joseph taking on a foreign characteristic. Did he really follow after foreign gods? We cannot be sure; it would seem to be unthinkable. But our narrator certainly leaves sufficient ambiguity for us to consider the possibility.

It is not necessary to take an either/or approach to these dreams. Yes, they are different from the dreams of Abraham and Jacob that the narrator unequivocally states are messages from God. Yes, they do reflect the character of the dreamer. However, the dreams of Joseph, the butler, the baker, and Pharaoh do for the most part come true. This is evidence that they are not pure inventions of the dreamer, that Joseph is not wrong when he says that in the dreams "God has shown . . . what he is about to do." The fact that the Egyptians are pagans does not preclude their receiving divine messages any more than Balaam is precluded from hearing that he must not curse the Israelites (Num. 22:12) just because he is a pagan.

The narrator's silence about the origin of these dreams is consistent with their ambiguous nature. Indeed, the narrator's silence on other key issues is one of the most salient features of this tale. This silence is part of a larger pattern in which the underlying intentions of all the characters, including God, are left open to interpretation. Thus the reader is very much in the position of Joseph himself: deprived of direct knowledge through revelation, he must fall back on the imperfect resources of interpretation, in which the interpreter always mingles something of himself with the meaning of the text. The refusal of the narrator to confirm an interpretation—to say that the dreams come from God—is not tantamount to a denial.[9]

Young Joseph: From Desire for Domination to Powerlessness

The power-laden character of Joseph's relationship to his entire family is evident from first to last in Genesis 37, the remarkably succinct account of how he seeks to reverse his subordinate position as a younger son among twelve and is rewarded by utter powerlessness in the pit into which his brothers throw him for his pretensions. The story begins with him as a helper to his older brothers in looking after their father's flocks. Immediately we are told that Joseph brought evil tidings of his brothers' doings to his father. The implication is that Joseph sought to ingratiate himself with his father by telling tales about his brothers' real or alleged (we never know) bad behavior. Joseph wins what his father, Jacob, had to steal from his father, Isaac—preferment within the family.

Referring to sibling rivalry, while formally correct, nevertheless underestimates the magnitude of familial tensions. They are both deepened and broadened by reference to past relationships, including conflicts among Jacob's wives. "The Leah-Rachel story," as Andriolo shows, "is a symmetric inversion of the Jacob-Esau story. The axis of this inversion is the common theme underlining the two narrations: competition among siblings." The younger, softer, more contemplative homebody, Jacob, with the help of his mother, Rebekah, seeks to supplant his older, coarser, hunter brother, Esau, and succeeds in doing so by deceiving his father with the aid of a goatskin to simulate Esau's hairy hands. Reversing this story, the elder sister, Leah, practices deception on her husband, Jacob, by pretending to be her younger sister, and later on buys the right to have sexual relations with her husband from her younger sister in exchange for mandrakes to eat. In the Jacob and Esau story, the elder brother sells his birthright for the proverbial mess of pottage. The goal of this competition, recalling God's promise to the patriarchs, is "to participate in the continuation of the Jewish lineage."[10] The difference, according to the customs of those days, is that while there can be only one male who continues the line, both sisters can legitimately perform that function. The question is whose sons will be preeminent.

If, according to custom, the eldest son becomes head of the family, why is there all this competition over the father's blessing? It is important to be first-born because that son receives either all or a double portion of the inheritance and is considered the leader of the family-clan-nation. The first-born is also evidence of the father's vigor and the mother's capacity to bear children and thus implies the continuity of that tribe. When God wants to show His concern for and protectiveness of the Hebrew people, He says, "Israel is My first-born son" (Exod. 4:22).

Evidently, being first-born carries a lot of weight. Yet if that status were fixed biologically, a little of the luster of Divine intervention in human life would be dimmed. One hardly needs divine aid in order to follow nature or custom. In fact, the Torah is full of instances in which the younger inherits, whether that be Solomon over Adonijah; David against his brothers; Joseph and Judah before Reuben, Simeon, and Levy; Isaac ahead of Ishmael; Abraham before Haran; and Abel over Cain. By working against custom, the Lord shows His powers. By working against the expected, Jacob and Joseph show their more limited power as well.[11] What is more, since Jacob has two wives, there are two candidates for the first-born, Reuben and Joseph, with Joseph coming from the best-loved wife.[12]

Now we are in a position to interpret the familiar statement about Jacob in Genesis 37:3—"Now Israel loved Joseph best of all his sons, for he was the child of his old age." As a literal explanation for Jacob's favoritism this is very weak. Benjamin, the youngest, was the child of Jacob's old age. Come to think of it, all of Jacob's children were born when he was, by our standards, quite old. Bush's suggestion that wisdom is supposed to accompany old age would make this statement into a belief that Jacob thought Joseph was wiser than his brother.[13] Perhaps Jacob saw in Joseph the same sort of imaginative and reflective character he believed himself to possess. Another clue is the change of the name Jacob to that of Israel, which could suggest that Jacob considered Joseph the one best suited to keep his family together.[14] Not likely. The reader is left to wonder whether Jacob's favoritism is a sign of his dotage or of his wisdom.

There are other clues to help explain the announcement that Joseph was the son of Jacob's old age. In the first instance of its use, Isaac is described as the son of Abraham's old age (Gen. 21:2-7). This phrase serves two purposes. One is to drive home the magnitude of Abraham's faith by demonstrating his willingness to test God's promise by offering up the only conduit through which that promise can be realized, his beloved son, Isaac. Another is to emphasize the God-given miracle that would allow a man as old as Abraham (100 years by the Torah's account), with an old wife to boot, to sire a child. *Midrash Tanuma* explains the emphasis on Abraham's old age as necessary to ward off rumors that his wife, Sarah, having previously stayed with Pharaoh (misled by Abraham to take her as his sister), might have been impregnated by him. Hence the necessity for repeating that Abraham was indeed the father of Isaac.[15] The concern about paternity—Are they God's people? Who is entitled to the land promised to the descendants of the patriarchs?—is never far from the surface of those who claim to be a people who have been chosen.

Another possible interpretation is to read the literal words "a son of old age to him" as moving from "old age" (in Hebrew, *zequnim*) to "old man" (*zaguen*), which, Kugel holds, "is practically a synonym in biblical Hebrew for 'sage' or 'wise man.' Following this line, the meaning of the phrase in question could be interpreted to be a 'son of wisdom' or, more prosaically, intelligent child. Thus the first century Bible (called Targum) of Onkelos in Aramaic reads in translation, 'And Jacob loved Joseph more than all his sons, *for he was a wise son to him.*'"[16] This favorable rendition of Onkelos suggests that it was Joseph's special qualities that led to this bond and downplays the possibility that it was his "bad reports" (Gen. 37:2) about his brothers that led his father to elevate him over them.

Yet we need look no further than the first clause of the sentence we have been perusing for an ominous sign. Have we not listened before to such anxiety-producing words—"Isaac favored Esau . . . but Rebekah favored Jacob" (Gen. 25:28)—as the beginning of a family feud in which deceit was piled on deceit, enmity on enmity, without end. The consequences of favoritism are horrendous. It is a particularly galling form of inequality when it takes place within the same family. No one in the audience to whom this sentence was first read would fail to recognize that it spells big trouble.

The previous sentence provides more familial context: "At seventeen years of age, Joseph tended the flocks with his brothers, as a helper to the sons of his father's wives Bilhah and Zilpah" (Gen. 37:2). Thus we are introduced to Joseph following sheep together with brothers who were the sons of the maids of Jacob's wives, Leah and Rachel. Given the competitive atmosphere within the family, the sons of the maids were undoubtedly of the lowest status,[17] but why Joseph chose to ally himself with them is not stated. Possibilities would be either that as a son of the favored wife he sought allies against the sons of the less favored wife or that his other brothers would not have him around. It is such circumstances that allow Hirsch to speak of Joseph as "a *motherless* and *brotherless youth*. All the others grew up in company with brothers and under the wing and influence of mother-love. Joseph [whose mother, Rachel, had died earlier] stood alone."[18] Perhaps, as Duane Christensen suggests, a play on words is intended "in the sense of 'shepherding his brothers' who in fact become the 'sheep.'"[19]

The sign of Jacob's preferment was his gift to Joseph of what has been variously translated as a coat of many colors, a long-sleeved robe, or a tunic with ornaments. Whatever it looked like, such a cloak was not only a visible sign of favoritism but also a symbol of leadership.[20] "When his brothers saw that their father loved him more than any of his brothers, they hated him so that they could not speak a friendly word to him" (Gen. 37:4). Rashi credits them at least with lack of hypocrisy in showing their anger outright.[21] Nevertheless, refusal to exchange greetings—or, as we might do, shake hands—portends a serious breach of relationship.

Who is at fault for this breakdown in family relationships? Joseph is outnumbered; Joseph is friendless; Joseph is the minority put down by the majority, indeed, by all his other brothers. "Motherless and brotherless" as he may be, as Hirsch's bathetic account has him, Joseph's behavior nevertheless instills doubts about his own responsibility. The image of a spoiled child willfully turning his father against his brothers and his brothers against him has caused consternation among commentators. They ask how it could fit in with the later images of Joseph the kind, the forgiving, the wise.[22] Philo attributes the brothers' hostility to envy, "which is ever the enemy of high success," which is true enough but not without warrant against a father's son who enjoyed his open partiality (Gen. 37:4).[23]

These efforts to make excuses for Joseph do not work because the text is loaded against him. The word *dibbah* in Hebrew conveys connotations of insinuating untrue reports, that is, of slimy slander.[24] "The view that holds Joseph responsible (partly at least) for other crimes committed by his brethren against him is old . . . ."[25] However hard he tries, for instance, Benno Jacob cannot excuse Joseph or Jacob. "Long robes," Jacob observes, "are worn by people who need not work. Jacob, with fatherly love, saw the future master in Rachel's first-born son. Showing this openly was a mistake."[26]

These already deteriorated associations between Joseph and his brothers were worn even thinner when he expressed out loud his will to power over them: "Once Joseph had a dream which he told to his brothers; and they hated him even more" (Gen. 37:5). Joseph went on to rub in his dreams of dominance:

"Hear this dream which I have dreamed: There we were binding sheaves in the field, when suddenly my sheaf stood up and remained upright; then your sheaves gathered around and bowed low to my sheaf." His brothers answered, "Do you mean to reign over us? Do you mean to rule over us?" (Gen. 37:6-7)

Everett Fox's translation brings out the poetic anger as if a chorus was complaining and predicting:

His brothers said to him:
Would you be king, yes, king over us?
Or would you really rule, yes, rule us?
From then on they hated him still more—for his dreams,
    for his words.[27]

The narrator leaves no doubt as to the brothers' response: "And they hated him even more for his talk about his dreams" (Gen. 37:8). This repetition of hate, hate, hate (Gen. 37:4,5,8), this crescendo of bad feelings, suggests violence is about to break out. The brothers' repeated question about being subordinated to Joseph is echoed on the occasion when Moses, witnessing a Hebrew being beaten by an Egyptian, kills the Egyptian and upon returning the next day chastises two Hebrews who are fighting, only to hear: "Who made you chief and ruler over us?" (Exod. 2:14). In both cases the meaning is the same: Joseph and Moses are assuming unwarranted authority over other Israelites without first achieving the legitimacy their acts require. Moses was vindicated by bringing the people out of bondage in Egypt and the law to a free people who accept its provisions. Joseph, who kept his family in Egypt, claims— but, as we will see, does not substantiate his claim—to be following God's will. And he leads his family into the Egyptian Diaspora, not toward the land of God's promises.

Boyhood Dreams of a Future High Administrator

Aside from its allusion to Joseph's future service in allocating Pharaoh's wheat during famine, the dream about the sheaves in the field is wishful thinking, imagined but not yet gratified. Nothing could be more blatant than the bowing down of the brothers' wheat to Joseph's wheat, an obeisance made worse by Joseph's insistent "Hear this dream" (Gen. 37:6). The progression of Joseph's images—binding, bolting, bowing— engenders exactly the reaction to what is inherent in them: hatred at the thought that one brother should rule over others, especially a young one, contrary to tradition.[28]

The bread out of which wheat is made is rightly called the staff of life; it sustains populations. The grains that make up the wheat are also seeds (hence the term "seed grain") that provide for the continuity of a people. Earlier in his history of Jacob's family, God promises to multiply his descendants so they become as numerous as "the dust of the earth" (Gen. 13:16). He might as well have said as numerous as grains of wheat. When wheat is on your side, you have a powerful ally, a point not lost on Jacob's sons, who undoubtedly grew up on stories of the Lord's promises to their family.

As if the bending sheaves were not enough for Joseph,

> he dreamed another dream and told it to his brothers, saying, "Look, I have had another dream: And this time, the sun, the moon, and eleven stars were bowing down to me." And when he told it to his father and brothers, his father berated him. "What," he said to him, "is this dream you have dreamed? Are we to come, I and your mother and your brothers, and bow low to you to the ground?" So his brothers were wrought up at him, and his father kept the matter in mind. (Gen. 37:9–11)

Joseph's demand for recognition—Hear! Look!—without earning it, in his brothers' estimation, angered them even more.

When Joseph says to Pharaoh that Pharaoh's two dreams are really one, the same is true of Joseph's dreams, each one about his coming dominance. These bowing down dreams represent what Joseph would like if the world were his to make over. Moreover, he tells both variations to his brothers, the second one in the hearing of his father. (The term "bow low" refers back to Jacob's efforts to placate his brother Esau by using the supplicating form—"he . . . bowed low to the ground seven times," Gen. 33:3—of a kind that animals use when met by overwhelming force or that the Chinese refer to in the word "kowtow.") According to the lore of the times, repetition of dreams, as Joseph would later reveal, was a sign that the dream was of divine origin and hence was destined to happen. In the minds of those who heard him, Joseph had raised the stakes of this little family spat considerably.

Jacob, not known for the moral training of his children (his sole remonstrance after the massacre at Shechem was that his sons had made trouble for him), nevertheless put Joseph down for his evident desire to exert power over his parents as well as his brothers. Ramban holds that Jacob rebuked Joseph for his conceit in even thinking such thoughts during the day so that he might dream at night of exercising control over his parents.[29] In short, the dream brings out what is already inherent in Joseph's desires.

The interpretation of the dream most favorable to Joseph is that the sun (his father), the moon (his mother), and the stars (his brothers) were willingly subordinating themselves to him. The most damaging is that this is an idolatrous dream in which Joseph takes the place of the Almighty, thereby worshipping himself. Self-worship is a characteristic of the Pharaoh, who is called the very incarnation of the sun god Ra.

Dreams (especially, in my estimation, daydreams) can be subversive. They can loosen the restraints of the status quo; they envisage futures not yet realized.[30] One can say that in Joseph's time dreams were also considered destabilizing in that they were a portent of a future that was different from the present. Dreaming of a desirable future does not seem to lessen the motivation of the dreamer to achieve that future. On the contrary, the belief that the dream will be realized, coupled with the implicit suggestion that more powerful forces are at work, is apt to be galvanizing. There is not all that much difference between foretelling the future, being energized by that forecast, and wanting it to turn out that way. No wonder Joseph's brothers, upon hearing his two dreams, and his repetition of them, thought he was too dangerous to let live.[31] In the future, the coupling of Joseph's remembering his dreams, together with his accusation of spying against his brothers (Gen. 42:9), will make more sense. In his youth, his public rendition of his dreams gave his brothers dangerous insights into his motives; later he will cloak them; older and warier, he would keep his aspirations to himself while tricking his brothers into revealing theirs.

After the narrator states that his brothers were angry at Joseph for what might be called his insubordinate dreams, we learn that Jacob took mental note of the dreams and his sons' reaction to them. Does this imply that Jacob kept Joseph's desire for dominion in mind? Does it signify that Jacob wondered whether Joseph might be in touch with some deeper or perhaps divine truth? Did the brothers, observing that their father might be taking this dream as a prediction of their future submission to Joseph, decide to take counsel by going at that point some eighty kilometers away to Shechem "to feed their father's flock"?

Shechem was redolent with violent memories. It was the place where two brothers, against the will of their father, slaughtered an entire community as retribution for the rape of Dinah. Going forward in time, Shechem was also the place where the Israelites, who refused to bear the onerous taxes of Solomon's son, Reheboam, broke up their confederation into what became northern and southern kingdoms. Shechem is a place of strong and independent actions with long-lasting consequences.

The Torah (Gen. 37:14) states simply that Jacob asked Joseph to find his brothers in Shechem and bring back word about how they and the flocks were doing.[32] What, exactly, did Jacob have in mind in giving Joseph this mission?

How could Jacob send his beloved son to Shechem of all places? Elie Wiesel has eloquently stated the problem of interpretation:

> And why did he not turn to God—he who never used to take a step without consulting Him—to obtain information if not intervention? There are only two possibilities; either Jacob was unaware of the hate his sons felt for Joseph—and then it is difficult to understand his blindness—or else he *did* know—and then one does not understand his passivity. What strange behavior for a father. Separated from his favorite son, he sank into a depression, was unconsolable, and yet he did nothing to find him or at least his mutilated remains.[33]

Wondering whether Joseph's behavior has divine warrant, Jacob may deliberately be sending him to the place of utmost danger to determine if God is really with him. If not, then the family faces a terrible problem in which a clever member seeks to establish his hegemony over the rest, not only against custom but also in contravention to God's will.

Sending Joseph to meet the fate God has in store for him is Jacob's replay of the Akedah, the binding of Isaac. God's promises to Abraham are conditioned upon obeying His laws. No pretense is made that this obedience will be easy. "Only in giving his present land could Abraham be shown another land," Turner interprets, "only in giving up his present kindred could he become the father of a great nation. . . . *Only in being willing to give up his only son* is he able to become the father of a multitude."[34]

Whether Joseph was oblivious to the increasingly stronger reactions he provoked, or whether he thought the force behind his dreams would come to his rescue, we cannot know. It is clear that things are not going too well for him; his brothers and his father are angry at him. Upon whom, then, can he call for support? He has reason to worry. Yet when his father sends him to Shechem, Joseph answers like one who is awaiting his call,

"I am ready" (Gen. 37:13), the exact Hebrew word used by Moses at the
burning bush.

In replying to his father, Joseph does not use the ordinary "I," *ani*, but
rather *anoki*, exactly the phrase found in "Am I my brother's keeper?"
(Gen. 4:9). To Lowenthal this usage implies that when Joseph becomes
the chieftain of the tribe, succeeding Jacob, "He wants indeed to become
'his brother's keeper.'"[35] Somehow a communitarian vision has been
transmuted into a hierarchical intention.

Joseph searches for his brothers to no avail. Finally a man finds him
wandering "in the field," *basadeh* in Hebrew, the term used to describe
the location of Cain and Abel when Cain murdered his brother (Gen. 4:8).
A very alert reader might have been reminded of this earlier occurrence
between brothers and seen it as a warning to Joseph. The man asks what
he is seeking, and Joseph replies (following the Hebrew order of the
words) "*My brothers* I seek" (Gen. 37:16). This phrase, too, should warn
us of impending doom, for in Genesis 4:9 Cain replies to the Lord's
inquiry regarding his brother's whereabouts, "I do not know; am I the
keeper of *my brother*?"[36]

Suspended "between his father's rebuke and his brothers' hatred,"[37]
wishing neither to return home nor necessarily to find his brothers, Joseph
is found wandering around by a man who just happened to know where
the brothers had gone. Whether the man who found Joseph and who just
happened to be able to direct him to his brothers in Dothan is a divine
instrument I cannot say. Perhaps he is the same man, the mysterious
stranger, who wrestled with his father, Jacob. He acts like fate itself.

As soon as his brothers get sight of Joseph, long before he comes close,
"they conspired to kill him" (Gen. 37:18). What they say to each other
is as human as it is revealing: "Here comes that dreamer!" (Gen. 37:19).
What they say next is as chilling as it is expected: "Come now, let us kill
him and throw him into one of the pits; and we can say, 'A savage beast
devoured him.' We shall see what comes of his dreams!" (Gen. 37:20).

Irritated beyond reason or moral considerations, the brothers, not
unlike their father, play a game of chance with life, implying that if indeed
their younger brother's dreams are destined to come true, he has nothing
to fear.[38] Speaking of Joseph in the ironical sense of those who justify
murder by saying that he who lives by the sword (or the dream) shall die
by it, Benno Jacob translates the brothers' mocking words in 37:19 as
"Mister Dreamer," spoken "mockingly, as if it were a profession."[39]

To emphasize the ruthlessness and determination of the brothers, the same root is used for killing with determined violence as when Cain kills Abel.[40] To accentuate the horror of what is happening, the brothers' insensitivity to Joseph's pleas, which we learn about only from their later confession, is demonstrated by the simple statement that in the midst of contemplated murder they sat down to eat. Twice in the following passage we are told that Joseph's coat was stripped off and that he was cast into a pit without water—that is, without means of sustaining life.

Yet the fact that Joseph's brothers peeled off his special coat of favoritism, though accurate enough, does not quite do justice to the narrative. Better, because of the stronger suggestion of compulsion, would be that his brothers made Joseph take off his coat. Best would be Lowenthal's portrait of the scene in which the brothers say only one word, "Undress!" (in Hebrew, *wayafshitu*, a causative verb), which has the right peremptory tone. That all this hatred is being directed at Joseph is emphasized by the use of his name twice instead of the pronoun the second time ("When Joseph came up to his brothers, they stripped Joseph of his tunic" Gen. 37:23). This locution, according to Chaninah Maschler, conjures up the image of a king being forced to remove his crown.[41]

The elder brother, Reuben, suggests that Joseph be left in the pit. Having slept with his father's concubine, taking what would be his by right but only after his father died—an impulsive act likely to lose him his place as first-born—Reuben tries to reassert his right to lead by saving his brother. His concern for Joseph and his desire for power are hopelessly entangled. It turns out that he is inept or unlucky.

Prefiguring his bid for power, Judah adds a new argument. Where Reuben cried "Shed no blood . . do not touch him yourselves" (Gen. 37:22), Judah, observing a caravan approaching, appeals to his brothers' self-interest, urging that Joseph be sold as a slave, for "he is our brother, our own flesh" (Gen. 37:27). Though Reuben's is the more worthy plea (he intends to restore Joseph to his father), Judah's is the more successful. This is so because it would be fatal for the brothers to return Joseph to his father. The least that would happen would be a charge of attempted murder. By selling Joseph, Judah keeps him alive while removing him from the scene. Let the dream lord be saved by his own powers.[42]

With the same sort of deception Jacob practiced on Isaac, goatskins being used in both cases, his sons slaughtered a kid, dipped Joseph's coat into the blood, and had it delivered to their father by someone else, asking

Jacob to whom the piece of clothing might belong. To their crimes of selling Joseph into slavery and deceiving their father, the brothers now add passivity (getting someone else to do their nasty work) in the face of evil.

The cloak covering up the skin of a goat with which Jacob deceived Isaac is used to deceive Jacob. When the brothers rip off Joseph's coat (barely concealing his lust for power), they use action verbs—kill him, throw him, devour him (Gen. 37:19), followed by the bursting out of anger over his deception: took the coat, slaughtered the goat, dipped it in blood (Gen. 37:31). Reuben and Jacob tear their clothes over Joseph, a sign of mourning for their broken dreams.

Jacob's sons deceive him about the fate of Joseph not by directly lying but by asking him a question about whether the robe dipped in blood belongs to his son, Joseph.[43] As the brothers hoped he would, Jacob assumed that Joseph had been eaten by a wild beast and immediately went into mourning, repeating twice that Joseph had surely been slain. Slain, surely, is Jacob's hope of passing on his dreams (and the power to fulfill them) to Joseph.[44]

Slavery terminates a family relationship, especially when one is sold into bondage by one's family. Instigator and victim, cause and effect, Joseph has played an integral role in this self-destructive family. Will Joseph in captivity learn better how to veil his thoughts and deceive his associates, or will he try to act so as to put family life onto a more mutually supportive plane? Is Jacob deceived, or has he sacrificed his son to test his faith? Twice sold, Joseph entered as a slave into the home of Potiphar, the chief steward and adviser of the Pharaoh.

Administrators Also Have Dreams

No student of administration or of dreams could ask for more: two dreams from a high-level administrator as a young man; two dreams from the chief of everything, and, in between, dreams from two top functionaries. The butler and the baker are not just household help; they are important figures in Egyptian administration.

It happened, the Torah tells us, that the Pharaoh's butler, or wine cupbearer, and his baker offended him so they had been confined in the house of the chief steward, where Joseph also was kept. He attended these formerly important officials. Because they gave drink and food to the

monarch (essential elements, which was no doubt why they were chosen
to appear in the story) and could easily poison him, they were powerful
but precarious, powerful because of their proximity to Pharaoh and
precarious because a whim or a misdeed might lead him to punish them
severely.

Now it is time to listen to the content of their dreams. The cupbearer
and the baker

> dreamed in the same night, each his own dream and each dream with its own meaning.
> When Joseph came to them in the morning, he saw that they were distraught. He asked
> Pharaoh's courtiers, who were with him in custody in his master's house, saying,
> "Why do you appear downcast today?" And they said to him, "We had dreams, and
> there is no one to interpret them." So Joseph said to them, "Surely God can interpret!
> Tell me your dreams."
>   Then the chief cupbearer told his dream to Joseph. He said to him, "In my dream,
> there was a vine in front of me. On the vine were three branches. It had barely budded,
> when out came its blossoms and its clusters ripened into grapes. Pharaoh's cup was
> in my hand, and I took the grapes, pressed them into Pharaoh's cup, and placed the
> cup in Pharaoh's hand." Joseph said to him, "This is its interpretation: The three
> branches are three days. In three days, Pharaoh will pardon you and restore you to
> your post; you will place Pharaoh's cup in his hand, as was your custom formerly
> when you were his cupbearer." (Gen. 40:5–13)

One may attribute to divine intervention the fact that Joseph was able
to give an immediate, successful interpretation, but I think this is just
Joseph's way of getting up his courage. An ancient commentary by B. R.
Hayya bar Abba contains a clue: "each dreamed both the dream and its
interpretation."[45] The phrase "each dream with its own meaning" also
suggests that the meaning was transparent in the telling. The threefold
mention of Pharaoh indicates the cupbearer's identification with his
master. The moving picture of the cupbearer's craft—budded blossoms
into clusters of grapes into juice—suggests in an instant the fulfillment
of the cupbearer's desires, as does the fact that he placed the cup with
the grape juice in the monarch's hand. In essence, the cupbearer is telling
himself that he deserves to be rewarded for his fidelity and his crafts-
manship, and he is.

Now listen to the other dream:

> When the chief baker saw how favorably he had interpreted, he said to Joseph, "In
> my dream, similarly, there were three open-work baskets on my head. In the
> uppermost basket were all kinds of food for Pharaoh that a baker prepares, and the
> birds were eating it out of the basket above my head." Joseph answered, "This is its
> interpretation: The three baskets are three days. In three days the Pharaoh will lift off

your head and impale you upon a pole; and the birds will pick off your flesh." (Gen. 40:16–19)

Obviously, Joseph was not sparing the poor fellow's feelings.

Comparing the two dreams, we see at once that the cupbearer personally participated in making the drink, whereas the baker speaks in a passive voice, as if the bread was prepared by others. Where the cupbearer succeeds in putting sustenance into his master's hand, the baker does not, inasmuch as birds ate it before it reached its destination. The former industrious, the latter lazy; the former husbanding his master's resources, the latter dissipating them. Given what we know and, more important, what the Hebrews mentioned in the Torah knew about Egyptian respect for the body of the dead, the punishment Joseph predicts (which comes true) is particularly severe.[46] Perhaps Skinner is correct in observing that the punishment fits the crime, since the baker should have tried to drive off the birds—that is, those who frittered away Pharaoh's substance.[47] Joseph's phrase "lift off your head" may be a pun intended to indicate the delicate position of those who serve people in high positions. The first rung up the slippery pole of success, as politicians are wont to say, is the first rung down, perhaps for Joseph too.

Without waiting for his interpretation of the butler's dream to be realized, Joseph, stating that he had been unjustly imprisoned, asks him to "think of me when all is well with you again, and do me the kindness of mentioning me to Pharaoh, so as to free me from this place" (Gen. 40:14). Since diviners were due a fee, and Joseph asked for none, he may have felt entitled to a little help. Given the wisdom on which this official was brought up, however, why should he remember, since Joseph in the dungeon is not in a position to do anything for him? The Hebrew term for not remembering means "complete forgetfulness."[48] It is the same term Joseph uses in referring to his father's house.

The Dreams of Pharaoh

Around two years later, after Joseph interpreted the administrators' dreams,

Pharaoh dreamed that he was standing by the Nile, when out of the Nile there came up seven cows, handsome and sturdy, and they grazed in the reed grass. But presently, seven other cows came up from the Nile close behind them, ugly and gaunt, and stood beside the cows on the bank of the Nile; and the ugly gaunt cows ate up the seven

handsome sturdy cows. And Pharaoh awoke.
He fell asleep and dreamed a second time: Seven ears of grain, solid and healthy, grew on a single stalk. But close behind them sprouted seven ears, thin and scorched by the east wind. And the thin ears swallowed up the seven solid and full ears. Then Pharaoh awoke: it was a dream! (Gen. 41:1-7)

Agitated, evidently worried, Pharaoh woke up the next day and "sent for all the magicians of Egypt and all its wise men; and Pharaoh told them his dreams, but none could interpret them for Pharaoh" (Gen. 41:8). Why not? It is hard to believe that such accomplished interpreters could not manage at least hypotheses about the meaning of an allegorical but not overly complicated dream. My guess, bolstered by how Joseph later handles himself before Pharaoh, is that the magicians and wise men feared telling Pharaoh bad news. Certainly the repetition of the adjectives "ugly" and "gaunt" and "thin" and "scorched" (or "diseased") does not bode well.

Pharaoh also considers himself divine, a demigod at least, possessing absolute power and responsible for the welfare of his people. Such dreams by such monarchs presumably reveal the bond between the ruler and the divine, thus convincing him that he is acting in a way that will turn out well and assuring his people that they will do well through their ruler.[49] The tone of his dreams must tell Pharaoh there is a threat to his kingdom or to him, and he is desperate not only to learn what it may be but especially how to take effective measures against whatever it is.

At that time the chief cupbearer, sensing an opportunity to raise himself in Pharaoh's eyes while now remembering to repay an old debt—his motives intertwined, as they are so often in the Joseph stories—tells Pharaoh about his and the baker's dreams and how Joseph divined their meaning. He adds, "and as he interpreted for us, so it came to pass" (Gen. 41:13). The phrase with which the cupbearer begins, "I must make mention today of my offenses" (Gen. 41:9), refers both to his original angering of Pharaoh and to his neglect of Joseph's request to be remembered to Pharaoh, the latter a real offense, the former an unwarranted accusation. It uses the same verb, "make mention" (*mazkir*), with the same root used by Joseph in asking to be remembered and by the narrator of the story in reporting that the cupbearer completely forgot.[50]

The slavery and imprisonment Joseph suffered came from his failure to remember, that is, to take into account his family's reaction to his own dreams. As a result, his passion for power became translated directly into his brothers' wish to kill him as soon as they saw him and perhaps into his father's willingness to send him to those he knew hated his favorite son. Now imprisonment has made his memory acute; Joseph remembers to anticipate the reactions of his audience. When Pharaoh calls, Joseph "rushes" (Gen. 41:14); whether to fulfill his or the Pharaoh's dreams remains open.

While in prison, Joseph has had a long time to ponder the nature of dreams, to learn that the trick is to understand the character of the dreamer who speaks more truly of his hopes and fears while sleeping than he can bring himself to do while awake.[51] The actualization of his interpretations of the dreams of the butler and the baker has given Joseph confirmation of the hypothesis that the dream reveals what is inherent in the dreamer. As for Pharaoh, Joseph has had an opportunity to study him through his servants, from Potiphar to the baker and cupbearer, and to understand what responsibilities he must be concerned about.

When Joseph is summoned to Pharaoh on the butler's recommendation, Pharaoh immediately retells his dreams, this time emphasizing the elements of disaster: "never had I seen their [the lean cows'] likes for ugliness in all the land of Egypt!" (Gen. 41:19). Joseph is prepared. He knows he needs to ingratiate himself with the Pharaoh by doing what his magicians and courtiers will not—telling him the bad news—yet he must simultaneously tie it to a positive plan of action that will get him out of jail and into the royal court. Joseph decides to give Pharaoh reason to believe that there is an optimistic interpretation behind the pessimistic one, an interpretation that will enhance Pharaoh's power.

Joseph's opportunity and ingenuity come by way of attributing dreams not to himself but to God, thus appearing self-effacing rather than power seeking, so that the same authority that brought the interpretation to Pharaoh must be solicited in order to determine what might be done to turn disaster into good fortune. That is why Joseph, going swiftly from his dungeon into new Egyptian clothes, complete with Egyptian haircut, says "Not I! God will see to Pharaoh's welfare" (Gen. 41:16).

His interpretation is that

Pharaoh's dreams are one and the same: God has told Pharaoh what He is about to do. The seven healthy cows are seven years, and the seven healthy ears are seven years; it is the same dream. The seven lean and ugly cows that followed the seven years, as are also the seven empty ears scorched by the east wind, they are seven years of famine. . . . As the land is ravaged by famine, no trace of the abundance will be left in the land because of the famine thereafter, for it will be very severe. As for

Pharaoh having had the same dream twice, it means that the matter has been determined by God, and that God will soon carry it out. (Gen. 41:25-32)

No need for Pharaoh to guess at the principle of interpretation as Joseph tells him exactly what it is twice, once by repetition and once by explaining the principle of doubling. Not only does Pharaoh dream two dreams on the same night, Ibn Ezra observes, and repeat those dreams to Joseph, but each dream is essentially the mirror image of the other.[52]

Before Pharaoh has a chance to think what to do, Joseph is on the spot, his instant recommendations giving Pharaoh no time to ponder whether they indeed come from the Almighty or from a mere mortal recently released from a dungeon.

Accordingly, [Joseph advises] let Pharaoh find a man of discernment and wisdom, and set him over the land of Egypt. And let Pharaoh take steps to appoint overseers over the land, and organize the land of Egypt in the seven years of plenty. Let all the food of these good years that are coming be gathered, and let the grain be collected under Pharaoh's authority as food to be stored in the cities. Let that food be a reserve for the land for the seven years of famine which will come upon the land of Egypt, so that the land may not perish in the famine. (Gen. 41:33-36)

A policy analysis subtly intertwined with its implementation, Joseph's interpretation is invented, but that does not necessarily mean it is divine. There would be no reason to hire anyone to do anything if in fact the Almighty had predetermined what was to happen. From the young man who wore his heart (and his will to power) on his sleeve, Joseph has come a long way in control and subtlety. Now he leads others to do what he wants in the belief that it is in their own interest.

I do not wish to leave the impression that the interpretation Joseph gave to Pharaoh's dreams is the only one possible. Not so. For instance, among Louis Ginzberg's *Legends of the Jews* are these interpretations. Perhaps the seven fat cows were the major defense cities of Egypt that were to be conquered by seven Canaanite nations. Naturally, they subjugated the Egyptians, who then became like lean cows. The meaning of the second dream would then be precisely the reverse of the first, namely, that Pharaoh's descendants would regain his fortified cities. Or Pharaoh might have seven good sons who were overwhelmed by seven evil ones, only in their turn to be conquered by their victims, the result being that Pharaoh would be restored to the throne.[53]

Joseph tells us that when a person has two similar dreams that means their realization is imminent. Caine adds that because Pharaoh has the same dream twice in one night, their realization is even more imminent.[54]

A dream together with its interpretation is only a prediction, a potential but not yet an actual event. Its realization depends in part, as we have seen, on the actions of the dreamer. But individuals do not operate alone; they are enmeshed in webs only very partially of their own making. When it is said in the Talmud (*Berachoth* 55B) that "Dreams follow the mouth," meaning that their interpretation is part of the meaning of dreams, the practicality of this generalization becomes evident: what other people do about your dreams or in response to them is part of their efficacy. This is the answer to the question that Munk raises: "How is it possible that the effects of a dream can be influenced in one way or another by the interpretation which friends or enemies or the dreamer give to it?"[55] The brothers' resistance unto death of Joseph's dreams contrasts nicely with Pharaoh's eagerness to place Joseph in charge of realizing his (and the Pharaoh's) dreams.

The insight we need into Pharaoh's dreams may be gained by asking how the interpretation Joseph gives serves him personally. We see more than a gain in manipulation; we also see a leap forward in self-control. Who will control whom is the next question to be decided. If Pharaoh's two dreams are one, as Joseph said, and his two dreams as a teenager were one, as his family realized, then interpreters who ruminate over both sets of dreams must agree with Seybold that, taken together, they are also "one: the weaker *unnaturally* dominates the stronger."[56]

Notes

1. Claus Westermann, *Genesis 37–50*, tran. John J. Scullion (Minneapolis: Augsburg Publishing, 1986), 78.
2. Walter Brueggemann, *Genesis: A Bible Commentary for Teaching and Preaching*, in the *Interpretation* series (Atlanta: John Knox Press, 1982), 302.
3. Nahum M. Sarna, *Understanding Genesis* (New York: McGraw Hill, 1966), 213.
4. See O. S. Wintermute, "Joseph Son of Jacob," *Interpreter's Dictionary of the Bible* 2 (1962): 981–986, at 983.
5. Benno Jacob, *The First Book of the Bible: Genesis*, His commentary abridged, ed. and trans. Ernest I. Jacob and Walter Jacob (New York: KTAV Publishing, 1974), 250; Sarna, *Understanding Genesis*, 212–13; J. Bergman, M. Ottosson, G. J. Botterweck, "Chalam," *Theological Dictionary of the Old Testament*, vol. 4 (Grand Rapids: William R. Eerdmans Publishing, 1980), G. Johannes Botterweck and Helmer Ringgven, trans. David E. Green, 421–32, see 423.

6. Johannes Pedersen, *Israel: Its Life and Culture* (London: Oxford University Press, 1926), 137, quoted in Leonard Mars, "What Was Onan's Crime?" *Comparative Studies in Society and History* 26, no. 3 (July 1984): 429-39.

7. Jacob, *Genesis*, 250.

8. *"Rashi" on the Pentateuch: Genesis*, trans. and annotated by James H. Lowe (London: Hebrew Compendium Publishing, 1928), 417.

9. I owe the interpretion in this paragraph to David Enelow.

10. Karin R. Andriolo, "A Structural Analysis of Genealogy and Worldview in the Old Testament," *American Anthropologist* 75 (1973): 1657-69; quote on 1667-68.

11. Benjamin Goodnick, "The Saga of the First Born," *Dor le Dor* 16 (1987): 170-178 at 173-74.

12. Samson Raphael Hirsch, *The Pentateuch Translated and Explained Vol. 1 Genesis*, trans. Esaac Levey, 2d ed. (New York: Bloch Publishing Co., 1963), 550.

13. George Bush, *Notes, Critical and Practical on the Book of Genesis*, vol. 2 (New York: Ivison and Phinney, 1859), 222.

14. For a related but somewhat different interpretation see Emanuel Feldman, "Joseph and the Biblical Echo," *Dor le Dor* 13 (1985): 161-66.

15. James L Kugel, *In Potiphar's House* (San Francisco: Harper, 1990), 72.

16. Ibid., 70, emphasis in original. Longacre's direct translation, "As for Israel he loved Joseph more than all his sons because a son of old age (or 'born leader') (was) he to him," comes close to Kugel's suggestion. (Robert E. Longacre, *Joseph: A Story of Divine Providence* (Winona Lake: Eisenbrauns, 1989), 211.)

17. See Yaakov ben Yitzchak Askenazi, *Tz'enah ur'enah The Classic Anthology of Torah Lore and Midrashic Comment*, trans. from the Yiddish by Miriam Stark Zakon (Jerusalem: Hillel Press, 1984), vol. 1 *Bereishis*, 178.

18. Hirsch, *Genesis*, 539.

19. Duane Christensen, "Anticipatory Paronomasia In Jonah 3:7-8 and Genesis 37:2," *Revue Biblique* 90 (1983): 261-63.

20. Sarna, *Understanding Genesis*, 212.

21. *"Rashi"*, 394-95.

22. John Peck, "Note on Genesis 37:2 and Joseph's Character," *The Expository Times* 82 (October 1970-September 1971): 342-43.

23. Philo, with an English translation by F. H. Colson, vol. 6 (Cambridge, Mass.: Harvard University Press, 1935), 143.

24. *"Rashi"*, 394; Peck, "Note on Genesis," 343.

25. Louis Ginzberg, *The Legends of the Jews*, Notes to Volumes I and II, From the Creation to the Exodus (Philadelphia: Jewish Publication Society, 1968), 341.

26. Jacob, *Genesis*, 249. In 2 Samuel, 13:18, the same word is used to describe the clothes worn by a princess. (See Westermann, *Genesis 37-50*, 37.

27. *In the Beginning*, A New English Rendition of the Book of Genesis, trans. with Commentary and Notes by Everett Fox (New York: Schocken Books, 1983), 151.

28. Westermann, *Genesis 37-50*, 38.

29. Ramban (Nachmanides), *Commentary on the Torah: Genesis*, trans. and annotated by Rabbi Dr. Charles B. Chavel (New York: Shilo Publishing, 1971), 453.

30. See Walter Brueggemann, "Dreaming, Being Home, Finding Strangers; and the Seminaries," *Mid-Stream* 26 (1987): 62-76, at 63.

31. See Sarna, *Understanding Genesis*, 213, for a parallel interpretation.

32. Ramban (*Mikra'ot Gedolot*) on Gen. 37:3, states that it was a custom of fathers to choose one of their young sons to serve them. The son would never leave the father

alone, especially when the latter reached an old age. That is also how Ramban explains why Joseph was at home with his father and not attending the sheep.

33. Elie Wiesel, *Messengers of God: Biblical Portraits and Legends* (New York: Random House, 1976), 156.
34. Laurence A. Turner, *Announcements of Plot in Genesis*, Journal for the Study of the Old Testament Supplement Series 96 (Sheffield: Sheffield Academic Press, 1990), 93.
35. Eric I. Lowenthal, *The Joseph Narrative in Genesis* (New York: KTAV Publishing House, 1973), 22.
36. This interpretation comes from Michael Hildenbrand.
37. Hugh C. White, "The Joseph Story: A Narrative which 'Consumes' Its Context," *Semeia* 31 (1985): 49–69; quote on 62.
38. See the discussion in Ramban, *Commentary on the Torah: Genesis*, 457.
39. Jacob, *Genesis*, 253. To murder, the brothers add deceit. The law had it that a shepherd was not liable if the animals in his charge were killed by wild beasts. The coat of undue favoritism would even the score by being used to deceive the gullible father who they believed had already been deceived about the qualities of his favorite son.
40. Nahum M. Sarna, *The JPS Torah Commentary: Genesis* (Philadelphia: Jewish Publication Society, 1989), 259.
41. Cited in Lowenthal, *Joseph Narrative in Genesis*, 25.
42. Plaut writes that "I Chr. 27:30 notes that Ishmaelites are camel drivers. But Judges 8 records that Gideon, after defeating the Midianites, requested the ear-rings of the loot. The text enters this telling parenthesis: 'For they (the Midianites) had golden earrings, because they were Ishmaelites.' (v.24). From this Ibn Ezra concludes that the terms are identical, and Abarbanel, going farther, states that Ishmaelites was a general gentilic word, Midianites a specific. Midianites are always Ishmaelites, he says, not vice versa. (En passant one may also note that in modern Hebrew *yishme'eli* means Arab or Bedouin.) They were, and are, that large group of people who were Israel's cousins.

Midianites, considered the descendants of the eponymous son of Keturah and Abraham, are also kinsmen of the Hebrews. Midian was that general area in northwest Arabia on the eastern shore of the Gulf of Akaba from which these nomads penetrated into Sinai (Nun. 10:29), Moab (Gen. 36:35), East Jordan (Num. 25:6-7 et al) and Canaan proper (Jud. 6:1-6, 33). They were traders and relatives, and could therefore easily be called Ishmaelites as the editorial comment in the old Gideon tale makes unmistakably clear." (W. Bunther Plaut, "Who Sold to Whom?" *Central Conference to American Rabbis* 15 (1968): 63–67; quote on 66. It has long been thought that the biblical account of Joseph being sold is confused, perhaps because the stories were woven together from tales told by separate writers. For conflicting interpretations, see White, "The Joseph Story"; Jacob, *Genesis*; and Edward L. Greenstein, "An Equivocal Reading of the Sale of Joseph," in *Literary Interpretations of Biblical Narratives*, vol. 2, Kenneth R. R. Gros Louis, ed. (Nashville, Tenn.: Abingdon, 1982), 114–25. Judah says "let us sell him to the Ishmaelites . . . . His brothers agreed" (Gen. 37:27); the narrator, "When Midianite traders passed by, they pulled Joseph up out of the pit. They [the brothers] sold Joseph for twenty pieces of silver to the Ishmaelites, who brought Joseph to Egypt" (Gen. 37:28). If these accounts are true, we have a coherent storyline; the brothers, following Judah's advice, intended to sell Joseph to the Ishmaelites but, before they could do so, the

Midianites found and sold him instead. But then the Midianites could not sell him again to Potiphar in Egypt. The narrator continues, "The Midianites . . . sold him in Egypt to Potiphar, a courtier of Pharaoh and his chief steward" (Gen. 37:36). Why are we left in doubt about who sold Joseph to whom? If we leave out the Ishmaelites, Judah is no longer suspect: "This overlap . . .," according to Robert Alter, "suggests that selling him into slavery is a virtual murder and thus undermines Judah's claim that by selling the boy the brothers will avoid the horrors of blood-guilt." (Robert Alter, *The Art of Biblical Narrative* (New York: Basic Books, 1982), 166–67.) The conflicting stories are successful in illustrating the hurry and confusion the brothers felt so that who sold Joseph to whom is part of blurred images. Whatever else may be in doubt, however, Joseph has been sold twice over by his brothers. Without quite saying so, Everett Fox's esteemed translation of Genesis suggests a simple solution. "The Hebrew," he writes, "has 'Medanites,' *court-official*." This translation makes sense of what happens next, namely, that Joseph was sold to a high court official. It also makes some sense of what has gone before, in that the similar terms, one standing for a people, Midyanites, and another for court official, are easily confused. As the story reads as follows: Midyanites pulled Joseph out of the pit and sold him to Ishmaelites who in turn sold him to minor court officials, that is, Medanites, who in turn sold him to their head man, Potiphar. (Everett Fox, *In the Beginning: A New English Rendition of the Book of Genesis*)New York: Schocken Books, 1983), 155.)

43. Williams, *The Bible, Violence, and the Sacred*, 56.
44. Feldman, "Joseph and the Biblical Echo," 162–63.
45. Jacob Neusner, *Genesis Rabbah: The Judaic Commentary to the Book of Genesis: A New American Translation*, vol. 3, Parashiyyot Sixty-Eight through One Hundred on Genesis 28:10 to 50:26 (Atlanta, Georgia: Scholars Press, 1985), 241.
46. S. R. Driver, *The Book of Genesis*, 3rd ed. (New York: Edwin S. Gorham, 1904), 328.
47. John Skinner, *A Critical and Exegetical Commentary on Genesis*, 2nd ed. (Edinburgh: T. & T. Clark, 1956), 463.
48. Sarna, *Understanding Genesis*, 280.
49. cf. Westermann, *Genesis 37–50*, 86–87.
50. Ibid., 88; Sarna, *Understanding Genesis*, 282.
51. In the name of Reb Jonathan, Samuel B. Nahmani said that "what is shown a man in a dream is something suggested by his own thoughts." This is true, Rabbah said, "by the fact that no dream is ever shown a man a date palm made of gold or an elephant passing through an eye of a needle!" (André Lacocque, *The Book of Daniel* (Atlanta: John Knox Press, 1976), 44. The quote is from Simon Talmud Berakot 55B. The Talmud with English translation and commentary, ed. by Rabbi Dr. A Zvi Ehrman (Jerusalem: El-Am-Hoza's Leor Ismel, 1982), 1015.
52. Ibn Ezra, *Commentary on the Pentateuch: Genesis (Bereshit)*, trans. and annotated by H. Norman Strickman and Arthur M. Silver (New York: Menorah Publishing, 1988), 379.
53. Louis Ginzberg, *The Legends of the Jews*, vol. 2, trans. by Henrietta Szold (Philadelphia: Jewish Publication Society of America, 1977), 66.
54. Ivan Caine, "Numbers In the Joseph Narrative," *Jewish Civilization: Essays and Studies* 1 (1979): 3–17, at 5.
55. Elie Munk, *The Call of the Torah, Volume II, Genesis, Part 2* (Jerusalem: Feldheim Publishers, 1969), 808.

56. Donald A. Seybold, "Paradox and Symmetry in the Joseph Narrative," in *Literary Interpretations of Biblical Narratives*, Kenneth R. R. Gros Louis, ed. (Nashville: Abingdon, 1974), 59–73, quote on 66; emphasis in original.

4

Fathers, Sons, and Brothers:
Joseph and His Family

In the Christian Testaments of the Twelve Patriarchs as in The Fathers, "Joseph is set forth as the exemplar of purity, righteousness, and that generous spirit of love, good will and forgiveness which good men must oppose to the envy and malice of their foes."[1] There are also those who see deficiencies in his character and wonder how the different sides of Joseph can be reconciled. Thus Humphreys asks,

> Is the stubborn, bullying "man, the lord of the land" of [Gen.] chapters 42–44 a model of friendliness or good manners? Is this brow-beating tyrant who plays with his victims like a cat with a mouse, and boasts of his power to divine and of his relationship to Pharaoh, a man of modesty? And how can we apply a term like "self-controlled" to a man who becomes violently angry one minute, runs out to cry the next, and finally breaks down completely when he can no longer continue the sham?[2]

One can, as Dahlberg does, view the Joseph stories as the reconciliation between a primeval conflict of brothers first seen in the stories of Cain and Abel.[3] Certainly, Genesis may be said to be about family conflict, whether between Isaac and his brother Ishmael or between Abraham and his brother-in-law Lot or between Jacob and Esau or between Joseph and his brothers or indeed among the brothers themselves. As the family is the microcosm of the society, therefore, endless strife appears to be the human lot.

Does Joseph set things up so that his father and brothers must come to him? Or do they come to him inadvertently as a result of the famine? The narrative makes it sound as if Joseph, personally, rather than one of his assistants, distributed rations to those who sought them. This is unlikely. Perhaps it was psychologically true that all this time he has lain in wait for his brothers. A Hebrew legend invents the necessary decree for Joseph to issue: "by order of the king and his deputy . . . be it enacted that he who desireth to buy grain in Egypt may not send some slave hither to do his bidding, but must charge his own sons therewith."[4] But this is not what the Torah says. Instead, we are told that Jacob took the initiative, telling his sons that there was not enough to eat in Canaan so they should buy food in Egypt. In addition, only ten sons went, because Jacob deliberately held Benjamin back, fearing something might happen to him, the only other son of his beloved Rachel. Before coming to Egypt, therefore, the brothers were reminded that their father's favoritism remained; it had merely been transferred to Benjamin. Thus their guilt regarding Joseph was already on the brothers' mind when they came into Egypt.

Joseph Tests His Brothers

The next thing we learn is that Joseph was the administrator "who dispensed rations to all people of the land. And Joseph's brothers came and bowed low to him, with their faces to the ground" (Gen. 42:6). Is this the fulfillment of Joseph's first dream in which his brothers' sheaves of grain bow down to his? A nice play, it turns out, on his power: for the wheat of Joseph-the-provisioner now stands when the wheat of his brothers is down so low there is no more. The once uncensored Joseph, however, is no more; the power-hungry but naive blurter-outer of personal desires expired in desert pits and Egyptian dungeons. Enter the self-controlled strategist.

Joseph "acted like a stranger toward them [his brothers] and spoke harshly to them" (Gen. 42:7).[5] In this abrupt sentence we learn that the tables have been turned. Whereas before they recognized his dreams of mastery when he did not, Joseph now recognizes his brothers, though they do not recognize him. Alter makes the comparison an ironic one in that the brothers' inability to recognize Joseph is parallel to "their earlier failure to recognize his true destiny."[6] Alter notes the play on words in which a profound difference emerges between the Hebrew *haker*, meaning "recognize," and the Hebrew *vayitnaker*, meaning "stranger." Between the recognition of the true feelings of one person by another and the recognition of one's own true feelings lies a small difference in words but a large one in life.

Joseph immediately recalls "the dreams that he had dreamed about them" (Gen. 42:9). But what exactly did Joseph recall? Is it, as Rashi states, that Joseph realized his first dream had come true in that his brothers had bowed down to him or, as the Ramban claims, that he realized that none of his own dreams had come true, for Benjamin and his parents were not there to bow down?[7] Thus Joseph had to devise a scheme to bring Benjamin and his father to Egypt to make his youthful dreams materialize. "Were it not for this consideration," Ramban muses, "Joseph would indeed be regarded as having committed a great sin: bringing anguish to his father, leaving him for many days in the position of being bereft and mourning for Simeon [to be discussed] and him."[8] In support of her claim that Joseph was not "a sadist who enjoyed inflicting pain on his brothers," Nehama Leibowitz observes that the text might have recapitulated the harms his brothers had done to Joseph but instead mentioned only his dreams.[9] Perhaps the narrator thinks that now that Joseph is in office his fixation on power is what matters.

Of course, Joseph had not entirely forgotten his dreams. Rather, as Bush states elegantly, "as God is said to remember his covenant or his promise when he begins to put them in execution, so this was an efficient remembrance on the part of Joseph, implying that he now began to put his dreams in a process of fulfilment."[10] Exactly so; for when it is said that God remembers the afflictions of the Hebrew people in Egypt, it is clear that He means to bring about His original plan of getting them to the land of promises.

This is "one of those rare moments in the Bible," Alter observes, "when a narrator chooses not only to give us temporary access to the inward experience of character but also to report the character's consciousness of his past." Whereas the prior episodes in the Joseph story are concerned with foreknowledge, this story is about "one's moral history, a way of working toward psychological integration."[11] Which past and what consciousness, the unresolved question is, does Joseph want to invoke? Is it that Joseph wishes to force them to come to grips with their past by confessing their sins against him, or that he wishes to come to grips with his inability to relate to them other than as inferiors?

"You are spies," Joseph tells his brothers immediately after he remembers his dreams, "you have come to see the land in its nakedness" (Gen. 42:9). Feldman sees that "The symmetry of the narrative is immaculate: they had accused him of bearing tales against them to their father, of harming them with his words; Joseph now accuses them of being spies, of carrying information about Egypt back into Canaan, to the enemy."[12]

After the brothers' heated denial that they have ever been spies, Joseph
repeats, in a narrative replete with doubling, that he does not believe
them, for "you have come to see the land in its nakedness!" (Gen. 42:12).
The surface reference is to the remote possibility that the brothers might
have been part of a team of spies seeking out weaknesses in Egypt's
defenses. That they would come to Joseph, thereby alerting him to their
nefarious purpose, rather than remaining inconspicuous, suggests the
made-up character of this charge. In fact, the only person who has been
seen naked, so that it could be said that others have seen him in the flesh,
is Joseph, who was left unclothed in the pit when the brothers took his
robe; Potiphar's wife also left him naked when she held on to his garment
as he fled from her. Now Joseph is determined to keep wearing royal
linen.

Jacob's sons explain that their family is composed of a father and
twelve brothers (not realizing how true that is) but that one is dead
(perhaps "dead to them") and the other remains with their father.[13]
Evidently, or so they wish Joseph to infer, no father would send all his
sons on a risky mission; one might as well suspect a doting father of
sending a beloved son to his enemies.

Fully in control of his emotions, Joseph decides to put his brothers to
the test by ordering them to bring their youngest brother Benjamin to him
as a sign that they have been telling the truth. "Else, by Pharaoh," Joseph
tells his brothers, "you are nothing but spies!" (Gen. 42:16). Would
Daniel have taken an oath by another god? What Hebrew in all the Bible
would take an oath by anything other than the God of his fathers? Indeed,
who would take an oath at all, seeing how the Torah warns against casual
oath-taking (cf. the story of Jephthah (Judg. 12), who ended up having
to kill his own daughter)? In his offhand manner, Rashi suggests that
whenever he was lying, Joseph swore on Pharaoh's life;[14] charming but
implausible. That this gifted interpreter felt obliged to defend Joseph tells
us that he badly needed a defense. "Had he said, 'As the Lord liveth,'"
Bush suggests, "his speech probably would have betrayed him."[15] Then,
again, Joseph did not have to take an oath at all.

To concentrate their attention, Joseph has his brothers confined to the
guardhouse for three days. Upon their release, he tells them to "Do this
and you shall live" (Gen. 42:18). By this statement he maintains his
Egyptian guise and reinforces his image of might, as if he were entitled
to dispense life and death. Even when Joseph goes on to assure the

brothers that he is "a God-fearing man" (Gen. 42:18), we do not know which god or whose god he means. Does this apparently unassuming phrase refer to the god of Pharaoh's vizier, whom the brothers see before them? Then they have little hope. "Could it be the God who has pity on the hungry and the poor?"[16] Then hope remains. Joseph says that it will be a sufficient test of truthfulness for one brother to remain in detention while the others bring the youngest to him.

Unaware that they are confronting a Hebrew speaker, the brothers draw the moral conclusion among themselves:

> "Alas, we are being punished on account of our brother, because we looked on at his anguish, yet paid no heed as he pleaded with us. That is why this distress has come upon us." Then Reuben spoke up and said to them, "Did I not tell you, 'Do no wrong to the boy?' But you paid no heed. Now comes the reckoning for his blood." (Gen. 42:21–22)

Alas, Reuben cannot even confess without adding exaggeration to his sins. As for the brothers' confession ("We looked . . . he pleaded . . . we paid no heed"), "The sinner is punished in the area in which he has sinned."[17]

Joseph now knows that his brothers feel guilty about what they did to him. But he cannot yet know whether their anger toward him has been turned toward his father's new favorite, his younger brother Benjamin. Momentarily—"he turned away from them and wept" (Gen. 42:24)—Joseph loses control. But he masters his emotions, as he has taught himself to do, and has his brother Simeon bound before all their eyes. Then the brothers receive their food, load up their donkeys, and leave, not knowing that Joseph has given his servant instructions that the money they paid him is to be put back at the top of each bag.

Why has Joseph done this? The variety of human motivation is never more evident than here. Returning the money his brothers paid is in one way a benevolent gesture, showing that whatever he is doing is not for pecuniary gain. Yet the money stands for other things as well. Having sold him for silver money (though that was hardly their chief motive), his brothers now stand accused by silver money. This is false money, false to those who receive it for selling their brother and false to those who use it to make an untrue accusation. Or is Joseph a psychologist who knows that, everyone being guilty of something, a false accusation is likely to trigger thoughts of what one feels really guilty of? Or is he returning hurt for hurt? Or might he even be returning the accusations against his mother, Rachel, for stealing her father, Laban's, idols? Or all of the above?

Turning to one another upon their extraordinary discovery of the money in their bags, the brothers say in unison, "What is this that God has done to us?" (Gen. 42:28).[18] Exemplifying the Hebrew belief that God is everywhere and that nothing can be hidden from Him, the brothers suspect they are being punished because their iniquity has been discovered. They are about, so they fear, to fall into the pit they had prepared for Joseph.

Leaving out their guilty revelations to one another, the brothers tell their father the story of what has occurred, ending with the Egyptian official's demand that Benjamin be brought to him. Two times in recounting this episode, and once in repeating Joseph's words, the brothers refer to honesty as the test. Yet they have been dishonest to their father about how and why Joseph disappeared. Perhaps that is why the very ones who had made a slave of their brother are in danger of becoming slaves themselves.[19] And what about the honesty of their interrogator?

Characteristically, with his now famous "woe is me" voice, Jacob wails that "these things always happen to me!" (Gen. 42:36). Seeking to reassert his leadership, the eldest son, Reuben, offers to allow Jacob to kill his sons, Jacob's grandchildren, if Reuben does not return from Egypt with Benjamin. This is promising too much. A vow to kill a man's grandchildren is not likely to appeal to him. Biding his time, Judah waits until Jacob realizes the family cannot continue without Egyptian food and then offers to stand surety with his father, who can hold him "guilty . . . forever" (Gen. 43:9). Thus Judah offers the only life that is his to give, his own.

Joseph Toys with His Brothers

Bowing to the inevitable, Jacob advises his sons to take double the amount of money they will need to buy food, in case more is asked of them, and he loads them with gifts for the high Egyptian official. In proper symbolic form, therefore, the brothers, now including Benjamin, take into Egypt the same sort of stuff as had the caravan that earlier brought Joseph into slavery in Egypt. Only now their younger brother is their master.

There is more to the story. When Jacob, pleading with Reuben not to take Benjamin, says "My son must not go down with you, for his brother is dead and he alone is left" (Gen. 42:38), it must have been hard for the brothers to hear that only the sons of his beloved Rachel matter to their father. The brothers are no longer acting out an earlier crime. Instead, Ackerman notes, "They are given a chance to commit a new one."[20] Who says history does not repeat itself or that criminals do not return to the scene of their crimes?

Benno Jacob is right when he says that to Jacob "Benjamin is a second Joseph."[21] Were we in doubt, the usual repetition is employed: as each one empties his sack before their father, they discover again that their moneybags have been disturbed and the money put back. When Joseph repeated his dream about the brothers bowing down to him in front of their father, that gave it a special poignancy. Now Jacob is allowed to experience the fear of recognition that something already latent in the context of his family life is about to happen, though without knowing that his sons have special reason to feel guilty. That is why he says: "If he [Benjamin] meets with disaster on the journey you are taking, you will send my white head down to Sheol in grief" (Gen. 42:38; in Hebrew lore, *sheol* is the home of the dead). How much of this grief is for what the brothers have done to one another and how much for what their father has half-knowingly done to them, Jacob does not say, for it was he who sent Joseph to brothers who were full of hatred.

The doubling increases. The brothers repeat the story of their encounter with the high Egyptian official. Judah states that if their father had not delayed sending Benjamin, he could have been back and forth two times. The brothers carry double the money with them. They see Joseph the second time. Life's choices, this doubling tells us, are made over and over. The future people of Israel will have to decide again and again whether to become Egyptian—that is, powerful but pagan—or remain Hebraic. Indeed, when the brothers see Joseph and bow low before him again, he asks about their father and inquires after Benjamin's presence so they will not suspect he already knows. So overtaken by emotion upon seeing Benjamin, "his mother's son" (Gen. 43:29), that he runs to another room and cries so hard he has to wash his face to wipe away the tears, Joseph is finding it more and more difficult to maintain self-control.

Joseph sees his brothers with Benjamin and has his steward invite them to lunch. Fearing they will be seized as thieves (had they not stolen their brothers' liberty?) inside Joseph's house, just as they had once used their younger brother's proximity to sell him into slavery, the brothers tell Joseph's steward about finding the money in their bags, all the while assuring him they had no intention of stealing. Telling them not to be afraid, the steward, like the unknown stranger who shows Joseph the way to his brothers, or the one who wrestled with Jacob—representatives all of God—remarks that "Your God and the God of your fathers must have put treasure in your bags for you. I got your payment" (Gen. 43:23). The charge of spying is dropped without a word more. Obviously, this locution has been made up for the steward by his master, who knows how to give his brothers the outward signs of the divine presence. The brothers are reminded that their God knows and sees all. But the only one they can see, and whom they undoubtedly fear, is the disguised Joseph. Simeon is brought out to his brothers, they are given water to wash their feet, they lay out their gifts, and they wait for the presence of the high official.

Joseph, "now in control of himself" (Gen. 43:31), orders the meal served. Immediately there appears an unusual structural differentiation: Joseph is served by himself, the brothers by themselves, and the Egyptians alone. "The Egyptians could not dine with the Hebrews," the narrator explains, "since that would be abhorrent to the Egyptians" (Gen. 43:32). Perhaps the Hebrews learned something about separation from the Egyptians. However Egyptianized Joseph has become, apparently he is still considered a Hebrew and therefore unfit to eat with. If Hebrew habits are an abomination to Egyptians, what will Egyptians do to Jacob's Hebrew family when they come to Egypt? And what will happen to them when Joseph is no longer around to offer protection?

Joseph arranged that the brothers be seated in the order of their age so that "the men looked at one another in astonishment" (Gen. 43:33), undoubtedly realizing that they had mysteriously been found out. Though they were thus arrayed by seniority, by far the largest portions of food were served to Benjamin. Whatever that mysterious force was, it did not favor the rules of primogeniture. As their father had preferred Joseph, the brothers now saw that even in Egypt their youngest, Benjamin, was preferred over them. The combination of law and custom, of giving precedence to the eldest son, is violated not only by the rise of Joseph and Judah and the consequent demotion of their older brothers but even at mealtime. I am not aware of other scenes in literature in which the youngest of a substantial group is treated as the guest of honor in the way that Benjamin is.[22]

Everyone, we are told, drank a good deal. The tone of their talk is peaceable enough so long as the brothers do not know they are speaking to Joseph. The Hebrew word *shalom* is repeated by both sides so the reader can understand that brothers who could not say a civil word to Joseph managed to go this far. Despite the merrymaking, Joseph is obviously sober enough to devise a plan for testing whether his brothers have actually undergone a change of heart. He once again has his steward fill their bags with food, topped off with the money they have brought to pay for it.

Thus the brothers' money, even when doubled, cannot buy them peace. The same money they received for selling Joseph into slavery he returns to them twice. This is both exceedingly generous—equivalent to the host who tells his guest "your money is not good here"—and exceedingly hostile, for if they cannot pay, even when they double their offer, they cannot lay claim to the staff of life. Money, which ought to be a neutral instrument of commerce, has been so contaminated by their behavior that they can no longer use it in trade.

Generosity is again intermixed with duplicity. Joseph instructs the steward to put his own silver goblet on top of Benjamin's bag, together with the money Benjamin has paid for his portion of the food the brothers again received from Pharaoh's storehouses. As soon as they leave the city, however, Joseph sends his steward after the brothers, instructing him explicitly to say: "Why did you repay good with evil? It [the silver goblet] is the very one from which my master drinks and which he uses for divination. It was a wicked thing for you to do!" (Gen. 44:4–5). "According to Egyptian law," Ginzberg tells us, "no one beside the king or the viceroy was permitted to use the silver cup, and therefore the stealing of the silver cup was a much greater crime to the ordinary theft."[23] Reasoning from the minor to the major premise, the brothers, bowing low, reply that they had already brought back from Canaan the money they had found in their bags on the first trip: "How then could we have stolen any silver or gold from your master's house!" (Gen. 44:8).

This is the second time they have tried and failed with the argument that "it stands to reason" they would not be spies or steal a goblet. But, we are led to understand, rationality of the usual kind does not matter. There is a different rationality that seeks to uncover human motivation.

The brothers add, as if their pledges were guarantors of their being honest men, "whichever of your servants it is found with shall die; the rest of us, moreover, shall become slaves to my lord" (Gen. 43:9). This offer is far too generous. It apes the Egyptians by proposing to do what no Israelite is allowed to do: sell himself and his brothers to another. Nevertheless, it is a sign that the brothers' sense of collective responsibility is growing.

However, collective responsibility does not square with a scheme whose purpose it is to separate Benjamin from his brothers so that their moral fiber can again be tested. Hence, the steward, replying that he accepts their proposition, actually narrows it to serve Joseph's purpose: "only the one with whom it is found shall be my slave, but the rest of you shall go free" (Gen. 44:10). Alas, the goblet turns up in Benjamin's sack. Understanding the implications of aligning their fate with Benjamin's, so they might all die together, versus leaving him to die alone, the brothers signal their choice: "they rent their clothes" (Gen. 44:13). This traditional sign of mourning indicates they felt as if they had killed either Benjamin or Jacob or both. Actually, it is neither Benjamin nor Jacob who has actually died; to the brothers, it is Joseph, before whom they are about to stand and bow down in a position of worship. The Joseph they knew really did die and reinvented himself as a high-ranking Egyptian.

Building on René Girard's analysis, Sandor Goodhart argues that the brothers "would substitute . . . Joseph for his dreams, and murder for his language."[24] We have seen that the brothers substitute their report that a wild animal killed Joseph for him. Goodhart adds that the brothers first substitute Reuben's and then Judah's suggestion for their own, after which they sit down for a meal in which "they substitute eating for dismemberment. What, after all, is eating itself but the substitution of food for the victim."[25] Needless to say, this vegetarian-egalitarian talk might be contemporary Californian but would not fit those ancient sheperds, the Hebrews. More appropriately, Goodhart argues that "What has happened is that Joseph, from his position as Egyptian viceroy, has restaged the sacrificial activity of the earlier sequence in its entirety." From here the language of substitution picks up: "Moreover," Goodhart continues,

> their victim (who is also their lord) is also their brother, identical to them by family origins and identical to Benjamin, the other son of Rachel, for whom Judah would now exchange himself. The disclosure of Joseph's identity is a demystification, in

short, of sacrifice: the identity of victim, master, and sacrificers, all as doubles, all as brothers. And in the context of Judah's offer it shows us the way out: to acknowledge our identity, which is to say our identicality with the other, that the other is the same, that the other is us.[26]

The fascination the Joseph stories have for René Girard is understandable in that he sees human culture as beginning with the effort to place society's difficulties on a scapegoat, the victim, a part for which Joseph appears to be particularly well-suited. When everyone else, the crowd in Girardian parlance, comes to understand they may be next, they seek to ritualize the violence through sacrifice. Jesus is the victim par excellence and Joseph his predecessor. Insofar as there is blame, Girard locates it in differences of status, language, wealth, and so on.[27] From my own cultural standpoint, Girard is attributing violence to hierarchy, that is, to differentiation, and nonviolence or lesser violence to greater equality of condition. In any event, the moral tension of the Joseph stories, without which they would lose their greatness, is precisely that the victim is guilty—he goads his brothers into violence—and that he exchanges roles with them, becoming their victimizer.

What warrant has Joseph for having his steward ask-tell the brothers, "Why did you repay good with evil?" (Gen. 44:4)? If Joseph has in mind the evil his brothers had done to him, there can be no question about it. But what good has he done for them? He did condescend to sell them grain and provide a free lunch, but insensitivity to their feelings when they were family members is not exactly doing good.[28] (Much later, in I Samuel 24:17, David addresses a similarly reproving expression to Saul when David had a chance to kill the king in a cave but did not.) Joseph's "good" is planting a goblet in a boy's sack and then accusing him of stealing it. This is a double lie, one for the prevarication itself and one for the resort to an object used in magic. Now Joseph's purpose is clarified: he is giving his brothers a lesson in villainy compounded, in how it feels to be falsely accused. Would it be true, however, to say that Joseph was entirely innocent before being thrown into the pit by his brothers? Like the rabbi who responds to a fete in his honor by replying, "About my humility you said nothing,"[29] of his own responsibility, Joseph is silent.

Returning to the city, the brothers prostrate themselves before Joseph. Reiterating essentially what has been said before, Joseph's question-statement is, "What is this deed that you have done? Do you not know that a man like me practices divination?" (Gen. 44:15). The method of divination referred to is called hydromancy: water is poured into a vessel or an object is thrown into a vessel containing water so that figures form in the moving liquid by which the diviner foresees the future. (Sometimes oil is thrown in to expedite the rippling effect.) Hydromancy was one of the practices of the magicians who were unable to help either Pharaoh or Nebuchadnezzar interpret their dreams. In Israel divination was outlawed (Deut. 10), and whether Joseph only wanted his brothers to believe that he, as a high Egyptian official, practiced this craft or whether he actually did so cannot be determined. Later Hebrew generations in exile heaped even greater ridicule upon the magic and idol worship of the pagan religions among whom they lived. When Ibn Ezra declares that "Joseph, of course, did not practice magic,"[30] he cannot mean that he knows from the text that this was so but rather assumes that Joseph remained a Jew and therefore was prohibited from such a practice. But, if Joseph had become thoroughly Egyptianized, performing divination (recall the great stress Judaism places upon performance of outward acts), he would be doing in Egypt just what Egyptians of his position did.

At the mention of divination the brothers are thrown off the track about Joseph's identity and feel even worse, as if through some pagan process their crime could be ferreted out (albeit a false crime substituted for the real one of years ago). Judah realizes there is no way of proving their innocence. He then leads the brothers in atoning for their past misdeeds as well as in acting properly in the present situation by declaring: "Here we are, then, slaves of my lord, the rest of us as much as he in whose possession the goblet was found" (Gen. 44:16). This is the lesson—leaders must identify their fate with their followers—that Moses would be taught.[31] This truly is collective responsibility. Neither Joseph nor his clone, Benjamin, nor any brother, will hereafter be singled out for punishment for the sins of the community.

The Fathers: Judah and Jacob

At that moment Judah establishes his leadership among his brothers by making a plea to Pharaoh's administrator to let Benjamin go back with his brothers while keeping him, if that is what is wanted, as a slave. The very fact that the speech is made, quite apart from its content, signifies a radical change: at least one brother is able to speak reasonably to

Joseph. The longest speech in the Book of Genesis deserves careful attention.

This all goes back to the time when Jacob lost his favorite son, Joseph. In a manner of speaking, Judah did try to save Joseph's life, but from Jacob's standpoint, as well for generations of rabbis, Judah did not do what he ought to have done, namely, bring Joseph back to his waiting father. To sell another person's liberty, the more so a brother's, is a grave offense.[32] Later, though Jacob recognizes Judah's preeminence among the brothers, he does not fully forgive him, as his blessing shows. Judah, we know, committed another wrong in regard to his daughter-in-law, Tamar. As Judah protected Shelah, his surviving son, by withholding him from Tamar, so Jacob resists sending Benjamin to Joseph because the father fears danger to the last son of his marriage to Rachel.[33] In each case there is a violation of collective morality: personal interest is indulged in the safeguarding of a surviving son instead of looking toward a common fate for the community.

When Judah says that Tamar is right, he comes to accept that his role in assuring the survival of his family must be played out in conformity to the moral law. Armed with this acceptance, Judah is able to counter with a more powerful argument Joseph's insistence that Benjamin is guilty of stealing and therefore must be his slave.

Many commentators say that Judah's speech is persuasive. But to whom? What Judah does is recount to Joseph the conversations about Benjamin between the brothers and their father, emphasizing the father's sorrow. His father will die if Benjamin does not return, and Judah cannot bear watching him grieve. Judah asks only to take Benjamin's place so his father will not suffer. Observing Benjamin's plight from the viewpoint of a father, Judah is able to identify with Jacob in a way he was not able to do before. Where heretofore Tamar took from Judah his pledge, Judah now pledges himself to Joseph in order to protect his father's favorite son.[34] Irony is a favorite tool of biblical writers. There is not only nobility in Judah's offer to become Joseph's slave, there is his own comeuppance, for the same Judah who once recommended selling Joseph into slavery, now offers to become Joseph's slave.[35]

"Please, my Lord," Judah begins his entreaty to Joseph, "let your servant appeal to my lord, and do not be impatient with your servant, you who are the equal of Pharaoh" (Gen. 44:18). The plea for patience may be just what it appears to be, namely, a request to be heard through to the end by buttering up the high administrator. It may also be an indirect way of saying that Pharaoh's high administrator, who is so exalted in status he need not fear the consequences, bears some responsibility for these events. Why "the equal of Pharaoh" is close to a demigod himself. This accusation in the form of praise shows subtlety. The edge is taken off the rebuke, however, by the reiteration of their relationship as "lord" and "servant."

At long last, Judah reveals in his own words (Gen. 44:20) that he is able to empathize with his father's preference for his youngest son, saying what the narrator said of Jacob's feelings about Joseph, namely, that Benjamin is "a child of his [Jacob's] old age . . . and his father dotes on him." This may be because "he alone is left of his mother" (Rachel died in childbirth), thus completing a double reference to Joseph. Judah's identification with Jacob is now complete down to the image of the grieving, gray-haired old man.

Yet there is no reason, really, for such words to appeal to an administrator of Pharaoh who has no personal connection with the people involved. Aimed at Judah's brother, Joseph, however, the constant reference to their father's grief was effective. Thus, "Joseph could no longer control himself before all his attendants, and he cried out, 'Have everyone withdraw from me!' So there was no one else about when Joseph made himself known to his brothers. His sobs were so loud that the Egyptians could hear, and so the news reached Pharaoh's palace" (Gen. 45:1-2). Is this a victory of Joseph over his brothers or a defeat, as they once again cause him to lose control?

The brothers listened, apparently dumbfounded, as Joseph revealed himself to them, albeit in a cutting way: "I am your brother Joseph, he whom you sold into Egypt" (Gen. 45:4). Joseph then explains that all of this is part of a divine plan to save the family and the people from whom they had come. Incredibly, "it was not you who sent me here, but God" (Gen. 45:8). If Joseph is not responsible for the bad things that happened within his family, if his brothers also are blameless, and his father deserves pity, then who is responsible?

When the brothers throw themselves on the ground before this Egyptian high administrator, right after his silver goblet has been found in Benjamin's bag, Joseph's first childhood dream is at last realized: all eleven of his brothers are bowing down to him. Even Joseph, when these dreams flitted across his mind on first catching sight of his brothers, gives signs that he is amazed at the working of providence. And when Judah begins his confession saying "Here we are, then, slaves of my lord"(Gen. 44:16), Joseph's hegemony could not be more complete. And that is the trouble. It is blasphemous for Judah to refer over and over to Joseph as "lord" and "my lord." It is idolatrous of Joseph to accept being referred to in such terms. It is idolatrous of the brothers to bow to him. In the Esther story, Mordecai will not bow to Haman, who held a post in Babylon equivalent to Joseph's in Egypt. Earlier, when the brothers entered Joseph's grand home, "they presented to him the gifts . . . bowing low before him to the ground" (Gen. 43:26). In commenting on this gesture, Westermann makes the important distinction that "mere prostration is submission but prostration with the presentation of gifts is homage."[36] To anticipate, if Joseph is not acting in the place of God, he sure has worked hard to get there.

Family Parallels

As Joseph is to his brothers—their deceit is mutual—so was his father Jacob to his father-in-law Laban. As Benjamin is endangered by being falsely called a thief so his mother Rachel was endangered by stealing her father's gods and then denying it. The parallels between the Jacob and Joseph stories are powerful. The most obvious similarity is their three-part plot structure. Both begin with deception of the father and treachery between brothers, which includes the threat of the murder of the younger brother (Esau threatens to kill his brother, Jacob, Gen. 27:41-42; Joseph's brothers talk of slaying him and casting him into a pit, Gen. 37:20). Neither story tells anything of the fortunes of the older brothers during the twenty-year separation from the younger brother in a foreign land and the eventual reunion of the estranged brothers.[37]

After Rachel gave birth to Joseph, Jacob asked Laban for permission to return with his wives and children and flocks to his homeland. But Laban, like Joseph the vizier, said, "I have learned by divination that the Lord has blessed me on your account" (Gen. 30:27), and he went on to ask what wages he desired to keep bringing these heavenly benefits. Jacob answered that he would take every spotted and speckled animal, and if he kept any that were not so marked, "they got there by theft" (Gen. 30:33). Jacob then schemed to have goats and sheep born spotted and speckled and further arranged that "the feeble ones went to Laban and the sturdy to Jacob" (Gen. 30:42). In other words, Jacob cheated Laban as he knew Laban was trying to cheat him. When Jacob told his wives Rachel and Leah what had happened, preparatory to asking them to leave their father and make their lives alone with him, he did not mention his own chicanery, saying merely, "God has taken away your father's live-stock and given it to me" (Gen. 31:9). Like father, like son; Joseph will soon claim that his family's quarrels had a divine purpose.

As Jacob fled in the night after having deceived his father, Isaac, in order to receive the main blessing, so he flees again by night, this time from Laban. In a few days Laban catches up with them and claims that Jacob has stolen his family idols. Jacob replies in the same vein as the brothers in regard to the silver goblet: "But anyone with whom you find your gods shall not remain alive!" (Gen. 31:32). The narrator then goes on to say that "Jacob, of course, did not know that Rachel had stolen them" (Gen. 31:32). They did not talk much in that family! As her father searches, Rachel, who is sitting on the statues, falsely tells him that she cannot get up because she is menstruating. To cap it all off, after reciting the immense effort he has made to bring prosperity to Laban, a statement both true and false, Jacob attributes the fact that he emerged so rich not to his own labor and ingenuity but to the Almighty: "Had not the God of my father, the God of Abraham and the Fear of Isaac been with me, you would have sent me away empty-handed" (Gen. 31:42). Like Jacob, like Joseph. But, also, like Laban the trickster, like Joseph, from Laban's divination to his false accusation of stealing.

There are telling differences between the two stories. The Jacob story is introduced and periodically marked by divine speeches that are either promises concerning the future or specific directions. The general out-come of the Jacob story is clear from the outset. Jacob will be the hero, will prevail over Esau, and will be the ancestor of a nation. The central motifs of departure and return are accompanied by divine assurances that these are legitimate decisions, and the major characters frequently as-cribe events to divine intervention. All is under the control of Yahweh, the God of his fathers. With Joseph, however, whether or not the dreams will turn out to be predictive is not clear at the beginning of the narrative. No communication between the God of his fathers and Joseph is ever mentioned; nor does Joseph even speak the name of the God of his fathers. Throughout the narrative, we wonder just who might be Joseph's

God. We are not told the end of the story until we are there, when Joseph tells us that "God meant it for good."

Joseph's brothers' attitude toward the past is similar to Jacob's: they all regard their past treatment of their brother as wrong. Because of past betrayal, Jacob expects revenge from Esau and Joseph's brothers from him. Jacob and Esau weep together, a sign of genuine reunion in which the past is forgotten. Joseph neither forgives his brothers nor declares that they have atoned for their past treatment of him, a point stressed at the close of the story after Jacob's burial. Joseph's brothers fear revenge and twice mention forgiveness of sin in their seemingly false statement to Joseph. Joseph's response carefully reassures them of safety but avoids any hint of forgiveness. God has brought good out of evil, but not forgiveness.

Joseph manages to accuse his brothers of stealing from him by planting his silver goblet in Benjamin's sack. The word for stealing contains the root *gnb*, which occurs only in four episodes in Genesis: when Jacob tells Laban that certain goats and sheep, if found among his flock, should be counted as stolen (Gen. 30:33); when Rachel steals Laban's idols (Gen. 31:19); and twice when Laban tells Jacob that he should not have stolen away secretly (Gen. 31:25–28). The author of Genesis is using this root word to underline the lengthening series of deceptions in Jacob's family.[38]

Would you trust a son of Jacob, perhaps his most clever son, to separate the work of his own design from the work of God? And when he attributes events to God's handiwork, would you believe him? Joseph assures his brothers that he will sustain all of them and their children (Gen. 50:21), an illustration of good will, surely, but also an unmistakable show of great power—almost, one might say, of divine power. Although Joseph interprets his whole history as being within the providence of God (Gen. 45:5, 7–8; 50:20), when one compares what he says elsewhere about God's workings, we find that he seems to be the one doing the work. Take, for example, Joseph's divinations through dreams. Joseph states that interpretations belong to God (Gen. 40:8), but then he goes on to do the interpreting. Perhaps the line is too finely drawn, but at least the ambiguity is unmistakable. My view is that Joseph has not changed. He still wants domination, even if he has to play God to get it.

Jacob and Joseph

Selling a person into slavery severs all bonds. In this sense, Joseph may no longer legally or morally be Jacob's son, for the father took part in this chain of events. It is no small thing for a Hebrew man to forget the house of his father, especially when forgetfulness implies that one no longer has something. Has Joseph decided to leave behind everything in his former life, his slavery, his troubles, his family, and his God? Is God, as Joseph implies in the naming of his sons, behind this forgetfulness or could von Rad be right in assessing the meaning of Joseph's being given an Egyptian name as his "being placed within the protective sphere of an Egyptian deity"?[39]

Noblesse oblige: the feeling is one of munificence presided over by the far-seeing, infinitely wise, and utterly benevolent Joseph. Now that he is in charge, and he lets everyone know he is in charge—"you must tell my father everything about my high station in Egypt" (Gen. 45:13)—Joseph showers goods and affection upon his family. He urges his father to come to him, he assures his brothers that he will provide for them and their families everything they might need in time of famine, and "he kissed all his brothers and he wept upon them; only then were his brothers able to talk to him" (Gen. 45:15). Family conversation, if not family peace, is at long last established.

Not to be outdone, Pharaoh promises to provide land and other good things. He urges Jacob and his sons to leave their belongings behind, as they will be entirely provided for when they come to Egypt. As if to accentuate his superiority, Joseph gives the brothers clothing, though he gives Benjamin several changes and three hundred pieces of silver, thus reinforcing his and his father's partiality. Joseph has now joined Pharaoh in giving Egyptian wares to Jacob's family. Daniel would not have approved.

Upon hearing the news that Joseph was alive and in a high position in Egypt, Jacob's "heart went numb" (Gen. 45:26). But upon being persuaded all this was true, he decided to go to Joseph in Egypt. Along the way he went to Beer-sheba

> where he offered sacrifices to the God of his father Isaac. God called to Israel in a vision by night: "Jacob! Jacob!" He answered, "Here." And He said, "I am God, the God of your father. Fear not to go down to Egypt, for I will make you there into a great nation. I Myself will go down with you to Egypt, and I Myself, will also bring you back; and Joseph's hand shall close your eyes." (Gen. 46:1–4).

This apparent deviation from the main story line reveals once more that Joseph may talk about God but God speaks directly only to Jacob. Always, Jacob was a person greatly in need of reassurance. What, exactly, is the nature of this reassurance, if that is indeed what it is? God tells Jacob that it is all right to go to Egypt, but Jacob is not commanded to go. That is a big difference. However awful life in Egypt will be, if Jacob chooses to go there, God will make it help fulfill His promise.

Taking an opportunity to gain the special loyalty that strangers entirely dependent on him might give, Pharaoh tells Joseph to choose from among his brothers "capable men" to put in charge of the king's livestock. Looking for trustworthy administrators, kings chose eunuchs and selected foreigners (often those especially odious to the local population, so they would have to rely on the good graces of their ruler for protection).[40]

"One of the surprises of the Old Testament," Argyle feels, "is the absence of any allusions in the prophets to the story of Joseph." Why, Argyle asks, do these prophets, concerned as they are with virtue, not

> appeal to the example of Joseph, the righteous man, afflicted and sold by his brethren, steadfast in resisting temptation, unjustly accused, arrested, imprisoned, humiliated, but afterwards exalted, the benefactor of others, tender-hearted, forgiving his brethren who had wronged him. His loving-kindness and mercy, his faithfulness and truthfulness, his righteousness and justice, were the very qualities for which the great ethical prophets stood.[41]

Joseph, I will say in greater detail later, is not exactly a radical criticizing existing rulers and institutions for treating their subjects' desires and needs as inferior to their own. On the contrary, he stands with existing authority, exemplified by the highest ranking patron, Jacob, his father; Potiphar, his master; the jailer, his keeper; and Pharaoh, his king. The prophets were confounded, I conclude, as we are, by the moral ambivalence of Joseph's legacy. They did not read him out of the Torah but neither did they glorify or teach his Egyptian brand of wisdom.

How did Joseph's inner journey begin? Did he learn from the master trickster, his father, Jacob? Like his father, Joseph is a survivor; he is good at overcoming adversity. Like his father as well, Joseph is gifted in deception; he manipulates Pharaoh as well as his family. One can always count on Joseph, as one could his father, to figure out the angles. The comparison ranges from the obvious fact that both men have brothers who tried to kill them to less obvious differences: Jacob married Rachel, who turned against her father's idol worship, while Joseph married Asenath, the daughter of the priest of On in the holy city of Ra, the Egyptian sun god. Commentators have disagreed forever about whether it was right for Jacob and later Joseph to be embalmed. It is a sign both of Joseph's Egyptianization and his identification with his father.

As Ginzberg summarizes the rabbinical commentators,

> The whole course of the son's life is but a repetition of the father's. As the mother of Jacob remained childless for a long time after her marriage, so also the mother of Joseph. As Rebekah had undergone severe suffering in giving birth to Jacob, so Rachel in giving birth to Joseph. As Jacob's mother bore two sons, so also Joseph's mother. . . . As the father was a shepherd, so the son. As the father served for the sake of a woman, so the son served under a woman. Like the father, the son appropriated his older brother's birthright. The father was hated by his brother, and the son was hated by his brethren. The father was the favorite son as compared with his brother, so was the son as compared with his brethren. Both the father and the son lived in the land of the stranger. The father became a servant to a master, also the son. The master whom the father served was blessed by God, so was the master whom the son served. . . . The father and the son were both blessed with wealth. Great things were announced to the father in a dream, so also to the son. As the father went to Egypt and put an end to famine, so the son. As the father exacted the promise from his sons to bury him in the Holy Land, so also the son. The father died in Egypt, there died also the son. The body of the father was embalmed, also the body of the son. As the father's remains were carried to the Holy Land for interment, so also the remains of the son. Jacob the father provided for the sustenance of his son Joseph during a period of seventeen years, so the son provided for his father Jacob during a period of seventeen years.[42]

Why this identity? Better still, what can these parallels tell us about the meaning of the Joseph stories? In the first chapter I raised the question of why the line of the patriarchs does not continue through Joseph but rather takes a circuitous route through Moses. A possible answer, we can now see, is that Joseph is essentially an extension of Jacob, the favored son acting out the unrealized dreams of the father. The kind of dominion for which Jacob longed could not be achieved within the confines of his extended family. There had to be a larger stage. Playing out Jacob's innermost longing through Joseph, however, revealed the temptation for the clever chief of clan to worship his own superiority. Joseph's second dream, in which his parents bow down to him, is not fulfilled, for his father is too canny and too tough—too much like his son—to be so easily manipulated.

Cautious to the last, even when apparently reconciled with his brother Esau, Jacob took no chances. When Esau suggested that he and his men accompany Jacob and his family, he excuses himself by saying, "My lord knows that the children are frail and that the flocks and herds, which are nursing, are a care to me; if they are driven hard a single day, all the flocks will die. Let my lord go on ahead of his servant, while I travel slowly" (Gen. 33:13-14). Esau countered by offering to give some of his armed men to accompany Jacob. "Oh no, my lord is too kind to me!" the wily one replied (Gen. 33:15). Tricky to the end, Jacob instead went to Succoth (the place for which the booths made on that holiday are named).

Unlike his son, Jacob is a whiner, with a considerable range. It varies from Job-like resignation when he realizes he must send Benjamin to Egypt (Gen. 43:14), to recriminations against an unkind fate, to a kind of worrying for its own sake. To Joseph, success is the best revenge, for when he gets to the top, he stays there. By contrast, top or bottom, Jacob continuously complains.

Before Jacob has a chance to greet him, "Joseph ordered his chariot and went to Goshen to meet his father Israel; he presented himself to him and, embracing him around the neck, he wept on his neck a good while" (Gen. 46:29). Since when do Hebrews use chariots to get around? Only when they think they are the boss (after all, in Exodus the Egyptians chased the Israelites in chariots). Shortly, Jacob will take steps to make sure that his son is disabused of these notions of dominance. The father greets the son of his dreams on a plane of equality. As for Jacob, even on his deathbed he is not finished playing games.

Noticing Joseph's sons, Jacob asks who they are and, upon being told, asks to bless them. The scene is quite touching: "And Israel said to Joseph, 'I never expected to see you again, and here God has let me see your children as well'" Gen. 48:11). Well said; yet the old man has one more trick in him. Jacob explains to Joseph how the Lord appeared to him and reiterated the promise of making his family a "community of peoples." This is easier said than done, but Jacob does his part: the two sons who were born to Joseph in Egypt Jacob will recognize as his own and therefore will be part of his inheritance. Those that come after, however, will be Joseph's responsibility. Aware of Joseph's drive to dominion, moreover, Jacob has arranged to teach his son a valuable lesson.

The stratagems these two old antagonists follow can be understood only by following the biblical account:

> Joseph took the two of them, Ephraim with his right hand—to Israel's left—and Manasseh with his left hand—to Israel's right—and brought them close to him. But

Israel stretched out his right hand and laid it on Ephraim's head, though he was the younger, and his left hand on Manasseh's head—thus crossing his hands—although Manasseh was the first-born. . . . When Joseph saw that his father was placing his right hand on Ephraim's head, he thought it wrong; so he took hold of his father's hand to move it from Ephraim's head to Manasseh's. "Not so, Father," Joseph said to his father, "for the other is the first-born; place your right hand on his head." But his father objected, saying, "I know, my son, I know. He too shall become a people, and he too shall be great. Yet his younger brother shall be greater than he, and his offspring shall be plentiful enough for nations." So he blessed them that day, saying, "By you shall Israel invoke blessings, saying: God make you like Ephraim and Manasseh." Thus he put Ephraim before Manasseh. (Gen. 48:13-20)

Now we understand the import of the Tamar and Judah story in which the twin who came first as determined by the red thread (Zerah) actually appeared second (after Perez); apparently this anomaly was rectified at Jacob's insistence. Perhaps the story should be read backward as ratifying the greater stature the Perezites, the progenitors of King David, achieved compared to their brother tribe, the Zerahites.[43]

Once more, but this time as a father should, Jacob reminds Joseph that he is not all powerful. Joseph may try to influence events, but higher forces will prevent him from doing so. If power means the ability to get what you want over the opposition of others, Jacob shows that Joseph lacks power. He is not divine. He cannot make the world the way he wants it. When Jacob blesses Joseph's two sons, but not in the usual order, he shows Joseph that he is still the one who hears God's voice. "The question," as von Rad rightly puts it, "about whether Joseph remained faithful to Yahweh . . . is not answered for the reader."[44]

The struggle between Jacob and Joseph continues into a contest over who shall have Benjamin. While an outside observer might think the father and the son had nothing left to fight about, they pull and haul over the one thing left to divide among them, Benjamin's affections. Once again a father and his son are competing over a younger son.[45] Though Benjamin is referred to as a lad, the list of his sons (Gen. 46:21) numbers ten; this is some kid! Obviously, the idea that a father of ten is somehow too young to leave his father will not wash.

Joseph is not a laggard in this competition. He maneuvers, as we have seen, with a major purpose in mind—to compel his brothers and father to send Benjamin to him. He has his silver divining cup planted in Benjamin's bag, thus establishing a legal right to keep him as a slave. Recall that upon taking his brothers to lunch, it is Joseph's catching sight of Benjamin, not of his brothers in general, that leaves him "overcome with feeling toward his brother and . . . on the verge of tears" (Gen. 43:30). Thus it is Benjamin who deprives Joseph of his self-control. Reasonable synonyms for the root *kmr*, for feeling, would be "yearn" or "warm" or "passionate." Besides giving Benjamin a much larger portion of food and money and other good things, Joseph, in the same passage just quoted, blesses him as if he were the man's father. Alone among the brothers, Benjamin is his full brother and the only one not responsible for his being sold into slavery.

Joseph blesses Benjamin by asking that God be gracious to him. His actual words bring to mind a lonely father bestowing favors upon a much dependent son: "May God be gracious to you, my boy" (Gen. 43:29). Jacob, when consenting that Judah take Benjamin to Egypt, asks for God's mercy (he calls Him El Shaddai, the family name for the Almighty; Gen. 43:13). "Together," Brueggemann asserts, "these two speeches bestow upon Benjamin the most profound blessing Israel has in its power to give."[46] But why is it Joseph's place to do what only a father can do for a son?

Why, in Franz Delitzesch's words, is it that "Jacob desires Joseph to put his hand under his thigh, and thus to assure him on the grounds of the covenant of circumcision made with Abraham, the actual proof of faithful love."[47] Steiner says that,

> There seems to be only one answer: that Joseph, because of his sale into slavery, is legally no longer Jacob's son. This selling is a renunciation of family solidarity with and responsibility for Joseph, and although the sale took place without the father's knowledge, it must affect the father as it does all other kinsmen. This would explain Jacob's deferential address.[48]

This interpretation would also explain why Jacob had to adopt Joseph's sons into the family and why he was able to exclude all who had came after the first two, as if he were entering into a contract for the first time. Jacob required a double oath from Joseph, then, because that is what would be required of a stranger.

The struggle between Joseph and Jacob over Benjamin is one in which the youngest son plays no part. He is entirely passive. Since he is the son of the wife-mother they have in common, it is a struggle over the future in which the tribe of Benjamin would hold the narrow strip of land between the southern kingdom of Judah and the northern kingdom. Each wishes to hold on to the future, each giving it his special stamp. The issue is whether the Hebrew people will become Egyptianized through Joseph or remain Israelites through Jacob.

The bittersweet blessings of Jacob (see Chapter 7) reflect a compromise. Joseph receives double the portion of the other brothers, and as long as he lives he is preeminent among his brothers in Egypt. But future leadership is given to Judah. Joseph is accepted, even honored, as would an Egyptian ruler who helped the Hebrew people in his time. But his example is not to be imitated.

Notes

1. The Rev. A. W. Argyle, "Joseph the Patriarch in Patristic Teaching," *The Expository Times* 67 (Oct. 1955-Sept, 1956): 199–201, quote on 200.

2. W. Lee Humphreys, *Joseph And His Family A Literary Study* (Columbia: Univ of So. Carolina Press, 1988), 180.

3. Bruce T. Dahlberg, "On Recognizing the Unity of Genesis," *Theology Digest* 24 (1976): 360–367, at 364–65.

4. Louis Ginzberg, *The Legends of the Jews*, vol. 2, trans. by Henrietta Szold (Philadelphia: Jewish Publication Society of America, 1977), 80.

5. The term translated as "acted like a stranger" to them is reflexive. Literally, it reads "he strangered himself" to them. As awkward as this phrase reads in English, the Hebrew is more powerful than the English. Joseph talks like an Egyptian, eats Egyptian food, wears Egyptian clothing, and now deliberately chooses to act Egyptian. Our narrator presents to us Joseph the Egyptian.

6. Robert Alter, *The Art of Biblical Narrative* (New York: Basic Books, 1982), 162–63.

7. Ramban (Nachmanides), *Commentary on the Torah: Genesis*, trans. and annotated by Rabbi Dr. Charles B. Chavel (New York: Shilo Publishing, 1971), 511–12.

8. Ibid.

9. Nehama Leibowitz, *Studies in the Book of Genesis* (Jerusalem: World Zionist Organization, 1972), 458.

10. George Bush, *Notes, Critical and Practical on the Book of Genesis*, vol. 2 (New York: Ivison & Phinney, 1859), 300.

11. Alter, *Art of Biblical Narrative*, 163.

12. Emanuel Feldman, "Joseph and the Biblical Echo," *Dor le Dor* 13 (1985): 161–66; quote on 165.

13. The text says "no more" (Gen. 42:13).

14. *"Rashi"* on the Pentateuch: Genesis, trans. and annotated by James H. Lowe (London: Hebrew Compendium Publishing, 1928) 439.

15. Bush, *Genesis*, 302.

16. Claus Westermann, *Genesis 37–50*, trans. by John J. Scullion (Minneapolis: Augsburg Publishing, 1986), 109–10.

17. H. Gunkel, quoted in Westermann, *Genesis*, 110.

18. We as the readers know it is Joseph who has done this to them, not the God of their fathers. Joseph is acting like a god. Joseph has now done more than just become an Egyptian. As a high-ranking Egyptian official, he has assumed, on his own, the position of God, which the brothers acknowledge verbally, if unknowingly.

19. *Soncino Chumash: The Five Books of Moses with Haphtaroth*, ed. by the Rev. Dr. A. Cohen (London: Soncino Press, 1966), 266.

20. James S. Ackerman, "Joseph, Judah, and Jacob," in Kenneth R. R. Gros Louis, *Literary Interpretations of Biblical Narratives*, vol. 2 (Nashville: Abingon Press, 1982), 85-113; quote on 94.

21. Benno Jacob, *The First Book of the Bible: Genesis*, His commentary abridged, ed. and trans. by Ernest I. Jacob and Walter Jacob (New York: KTAV Publishing House, 1974), 289.

22. Westermann, *Genesis*.

23. Ginzberg, *Legends of the Jews*, vol. 5, fn 256, 352.

24. Sandor Goodhart, "'I am Joseph': René Girard and the Prophetic Law," in *Violence and Truth: On the Work of René Girard*, Paul Dumouchel, ed. (Stanford University Press, 1988), 53-74, quote on 69.

25. Ibid.

26. Ibid., 73.

27. The best account I have read is James G. Williams, "The Innocent Victim: René Girard on Violence, Sacrifice, and the Sacred," *Religious Study Review* 14, no. 4 (October 1988): 320-326. See also René Girard, *Violence and the Sacred* (Baltimore: Johns Hopkins University Press, 1977).

28. If Joseph is referring back to the rape of Dinah at Shechem, when several brothers from her mother requited that peoples' desire to live peaceably among them (while marrying Dinah to their son) with a mass slaughter, the question might make more sense. Simeon and Levi's reply to Jacob's reproof at that time was another answer-question, "Shall our sister be treated like a whore?" (Gen. 34:31). Jews have been answering questions with questions for a long time. The answer for those who disagree with mass slaughter must be "no" but that an individual act does not justify treachery and murder against a whole people. Dinah had been taken by force, but the men of Shechem offered to set things right in a generous way. Now try the aphorism raised in Proverbs 14:29: "he that is slow to wrath is of great understanding; but he that is hasty of spirit exalteth folly." Perhaps, as the wife-sister stories suggest, an extreme penalty is applied to foreigners who take Israelite women.

29. I am indebted to Nelson Polsby for this joke.

30. Ibn Ezra, *Commentary on the Pentateuch: Genesis (Bereshit)*, trans. and annotated by H. Norman Strickman and Arthur M. Silver (New York: Menorah Publishing, 1988), 395.

31. See Aaron Wildavsky, *The Nursing Father: Moses As a Political Leader* (University of Alabama Press, 1985).

32. See the discussion in Calum M. Carmichael, "Some Sayings in Genesis 49," *Journal of Biblical Literature* 88 (1969): 435-444; at 438.

33. See also Sarah Ben-Reuven, "I will be the Pledge and you may require him of my hand," *Beth Mikra* 33 (1987/88): 337-38.

34. Gerhard von Rad, *Genesis: A Commentary* (Philadelphia: Westminster, 1972), 394-95; Ben-Reuven, "I will be the Pledge," 338.

35. Nahum M. Sarna, *The JPS Torah Commentary: Genesis* (Philadelphia: Jewish Publication Society, 1989), 307.

36. Westermann, *Genesis*, 125.

37. Peter D. Miscall, "The Jacob and Joseph stories as analogies," *Journal of Studies in the Old Testament* 6 (1978): 28-40.

38. See Siegfried Raeder, "Die Josephsgeschichte im Koran und in Alten Testament," *Evangelische Theologie* 26 (1966), 169-190, at 175. Michael Hildenbrand helped

me analyze the occurrence of this root. I do not include repetitions of the same theme, i.e., about Jacob's stealthy departure.

39. von Rad, *Genesis*, 373.
40. Stalin had much the same purpose in mind when he selected Polish Jews to run the secret police in that country after the Second World War. See John Clark and Aaron Wildavsky, *The Moral Collapse of Communism* (San Francisco: Institute for Contemporary Studies, 1990).
41. Argyle, "Joseph the Patriarch," 199.
42. Ginzberg, *Legends of the Jews*, vol. 2, 4-5. For further parallels between father Jacob and son Joseph, see Yaakov ben Yitzchak Askenazi, *Tz'enah Ur'enah. The Classic Anthology of Torah Lore and Midrashic Comment*, trans from the Yiddish by Miriam Stark Zakon (Jerusalem: Hillel Press, 1984), vol. 1. *Beveishis*, 175ff; *"Rashi"*, 392-93; Humphreys, *Joseph and His Family*, 38.
43. K. Luke, "Two Birth Narratives in Genesis (Gen. 25:19-26; 38:27-30)," *Indian Theological Studies* 17 (1980): 155-80; at 173.
44. von Rad, *Genesis*, 436-37.
45. Westermann, *Genesis*, 105.
46. Walter Brueggemann, *Genesis: A Bible Commentary for Teaching and Preaching*, in the *Interpretation* series (Atlanta: John Knox Press, 1982), 341.
47. Quoted in Franz Steiner, "Enslavement and the Early Hebrew Lineage System: An Explanation of Genesis 47:29-31; 48:1-16," in *Anthropological Approaches to the Old Testament, Issues in Religion and Theoleoy 8*, Bernhard Lang, ed. (Philadelphia: Fortress Press, 1985), 21-25; quote on 22.
48. Ibid.

5

The Egyptianization of Joseph Compared to the Hebraicization of Daniel and Esther

Joseph and Pharaoh have at least one thing in common: they believe the divine is active in human affairs. He is not only up there but down here. The difference, supposedly, is that Pharaoh considers himself one of the gods, while Joseph believes that neither he nor Pharaoh is divine. The difficulty with this interpretation is that the difference between them in this respect is continually narrowed by Joseph's behavior.

To begin with, the first thing that Joseph does upon being called to the audience to hear Pharaoh's dream is revealing. Though on special occasions Egyptians might paste on false beards, they shaved not only their faces but also their heads. Only foreigners and people of inferior ranks are pictured wearing beards.[1] Hebrews, by contrast, grew beards and wore them as part of their badge of identity.[2] "In ancient Israel," Lynn M. Bechtel writes, "a man's beard was a symbol of his dignity and vitality, particularly his sexual vitality." That is why, when King David's ambassador to the Ammonites had half their beards cut off, this shamed them and thus belittled the king for whom they stood.[3] As Bechtel has it, "A further complication of the shaming action was the men's necessary exclusion from the Israelite community."[4] Before they could rejoin the community, David had them wait in a town along the way. The relationship between the male beard and community membership makes more poignant Joseph's voluntary shaving of his own beard, thereby severing himself from the Jewish community and joining the Egyptian.[5] That Joseph immediately cut his hair and put on Egyptian clothes tells us that he has chosen assimilation.

In order to understand Joseph's developing relationship to Pharaoh, we must have before us the entire text explaining how Joseph became a high-ranking official. When Joseph outlined his recommendations for

119

dealing with the predicted years of famine, his plan pleased Pharaoh and his retinue:

> And Pharaoh said to his courtiers, "Could we find another like him, a man in whom is the spirit of God?" So Pharaoh said to Joseph, "Since God has made all this known to you, there is none so discerning and wise as you. You shall be in charge of my court, and by your command shall all my people be directed; only with respect to the throne shall I be superior to you." Pharaoh further said to Joseph, "See, I put you in charge of all the land of Egypt." And removing his signet ring from his hand, Pharaoh put it on Joseph's hand; and he had him dressed in robes of fine linen, and put a gold chain about his neck. He had him ride in the chariot of his second-in-command, and they cried before him, "Abrek!" Thus he placed him over all the land of Egypt.
>
> Pharaoh said to Joseph, "I am Pharaoh; yet without you, no one shall lift up hand or foot in all the land of Egypt." Pharaoh then gave Joseph the name Zaphenath-paneah; and he gave him for a wife Asenath daughter of Poti-phera, priest of On. Thus Joseph emerged in charge of the land of Egypt. (Gen. 41:38–45)

The Egyptians will be expected to conduct themselves as Joseph directs. Is the administrator for the great god Pharaoh not a lesser god? The literal meaning of "by your command shall all my people be directed" is "on your mouth shall all my people kiss," suggesting at least the homage due to royalty. This feeling is solidified by giving Joseph the gold chain of command and having him ride in the chariot of Pharaoh's second in command where the people, seeing him, were required to cry out *Abrek!*, meaning something like "kneel down" or "bow the knee."[6] Joseph is not being initiated into just any political system but rather a steep hierarchical order that justifies vast inequalities based on birth and position. The ring carries with it the rights to use Pharaoh's seal, which, impressed upon wax, signified his authority. Is it also a sign that Pharaoh's values are imprinted on Joseph? The gold that so amply circles Joseph's neck bespeaks high status. Is it also, we may ask, a chain by which Joseph is held fast to Pharaoh?[7]

The turnaround is now complete. "The Hebrew slave who was once in charge of Potiphar's household," Davidson writes, "is now come, through imprisonment, to be in charge of Pharaoh's household."[8] Soon he hopes to be in charge of his own household. Indeed, with the name of the father of his new wife, Poti-phera, but a play on the name of his old master, Potiphar, Joseph has succeeded in having sex with a high-ranking Egyptian woman but legally and on his own terms.

We know that a change of clothes signifies a change of power for Joseph. Does it also portend a change of allegiance? When Pharaoh places his signet ring on Joseph's hand he is repeating the action of Judah, who gave his ring, carrying his personal seal, to Tamar in exchange for intercourse with her.[9] Is Joseph also prostituting himself? Worse yet, is Joseph taking orders from a person who thinks of himself as divine?

In urging Pharaoh to take steps to implement the plan of action necessary to avoid famine, Joseph uses the same Hebrew expression, *elohim-ahseh* he used on three other occasions in regard to a forthcoming divine act. Sarna says "deliberately," "as though to imply that Pharaoh was the human counterpart of God."[10] This is close to idolatry. As if to take up this charge, Judah, later pleading with Joseph, refers twice to him as if he were a Pharaoh, "my lord" (Gen. 44:18). Later still, when Joseph tells his brothers he is their leader and talks about his high status, he refers to himself as "father to Pharaoh." This title was common enough in those days—possibly equivalent to the "vice presidents" that corporations throw around so freely nowadays—but, nevertheless, for a Hebrew such an epithet was fraught with the danger of violating what was to become the first commandment.[11] Did Joseph, the question is, recognize Pharaoh as his substitute father?[12] Or as a god?

By having Joseph dressed "in robes of fine linen" (Gen. 41:42), a very expensive material, Pharaoh not only showed Joseph a mark of favor but also made sure he would be recognized everywhere as a high official.[13] Think back to Joseph's long-sleeved coat; think again of Joseph's garment in the hands of Potiphar's wife: clothes have been his undoing. On the surface, the linen robes suggest a break with the past and a richer future. But then Joseph never did do well with rich clothes that singled him out as an object of attention.

In ancient times it was believed that a person who could name a thing could control it. That is one reason why God resists being named, so the divide between the holy and the human, between self-worship and worship of the Absolute, is maintained. But patrons can change the name of mere mortals, often signifying a promotion, as when Moses alters Hoshea to Joshua.[14] God changed Jacob's name to Israel and Abram to Abraham, indicating a new destiny if not necessarily a wholly new character; Pharaoh does the same thing to indicate the break toward the better in Joseph's life.[15] Presumably the renamed accepts the right of the renamer to alter his status. If Joseph is, indeed, as Christians say today, born again, Pharaoh is his father and mother, giving birth to his new Egyptian persona. In this tradition, Pharaoh "gave Joseph the name Zaphenath-paneah," variously defined as "he who reveals that which is hidden"[16] or Egyptian for "God speaks, he lives" or "creator of life."[17] Fox translates Joseph's Egyptian name as "The God Speaks and He Lives" as an appropriate name to the story: "Yosef lives, and through him, so do Egypt, his family, and the future People of Israel."[18]

Besides giving Joseph his new name, Pharaoh also chooses a wife for him, Asenath, daughter of the priest of On. Joseph is not merely marrying an Egyptian woman but a woman whose family belongs to the priesthood. As Joseph rises in status, questions about his fidelity to the religion of his original family grow. His language, food, clothing, customs, and wife are now Egyptian.

Pharaoh's investiture of Joseph runs parallel to a Hebrew ceremony for captive women. When God, to whom all victories are credited, brings Israel a military victory and its soldiers see a woman captive they would like to marry, a specific process is made mandatory: "you shall bring her into your house, and she shall trim her hair, pare her nails, and discard her captive's garb" (Deut. 21:12-13). What the woman has to say about all this is not specified.

As best as can be determined, Joseph was among the elite of Egyptian officials, though not necessarily the highest below Pharaoh. He administered the personal estates of Pharaoh, helped build government warehouses in which to store food, distributed food during famine, and collected agricultural taxes. Thus he would have had titles like Overseer of the Granaries of Pharaoh, Great Steward of the Lord of the Two Lands, Great Chief in the Palace, Royal Seal-Bearer, Foremost of Courtiers, and Chief of the Entire Land.[19]

While waiting for the years of famine, Asenath bore Joseph two sons. Their names are indicative of Joseph's thought vis-a-vis Egypt. His first-born, Manasseh, carried a name that meant "God has made me forget completely my hardship and my parental home." His second-born was called Ephraim, "meaning 'God has made me fertile in the land of my affliction'" (Gen. 41:51-52). The first-born's name indicates cooptation by Egypt. The second-born's could be applied to the increase of the Hebrew people under a later Pharaoh, or it could just signify the growth of Joseph's wealth and power.

Though von Rad tries to rescue Joseph's reputation by saying that "forget" in regard to forgetting his ancestral home means "to have something no longer," neither the text nor the rabbis would have it.[20] It would be more apt to translate the term as "to want something no longer."

A neat defense is given by Philo and others who claim that Joseph did not get in touch with his father because he would have had to tell him about his brothers' effort to kill him or to sell him into slavery.[21] Maybe. Stronger still would be the rationale that if Joseph had contacted his father, without waiting for his father to come to him, Joseph could not have been certain of his brothers' peaceableness or their truthfulness. Suppose the brothers said that they were also surprised to see Joseph alive, being fooled by his torn robe? It would still be ten to one against Joseph. The Ramban indelicately asks, "How was it possible that he did not send a single letter to his father to inform him of his whereabouts and comfort him, as Egypt is only about a six-day journey from Hebron?"[22] No decent son would fail to inform his parents of his whereabouts, especially if he were successful, unless he wanted to separate himself from them and perhaps his new friends from his old family.

"By these new connections," von Rad concludes, "Joseph has become completely Egyptian."[23] Consider in this context the remarkable treatment of the death of Jacob some years later. Although Joseph honors Jacob's request to be buried in the grave he had prepared in Canaan where his wife and father and grandfather were also buried, Joseph mixes it with a bow to the Egyptian method. He orders his father embalmed, which is not the way of the Israelites, whose customs feature a quick burial in a shroud ("dust to dust") until this day. Worse, "Embalming a corpse in ancient Egypt," Ward informs us, "was purely a priestly function."[24] In effect, Joseph handed the preparation of his father's body for burial over to Egyptian priests. No wonder Jacob insisted he should be buried in the land promised to him and his forefathers.

The entourage was large, noisy, and remarkable in its composition. The Egyptian turnout is what might be expected for a royal death: "all the officials of Pharaoh, the senior members of his court, and all of Egypt's dignitaries" (Gen. 50:7). "The twofold 'all' is deliberate exaggeration."[25] There was also a large military contingent including horsemen and chariots, the very kind that pursued the Israelites in the desert in the course of their exodus from Egypt hundreds of years later.[26]

Military protection may have been prudent in view of the local circumstances and the rank of the people involved; a military escort may also have been a mark of royal respect; yet this guard of honor may also have served to prevent the Israelites (by then an important part of Egyptian administration) from failing to return to Egypt. As the narrator informs us that the households of Joseph, his father and his brothers all came with the funeral procession, we also learn that "only their children, their flocks, and their herds were left in the region of Goshen" (Gen. 50:8). Were they being held hostage? And was this remarkable funeral procession, which mourned for seven whole days in "a very great and solemn lamentation" (Gen. 50:10), part of the Egyptianization of the Israelites? The local inhabitants must have thought so, for they are quoted as saying, "This is a solemn mourning on the part of the Egyptians" (Gen. 50:11).[27]

"After burying his father, Joseph returned to Egypt, he and his brothers and all who had gone up with him to bury his father" (Gen. 50:14). Has Joseph, then, buried his father twice, in his body and a second time for the end of his heritage? Do Jews return to Egyptian ways or do they depart from them?

The Pharaoh who elevated Joseph to a high rank was no one's fool. He needed help and he took it where he could find it. He rewarded that help generously. If Joseph remained loyal to Pharaoh, these honors and perquisites would be maintained. Were Joseph disposed to be disloyal, however, Pharaoh had taken care to entangle him in a series of relationships and commitments so warm and supportive yet so confining that he would find it difficult to act against the ruler's will. The Pharaoh was too wise to command a powerful personality like Joseph to do as he was told. Instead, the Pharaoh acts so Joseph will want to do as much and more for him than he could do for himself.

Upon hearing that Joseph's brothers were coming to Egypt, Pharaoh and his court reacted enthusiastically, offering them every assistance and assuring them that "you shall live off the fat of the land" (Gen. 45:18). Indeed, Pharaoh is so enthusiastic he bids Joseph provide wagons for the brothers, encourages them to take their wives and children, "and never mind your belongings, for the best of all the land of Egypt shall be yours" (Gen. 45:20). Most of these belongings would consist of clothes and bedding and cooking utensils, precisely those items that remind a people, especially a Hebraic people, of their way of life. To help the process of Egyptianization along, Joseph provides his brothers with Egyptian clothing: "And to his father he sent . . . the best things of Egypt" (Gen. 45:23). Now they were being told both by Pharaoh and by Joseph to leave behind their distinctive marks.

What else did Joseph give his brothers? The kind of advice that children have resented from time immemorial, especially when proferred by a sibling with an air of condescension: "Do not be quarrelsome on the way" (Gen. 45:24). Among the new state of affairs the brothers are to experience in Egypt will be a brother who acts with the right of a father. Joseph instructs his brothers like a father or a teacher when he says:

> So when Pharaoh summons you and asks, "What is your occupation?" you shall answer, "Your servants have been breeders of livestock from the start until now, both we and our fathers"—so that you may stay in the region of Goshen. For all shepherds are abhorrent to Egyptians. (Gen. 46:33-34)

To ensure conformity with his views, Joseph selects only five of his brothers to come before Pharaoh. But the brothers do not speak as instructed. Instead "they answered Pharaoh, 'We your servants are shepherds, as were also our fathers'" (Gen. 47:3). Through this little bit of disobedience, passive resistance really, the brothers indicate they do not wish to be Egyptianized but rather to live as their fathers have done. It is Pharaoh who follows Joseph's line by offering to put the brothers in charge of his livestock, meaning cattle, rather than sheep. "The grant has a price," Brueggemann comments, "it is to join the royal world."[28]

Pharaoh, in sum, marries Joseph to Egypt. Pharaoh puts his signet ring on Joseph's hand as a husband would on a bride. He dresses him in finery and gives him jewelry, the gold necklace of office, as befits a bride. He gives him a new name as a wife takes on the name of her husband. By marrying Joseph to the family of his god, Pharaoh seeks supremacy over both the man and his God. Pharaoh marries, clothes, adorns, and names Joseph, everything, it seems, but literally giving birth to him as a new Eqyptian man.

It is hard to know how his father and brothers regarded the Egyptianization of Joseph, whether as securing their survival or as threatening their identity. As a youth, Joseph was hardly aware of the hostile interpretation his family would give to his dreams. In captivity he became not the dreamer per se but the controlled interpreter making his own dreams come true through divining the dreams of others. Perspective on Joseph's ability as an interpreter of dreams and as a guardian of his people may be gained by distancing ourselves from the scene we have been studying. Going ahead in time to Israel in exile via the Book of Daniel, we find an author alert to the precarious nature of Joseph's claims, but even more so to the un-Hebraic character of Joseph's actions.

The Book of Daniel as a Satire on Joseph

The serious purpose of the first part of the Book of Daniel is to contrast the behavior of Daniel and his friends, taken in captivity from Jerusalem to Babylon and trained in the sciences of the local wise men, with that of Joseph.[29] For Daniel defends the ways of his people and his God down to the food and customs that, in Judaism, are ordained by God. Even when as apprentices to the prince of the eunuchs, who gave them new names as Pharaoh did to Joseph, they are told they must eat the food the king provides for them, Daniel and company insist on eating grains and vegetables to avoid transgressing the Torah's dietary proscriptions. They recognize that getting used to foreigners' food is a step toward accommodation to their values.[30]

Strong language is used: "But Daniel purposed in his heart that he would not defile himself with the portion of the king's meat, nor with the wine which he drank: therefore he requested of the prince of the eunuchs that he might not defile himself" (Dan. 1:8). Just to make sure the parallel cannot be missed, we are told that, as happened with Joseph in regard to his masters (Potiphar, the jailer, and Pharaoh), "Now God had brought Daniel into favour and tender love with the prince of the eunuchs" (Dan. 1:9). Their keeper, though favorable to them, fears that they will not do well on this less sumptuous diet and that he will therefore get into trouble with the king. Daniel prevails on him for a trial, and it turns out that their vegetarian diet makes them look even better.

The Book of Daniel is roughly divided into two quite different parts. The first six chapters, which I am using here, comprise tales of court life in Persia during the Babylonian captivity, together with a storyline of an unmistakable kind—foreign influences are evil but may be overcome by the faith of the fathers.[31] The last five chapters can be characterized as an apocalypse, a collection of fantastic visions related to the end of the world in which struggles are carried on between evil powers that are decided by the glorious intervention of God. In the end of days, the righteous are reborn and the rule of God is inaugurated. When the official Jewish text of the Bible was fixed, roughly in the first century, most apocalypses were omitted because the Pharisees considered them idolatrous. "According to Rabbi Akiba, consulting an apocalypse would cost the reader his part in the world to come."[32] A compromise was made by including Daniel among the Writings, an expression the rabbis used to indicate that it was not holy. (The exact expression is that such Writings would "not defile one's hands; not being holy there was no need to wash one's hands before reading it."[33]) I treat the first part (without pretending to understand the second) as a polemic against Joseph's surrender to foreign ways by indicating, in the person of Daniel, what Joseph ought to have done.

From one point of view, the relationship between Joseph's and Daniel's stories can be aptly summed up by a line from the hit song of the musical *Annie Get Your Gun*: "Anything you can do, I can do better." So Joseph interprets Pharaoh's dreams after being told what they are; anybody can do that. Daniel not only interprets a king's dream but first reconstructs it in precise detail for Nebuchadnezzar, who had—to his dismay—forgotten what it was. The phantasmagoric character of this dream and its intricate patterns serve as a strong counterpoint to Pharaoh's oversimplified dreams, stripped of all but the barest facts, which Joseph interpreted. Joseph's Pharaoh was disappointed with his magicians and advisers for failing to come up with any interpretation. Daniel, however, by dint of his retrodiction of what Nebuchadnezzar's first dream was and his prediction of how it would be realized, saves all the wise men of Babylon, whom the king had ordered to be put to death because of their failure to guess what he had dreamed.

Joseph is taken out of the pit and sold into slavery; not much talent required there. Daniel goes into a pit, the famous lion's den, and emerges unscathed. For good measure, his three companions, Shadrak, Mesach, and Abed-nego, fall into a fiery furnace and come out unharmed, while the guards who attempted to throw them in perish from the heat outside the furnace. One is left with the impression, after reading Daniel, that anyone could do what Joseph did.

The parallels of Daniel to the Joseph stories were undoubtedly meant to be evident from the first. Daniel and his brothers are identified as children of Judah (read "Jacob"). They are renamed by the prince of the eunuchs as Joseph was by Pharaoh. And like Joseph they were found by the king to be "ten times better than all the magicians and astrologers that were in all his realm" (Dan. 1:20). The times when the Book of Daniel changes from Hebrew to Aramaic stand for the influence of foreign tongues, much as the Joseph stories emphasize his fluency in Egyptian.[34] Both Joseph and Daniel get new clothes and gold collars and are promoted. Even the fear of lions devouring these children of Israel harks back to the false story that Joseph was torn apart by a wild beast, as Jacob reminds Judah through the patriarch's mixed blessing.

Should any doubt remain, the redoubtable Rosenthal in his 1895 article "The Joseph Stories and the Books of Esther and Daniel Compared" (in German) reveals numerous examples of similar phraseology: "Compare Gen. 41:15 'I have dreamed a dream and there is none to interpret it and I have heard about you, that you can understand a dream to interpret it.' and Dan. 5:15-16 'But they could not tell the interpretation of the word. And I have heard about you that you can interpret and solve difficult problems.'"[35]

In all the Bible, only two Jews, Joseph and Daniel, interpret dreams. To indicate that this is not what Jews are supposed to do, both interpretations concern dreams of foreign rulers and in both cases the interpreters attribute the powers they possess to God.[36] Robert Gnuse finds the following similarities in the two sets of dreams: in both (1) a man of God decodes symbols only with divine help, (2) the interpreter is a young Jewish prisoner in a foreign land, (3) professional dream interpreters have failed the ruler, (4) God brings the dreams to pass, and their interpretation is said to be certain, (5) the young man is elevated from his lowly position, and (6) the heathen praise God.[37]

When Nebuchadnezzar dreamed a second dream, Daniel did not do what Joseph did, tell the king the bad news by framing it in the context of good news, thus hoping to gain employment at court. Rather Daniel told his king off, to wit: "break off your sins by righteousness, and thine iniquities by shewing mercy to the oppressed; if it may be a lengthening of thy tranquillity" (Dan. 5:27). To the king's son, Daniel told the meaning of the writing on the wall to the effect that Belshazzar would be driven from office, prefacing his remarks with excoriation of the son's behavior (Dan. 5:23).

A major point of both the Daniel and Joseph stories is to show that God's will rules mankind. The parallel between the two stories is buttressed by countless similarities of structure. There are, however, important differences that should be reemphasized. Joseph is a self-promoter; Daniel promotes his God. While Daniel becomes ruler of the province of Babylon, he makes no move toward getting it.[38] Most important, the Book of Daniel tells the reader over and over that Daniel and his brothers remain faithful to God. This is done in two effective ways. They respond to or even seek challenges by placing their lives in the hands of God, so as to show His saving powers. And they defend their customs as part of their faith. In Judaism, a religion in which observance is given far more emphasis than in most others, this is no small matter.[39]

Were Joseph's fidelity to Yahweh presumed, however, as authors closer to the time and scene would have known, there would have been no need to demonstrate again and again what real faith required. There came the time, for instance, when those opposed to Daniel got the king to sign an irrevocable decree to the effect that anyone who made petition to any man or god for the next month should be cast into the lion's den. The first thing Daniel does upon verifying this decree is something Joseph never does: he prays to God. Moreover, he opens wide his windows and prays toward Jerusalem three times a day "as he did aforetime" (Dan. 6:10). Daniel presumably could have kept his prayers to himself, but he did not, at the risk of his life. Joseph never prays.

Though Dwight MacDonald notes in his anthology of parodies that "Parody seems not to have appealed to the ancient Hebrews or the early Christians; at least there is no trace of it in either the Old or the New Testament," Daniel presents an exaggerated version of the same tale. The story of Daniel is a satire in the usual sense of the term—something that ridicules human vice or folly with the intent to bring about improvement. Daniel is also a parody on Joseph in that the vice and the folly are constituted by Joseph's assimilation to the ways of the Egyptians—their food, their clothing, their names, all of which Daniel rejects—and hence to their destructive powers. Where Joseph helps his Pharaoh become more powerful—more wealth and land, and more dependent subjects— Daniel pointedly tells off his king in the name of God's higher morality. The joke is on the Josephs of this world to help their sovereigns and thus their people by making them more moral rather than necessarily more powerful.

Esther and Mordecai versus Joseph

What, to reiterate a major question of the Joseph and the Daniel stories, should a high-ranking Hebrew do when working for a foreign ruler? Esther uses her beauty and her conjugal relation with King Ahasuerus to save her people from destruction. She is also discreet; at her cousin Mordecai's urging, she reveals neither "her kindred nor her people"

(Esther 2:20). What she attempts is dangerous for her and for her people. Games played at high levels tend to have high stakes.

Esther had been chosen to serve as queen from among the virgins of the land of Babylonia, where Jews had been brought in their captivity, to replace the independent Queen Vashti. Her dilemma comes when Haman, the court adviser, enraged by Mordecai's refusal to bow down to him as if he were a pagan god, persuades the king to send commands "to destroy, to kill, and to cause to perish, all Jews both young and old, little children and women, in one day . . . and to take the spoil of them for a prey" (Esther 3:13). A minor court official and Esther's guardian, Mordecai, like Jacob upon being shown evidence of Joseph's death, "rent his clothes." Unable to persuade Mordecai to cease mourning, Esther sends him a messenger who returns with his request that she plead for her people before the king. Reminding Mordecai of what he already knows—that unauthorized people who come before the king are put to death unless he points his golden scepter at them—Esther hesitates. His answer deserves recording:

> Think not with thyself that thou shalt escape in the king's house, more than all the Jews.
>
> For if thou altogether holdest thy peace at this time, then shall there enlargement and deliverance arise to the Jews from another place; but thou and thy father's house shall be destroyed: and who knoweth whether thou art come to the kingdom for such a time as this? (Esther 4:13-14)

Acting under stress, Mordecai still exudes serene confidence that God's promises will be kept no matter what. He appeals not only to Esther's fidelity to him but to her self-interest through her identification with other Jews. The court Jew may be favored, but her fate is still aligned with her peoples'. His appeal rises above the ordinary because Mordecai gives Esther a sense of her mission.

The Book of Esther is remarkable among the Writings in that it contains no mention of God or religion (though his will to keep the commandments is evidently what makes Mordecai refuse to bow to Haman and later to the king, and what gives Mordecai hope of deliverance).[40] No thought is given to appeal to other Jewish communities. Instead, Esther takes charge, fasts for three days while advising the Jews of her city to do the same, and plans to see the king uninvited, saying, "If I perish, I perish" (Esther 4:16), a repeat of Jacob's fear of losing Benjamin: "If I am to be bereaved, I shall be bereaved" (Gen. 43:14).[41]

As Jacob said that he loved Joseph more than his other sons, so was it said that the "king loved Esther above all the women" (Esther 2:17).

Queen Esther comes to King Ahasuerus. He points the golden specter toward her, indicating his high regard, and she tells him to come to a feast and invite Haman. Overjoyed that he is dining alone with the king and queen, ecstatic at the extent of his preferment and the riches that will flow therefrom, Haman nevertheless can take no pleasure in his fabulous fortune "so long as I see Mordecai the Jew sitting at the king's gate" (Esther 5:13). In a sentence, a feeling of murderous envy is created among people who, no matter how much they have, cannot be happy if others are doing well. The narrator does not call him "the Jews' enemy" (Esther 3:10) for nothing. Haman's wife and advisers pick up what is manifest in his thoughts by counseling him to build a high gallows on which to hang Mordecai.

Unlike the Joseph stories, the Book of Esther has no dreams, but there is the equivalent in a restless night the king spends. He has the history of the kingdom read to him and discovers that Mordecai had earlier saved his life by informing him of a plot against him. So the king orders Haman to get out royal clothes, which his chief adviser thinks must be for him. Instead, in this story of a wicked man who is punished by his own devices, the king orders Haman to dress Mordecai in royal garb and crown and put him on a horse so he can display the king's favor. The first thing that Pharaoh did to Joseph after he emerged from prison was to have his clothes changed to royal finery.

At the second banquet to which she invited them, Queen Esther informs Ahasuerus that Haman wants to have all the Jews of the kingdom killed through kingly command. Furious, the king spots Haman in the palace garden apparently trying to rape Esther, though actually the bad man was pleading for his life. "So they hanged Haman on the gallows that he had prepared for Mordecai" (Esther 7:10).

There can be no doubt, as Ludwig Rosenthal demonstrated in 1895, that there are many parallels between the Esther and Joseph stories, including similar wordings. For instance, the language Joseph uses in spurning Potiphar's wife is paralleled in the phrases by which Mordecai refuses to bow down to Haman as the king commanded: "And much as she coaxed Joseph day after day he did not yield to her" (Gen. 39:10); "Now it came to pass when they [the king's servants] spake daily unto him [Mordecai], and he hearkened not unto them" (Esther 3:4).

The linguistic influence is indicated chiefly in the use by the author of the Book of Esther of expression and figures of speech that only appear in the story of Joseph. Here are some of them:
a) "for so are fulfilled the days of those who are embalmed" (Gen i,3); "for so are fulfilled the days of their anointing" (Esther ii, 12). . . .
Consecutive appearance of parallel introductory formula in corresponding groups of verse in both stories:
"let the king appoint officers . . over all the countries of his kingdom"
"let every young virgin of goodly appearance be gathered."
"And the matter was pleasing in the eyes of the king." (Esther ii, 3-4)
"let Pharaoh . . . appoint officers over the land . . ."
"let all the food of the good years be gathered."
"And the matter was pleasing in the eyes of Pharaoh." (Gen. xli, 34-37)[42]

Q.E.D.

There is much in the Esther and Joseph stories that resonate with Egyptian and Hebrew wisdom literature. Mordecai and Joseph are successful, we are told, because they follow God's commands. By refusing Potiphar's wife, Joseph obeys the wisdom of those who warn against the wiles of foreign women.[43] Consider Proverbs 16:14, "The wrath of a king is as messengers of death: but a wise man will pacify it." The ancient Egyptian vizier Ptah-Hotep advised: "With him who is more exalted than thou, call not. With him who is stronger than thou [contend not; for he will take] of thy portion and [add it to] his."[44] However, Mordecai refuses this advice in regard to earthly rulers, hardly a way to get on in this world.

The strategic use of Esther's beauty and charm to serve her people, to which the text often calls attention, has ample precedent. Tamar and Ruth have gone before her. One difference, however, is that Esther used the legally acceptable route of marriage. By marrying out of her faith, however, albeit to a king, she may have created a precedent of dubious value to those who wish to keep their people intact. There is a Talmudic discussion (b.Sanhedrin 74b) about whether Esther should have committed suicide before submitting to the King's embrace. The verdict was no.[45]

An addition to the traditional Hebrew text of the Book of Esther, contained in the Septuagint, may have been intended to meet this concern. There she says, "I abhor the couch of the uncircumcised, and of every stranger." To make sure that her intent is not missed she claims she had relations with the king out of necessity, for, she prays, "I abhor the symbol of my proud station [the crown], which is upon my head in the days of my splendour: I abhor it as a menstruous cloth, and I wear it not in the days of my tranquility." Like Daniel, she does not eat the king's food or drink his wine or rejoice.[46] That, I think, is the complete orthodox Esther.

Suppose we read the story of Esther as a manual on how Jews might survive as a minority subject to persecution under foreigners.[47] Haman presents the king with a plan to benefit himself by killing Jews, seizing their property, and selling the proceeds. David Daube shows that Esther and Mordecai also claim to promote royal self-interest by offering a plan of taxation under which the revenues Haman had promised would be restored to the king.[48] Thus the Book of Esther ends with King Ahasuerus levying a tax and elevating Mordecai into high position.

In support of Daube's thesis, which rescues the last part of Esther from the near-universal charge of being unconnected with what has gone before, are the frequent references to the king's pleasure. Ahasuerus is not a fellow to be satisfied with a little merrymaking: his banquet lasts six months. The moral is summed up by Jones' statement of the purpose of the Book of Esther: "demonstrating that a Jew can be a civil servant and can successfully refuse to give what he considers excessive honor to a Gentile superior."[49] As W. Lee Humphreys puts it, "The tale does not permit any tension to develop between their double loyalty to king and co-religionists; the actual benefit of each party coincides."[50]

The purpose of the Book of Esther may be seen in the light of the benefit accrued to the king because of his good treatment of the Jews. The book "as it lies before us is supplying to the heathen powers-that-be a program for a sensible treatment of the Jews. . . . Indeed, that ruler will do best whose fiscal affairs are run by a court-Jew or a pair of them."[51] We find that Joseph also benefits those over him when they treat him well.

Both Joseph and Esther are victorious in part because of careful planning. There is no sense that they should be ashamed to have deceived those who would harm them or to have connived so as to gain the good favor of the kings that rule in their countries. If one has to cohabit with foreigners they should presumably be high up enough to help preserve one's people. No hint is given that high places should be abandoned; rather, they are to be used for the benefit of the kingdom and of one's people.

The lesson of Esther for the Joseph stories is that it is not necessary to adopt foreign customs or to bow to foreign gods in order to rise to high places. The most telling comparison is intended. Compare the elevation of the wicked Haman with that of the presumably noble Joseph:

> And the king took his ring from his hand, and gave it unto Haman . . . the Jews' enemy (Esther 3:10).

> And Pharaoh took off his ring from his hand, and put it upon Joseph's hand. (Gen. 41:42)

My verdict in comparing the morality of the protagonists in the two stories is Esther and Mordecai, yes, Joseph, maybe.

Hanging Haman on the gallows he constructed for Mordecai does more than satisfy general ideas of justice; it fulfills what might be deemed the principle of the false witness in which the Israelites are told that "you shall do to him as he schemed to do to his fellow" (Deut. 19:19). Unfortunately for the descendants of the sons of Israel—are the Israelites oppressed in Egypt because Joseph oppressed the Egyptians?—the same teaching applies to their own people.

Notes

1. S. R. Driver, *The Book of Genesis* (London: Methuen & Co., 1904), 341.
2. Eric I. Lowenthal, *The Joseph Narrative in Genesis* (New York: Ktav Publishing House, 1973), 49.
3. Lynn M. Bechtel, "Shame as a Sanction of Social Control in Biblical Israel: Judicial, Political and Social Shame," *Journal for the Study of the Old Testament 49* (February 1991): 49–76, quote on 69.
4. Ibid., 707.
5. For a person to feel ashamed, there must be community presence in some violation of community mores (Bechtel, "Shame as a Sanction of Social Control," 74–76). Judah reflects a fear of being shamed when his emissary cannot find the prostitute with whom he had intercourse the day before in order to give her her fee and redeem the pledges he left with her. For "Judah said, 'Let her keep them [his pledges, his seal, cord, and staff], lest we become a laughingstock'" (Gen. 38:23).
6. Nahum M. Sarna, *The JPS Torah Commentary: Genesis* (Philadelphia: Jewish Publication Society, 1989), 286; the *Torah*, 76.
7. Decoration with gold chains or gold collars was the usual way of rewarding officers who pleased the king. They were sometimes thrown down to the recipient from his throne by the king himself or given to servants to distribute. This distinctive honor was called "receiving gold." The cloth was plain white but necessary color was added by embroidered fittings, by elaborate collars of semi-precious stones, and by an abundance of jewelry of which the gold chain placed about Joseph's neck was an example. (Albert Edward Bailey, *Daily Life in Bible Times* (New York: Charles Scribner's Sons, 1943), 68.)
8. Robert Davidson, *Genesis 12–50* (Cambridge: Cambridge University Press, 1979), 247.

9. W. A. Ward, "The Egyptian Office of Joseph," *Journal of Semitic Studies* 5 (January-December 1960): 144-150.
10. Sarna, *Genesis*, 285. The verses mentioned are 25, 28, and 32.
11. Ward, "Egyptian Office of Joseph," 149.
12. "The term 'father to Pharaoh' can only be the equivalent of the Egyptian title God's Father; God, in this title, always refers to the living king" (Ward, "Egyptian Office of Joseph," 144-50; quote on 149).
13. *"Rashi" on the Pentateuch: Genesis*, trans. and annotated by James H. Lowe (London: Hebrew Compendium Publishing, 1928) 429.
14. The *Soncino Chumash: The Five Books of Moses with Haphtaroth*, ed. by the Rev. Dr. A. Cohen (London: Soncino Press, 1966), 258.
15. See Davidson, *Genesis 12-50*, 247.
16. *Soncino Chumash*, from the Targum, 258.
17. The *Torah*, 76.
18. Everett Fox, *In the Beginning: A New English Rendition of the Book of Genesis*, Translation With Commentary and Notes by Everett Fox (New York: Schocken Books, 1983), 171.
19. Ward, "Egyptian Office of Joseph," 146-47, 150.
20. Gerhard von Rad, *Genesis: A Commentary (Philadelphia: Westminster, 1972)*, 379. See also Davidson, *Genesis 12-50*, 248, who argues that the next chapter would show that "Joseph was far from forgetting his father's family."
21. Louis Ginzberg, *The Legends of the Jews*, vol. 5, trans. Henrietta Szold (Philadelphia: Jewish Publication Society of America, 977), 365, fn. 370.
22. Ramban (Nachmanides), *Commentary on the Torah: Genesis*, trans. and annotated by Rabbi Dr. Charles B. Chavel (New York: Shilo Publishing, 1971), 513. The lame excuse that Ramban offers for a Jewish boy who would not call home is that Joseph somehow understood that the bowing down of his brothers and father could not possibly be accomplished in their homeland but only in Egypt after he became successful.
23. von Rad, *Genesis*, 379.
24. William A. Ward, "Egyptian Titles In Genesis 39-50," *Bibliotheca Sacra* 14 (1957): 40-59; quote on 56.
25. Claus Westermann, *Genesis 37-50*, trans. John J. Scullion (Minneapolis: Augsburg Publishing, 1986), 200.
26. Bruce Vawter, *On Genesis: A New Reading* (Garden City, NY: Doubleday, 1977), 471.
27. No doubt Gibson is correct when he notes that the adulation of Joseph "was distinctly un-Hebraic. It was almost as if the divine honor that in Egyptian belief belonged to the Pharaoh as a son of the gods were being transferred to him. Was the storyteller not overdoing it? What could he be getting at?" (John C. L. Gibson, *Genesis*, vol. 2 (Philadelphia: Westminster Press, 1982), 262-63.
28. Walter Brueggemann, *Genesis: A Bible Commentary for Teaching and Preaching* (Atlanta: John Knox Press, 1982), 357.
29. Since they are put in charge of the master of the eunuchs, Daniel and his friends may have been castrated. In any event, they are portrayed as celibate. (André Lacocque, *The Book of Daniel* (Atlanta: John Knox Press, 1976), 31-32.
30. H. L. Ginsberg, quoted in Lacocque, *Book of Daniel*, 31.
31. See Lacocque's introduction to *Book of Daniel*, 1; see also H. L. Ginsberg, "The Composition of the Book of Daniel," *Vetus Testementum* 4 (1954): 246-75; and H.

L. Ginsberg's *Studies in Daniel* (Text in Studies of the Jewish Theological Seminary of America, vol. 14) New York, 1948, Studies 2 and 4 and addenda to Section 4.

32. Lacocque, *Book of Daniel*, 6.
33. Ibid.
34. Ibid., 13.
35. Ludwig A. Rosenthal, "Die Josephsgeschichte, mit den Buchern Ester und Daniel verglichen," *Zeitschrift fur die Atestament Liche Wissenschaft* 15 (1895): 279-80.
36. Nahum M. Sarna, *Understanding Genesis* (New York: McGraw Hill, 1966), 218-19.
37. Robert Gnuse, "Dreams and their Theological Significance in the Biblical Tradition," *Currents in Theology and Mission* 8 (1981): 166ff.
38. John C. L. Gibson, *Genesis*, vol. 2 (Philadelphia: Westminster Press, 1982), 259.
39. von Rad, *Genesis*, 436-37, italics added.
40. S. Talmon, "'Wisdom' In the Book of Esther," *Vetus Testamentum* 13 (1963): 419-55; see 428-30; and the references cited there.
41. On this idem-per-iden construction, see G. S. Ogden, "Idem Per Idem: Its Use and Meaning," *Journal for the Study of the Old Testament* 53 (1992): 107-120
42. The verbs describing the bestowing of royal honours are identical:

Esther viii 2,7
wayyasar ("and he took off")
wayyittenah ("and he put it")
wayyalbesh ("and he clothed")
wayarakivehu ("and he caused him to ride")
wayiqra lefanaw ("and he cried before him")
Gen. xli 42-43
wayyasar ("and he took off")
wayyitten 'ota ("and he put it")
wayyalbesh ("and he clothed")
wayyarkev ("and he caused him to ride")
wayyiqre'u lefanaw ("and they cried before him") Moshe Gan, "The Book of Esther in the Light of the Story of Joseph in Egypt," *Tarbits*, 31 (1961), 144-149. Scholars disagree as to whether the Book of Esther refers to the early Persian period, under the Cyrus the Great, 559-530, as Josephus thought, or Xerxes I or in the later Persian period. Gunkel prefers Darius II and Hoshander Artaxerxes II, 404-358. There is also no agreement on whether Esther refers to real historical events or is a "clever literary fabrication which is but a disguised report on historical facts that came to pass in Hellenistic or in Roman times and were retrojected into the Persian period for reasons of political expediency." (Talmon, "'Wisdom' in the Book of Esther," 420.

43. Charles T. Fritsch, "God Was With Him," A Theological Study of the Joseph Narrative, *Interpretation* 9 (1955): 22-34; see 33.
44. Cited in Talmon, "'Wisdom' in the Book of Esther," 447.
45. Yehuda T. Radday, "Esther With Humour," in Yehuda T. Radday and Athalya Brenner, *On Humour and the Comic in the Hebrew Bible* (Almond Press, 1990), 295-313.
46. "Esther, additions at the end of Chapter 4," *The Sepuagint Version of the Old Testament with an English Translation* (Grand Rapids: Zondervan Publishing House, 1970), 657.

47. Bruce William Jones, "Two Misconceptions about the Book of Esther," *Catholic Biblical Quarterly* 39 (1977): 171. He quotes W. Lee Humphreys, "A Life-Style for Diaspora: A Study of the Tales of Esther and Daniel," *Journal of Biblical Literature* 92 (1973), 211-23.
48. David Daube, "The Last Chapter of Esther," *Jewish Quarterly Review* 37 (1946-7): 139-47; 141-44.
49. Jones, "Two Misconceptions," 178.
50. Humphreys, "Life-Style for Diaspora," 215.
51. David Daube, "Damnum and Nezeq," *Rechtshistorisches Journal* 8 (1989): 275-285.

6

Joseph the Administrator

"There is none so discerning and wise as you," Pharaoh says of Joseph. The two men appear to be well matched; both expect to become better off as a result of their meeting. The wisdom referred to is administrative. As Westermann says, "the 'wise and intelligent' man described here is the one who is capable of planning and carrying through important economic measures."[1] "The reason for the Pharaoh's choice," Coats writes, "does not lie primarily in Joseph's ability to see into the future, but in his ability to administer an office of power like the one he recommended."[2]

After the seven years of abundance passed and the seven years of famine began, in accord with Joseph's interpretation of Pharaoh's dreams, there was famine everywhere in the known world. As Egyptians became hungrier, they appealed to Joseph as the person Pharaoh had designated to distribute food. As the famine worsened, Joseph took money for foodstuffs, filling the Pharaoh's coffers, until the money ran out. The entirety of Joseph's administration is described in the following passages:

> Joseph gathered in all the money that was to be found in the land of Egypt and in the land of Canaan, as payment for the rations that were being procured, and Joseph brought the money into Pharaoh's palace. And when the money gave out in the land of Egypt and in the land of Canaan, all the Egyptians came to Joseph and said, "Give us bread, lest we die before your very eyes; for the money is gone!" And Joseph said, "Bring your livestock, and I will sell to you against your livestock, if the money is gone." So they brought their livestock to Joseph, and Joseph gave them bread in exchange for the horses, for the stocks of sheep and cattle, and the asses; thus he provided them with bread that year in exchange for all their livestock. And when that year was ended, they came to him the next year and said to him, "We cannot hide from my lord that, with all the money and animal stocks consigned to my lord, nothing is left at my lord's disposal save our persons and our farm land. Let us not perish before your eyes, both we and our land. Take us and our land in exchange for bread, and we with our land will be serfs to Pharaoh; provide the seed, that we may live and not die, and that the land may not become a waste.

So Joseph gained possession of all the farm land of Egypt for Pharaoh, every Egyptian having sold his field because the famine was too much for them; thus the land passed over to Pharaoh. And he removed the population town by town, from one end of Egypt's border to the other. Only the land of the priests he did not take over, for the priests had an allotment from Pharaoh, and they lived off the allotment which Pharaoh had made to them; therefore they did not sell their land.

Then Joseph said to the people, "Whereas I have this day acquired you and your land for Pharaoh, here is seed for you to sow the land. And when harvest comes, you shall give one-fifth to Pharaoh, and four-fifths shall be yours as seed for the fields and as food for you and those in your households, and as nourishment for your children." And they said, "You have saved our lives! We are grateful to our lord, and we shall be serfs to Pharaoh." And Joseph made it into a land law in Egypt, which is still valid, that a fifth should be Pharaoh's; only the land of the priests did not become Pharaoh's. (Gen. 47:14–26)

Bit by bit, Joseph took all the resources of the Egyptian population: first their money, then their livestock, and then their land. In desperation, they offered to become "servants to Pharaoh" if only his agent, Joseph, would provide them with seed. In addition to the money that went through Joseph's hands into Pharaoh's treasury and the vast store of animals, Pharaoh now had all the land in his own private domain, except for that held by priests. Joseph giveth and taketh away; no wonder the Egyptian serfs referred to him as "my" or "our lord." It is possible, as von Rad contends, that a stronger word than "serf"—that is, "slave"—better fulfills the intention of the writer.[3]

"This is a story," Caine concludes, "in which the pagan potentate is depicted as benign, while the Hebrew hero, normally bearer of a high moral standard, is seen as behaving in a way that offends God."[4] Pharaoh is benevolent in allowing Jacob's family to settle by themselves and to occupy important administrative positions. At the same time that Pharaoh is positively beaming at the Israelites and Joseph is providing them with what Israelis today call *protexsia*, privileged access to officialdom, the Israelite grand administrator is leaning hard on the Egyptians. There is a hint of bargaining. The Egyptian landholders insist their money is gone. If so, Joseph replies, suggesting that this may not be the whole truth, he will take payment against the value of their livestock. That is why, when they come to him the next year, the Egyptians say they are not trying to hide their desperate situation. Joseph is deliberately screwing them down.[5]

How, in Egyptian terms, was a good administrator supposed to behave? In a protective and nurturing manner, we may say. These are the words Ameni, the nomarch of the Oryx-nome, had inscribed on his tomb:

There was no citizen's daughter whom I misused, there was no widow whom I oppressed, there was no peasant whom I repulsed, there was no herdsman whom I repelled, there was no overseer of serf-labourers whose people I took for [unpaid] imposts, there was none wretched in my community, there was none hungry in my time. When years of famine came, I plowed all the fields of the Oryx-nome, as far as its southern and northern boundary, preserving its people alive, and furnishing its food, so that there was none hungry therein. I gave to the widow as to her who had a husband; I did not exalt the great above the small in all I gave. Then came great Niles, rich in grain and all things, but I did not collect the arrears of the field.[6]

Caine's judgment is severe but, I think, warranted: "He who had himself been sold, then sold others, had his people sold."[7] As Joseph did not remember his obligations to the Egyptians, so a future Pharaoh would not remember him.

Counting the ruler's wealth in the slavery of his people is extraordinary. Since Pharaoh, the father-protector of his people, had the substance required in his storehouse, it would have been proper for Joseph, acting for him, to have kept the people whole, land as well as livestock. It is as if the Pharaoh were not a hereditary ruler with extensive holdings but a vast mercantile company whose purpose it was to exact all that it could from its suppliers. "Leave no cash on the table" is not a good adage for the supposed protector of his people. The question is not one of capitalism; indeed, under Joseph, there could be no future capitalism because there would be no capitalists. When one player has all the properties, even the game of Monopoly is over. Yet no justification was offered for these confiscatory acts.

The rationale for leaving land for the priests makes no sense. While they may well have depended on the land for their livelihood, so did the peasants. Besides, if there were famine in all the land of Egypt, what did the priests live on? As far as we know, Joseph was the only source of food. For Joseph to take from Egyptian farmers is a wrong done to them. For Joseph to exempt the priests of a pagan religion is a wrong to his religion.

And worse was yet to come. On top of Joseph taking the land, even more extraordinary, "he removed the population town by town, from one end of Egypt's border to the other." This is the same action that Sennasacherib threatened Israel with in Isaiah's time (Isa. 36:10). The usual purpose of such forced uprootings and dispersals was to remove people's attachment to their ancient land as well as to demonstrate to them that they are no longer in possession. It is a vast cruelty. The parallels in our own time we owe mostly to Stalin, though he gave nothing in return. What can explain it?

Had Pharaoh done this by himself, we might not think anything of it; after all, his whims were law and he might deem the subjection of his people insufficient and therefore seek means of compelling them to be more obedient. Nor, since he thought of himself as a god, would he have reason other than his own will to listen to the voice of the people who, the Torah tells us, were pathetically grateful for having their lives saved. We do know that irredentist movements are often more nationalist than those on the mainland and that leaders born outside the main centers of power—like a Hamilton or Napoleon or Hitler or Stalin—are often more nationalist or royal than the king. But for Joseph to be the main actor, not an accomplice, tries our understanding.

Joseph's rationale for his behavior as chief administrator must have been the same as the one he later gave to his brothers, namely, that all this was part of a divine plan to keep the Hebrew people alive so that they might one day return to their native land. Perhaps we can extend this rationale to keeping the Egyptian people alive, albeit to emerge in much worse circumstances. But this is to make God an accomplice to immoral behavior.

Did these unfortunate events occur because of the normal workings of the Egyptian economy in difficult times? Egyptian farmers received governmentally set prices for their food in the seven years of abundant harvest. I infer this from Joseph's recommendation to Pharaoh: "Let all the food of these good years that are coming be gathered, and let the grain be collected under Pharaoh's authority as food to be stored in the cities" (Gen. 41:35). Why, then, was this money not sufficient to tide them over the seven lean years? In part, the answer must be that they used it up for ordinary living. But why did they run out of money so soon? Was the surplus of the first seven years bought at a discounted price? Did Joseph use his position to buy low and sell high? There are suggestions in the text that Joseph rationed the food by administrative means so that, for instance, buyers would not purchase more than their families could eat. But that does not reach the question of price. Were Egyptian farmers not informed of the coming famine, or did they not believe the warning? We cannot know, but this elementary economic analysis does suggest that market forces could not have been all that were at work to make Egyptian landholders into serfs to Pharaoh.

Joseph left the system into which he was elevated less humane than it was by making Pharaoh more powerful than he had been. In cultural terms, Joseph helped change an inclusive hierarchy, in which there was a place for a multitude of landowning farmers, into an exclusive hierarchy, narrow and steep, in which only a single hierarch rules. What, I ask, did Joseph owe to Pharaoh? Because he accepted his boss's terms, Joseph owed him fidelity. He would work for Pharaoh and not to enrich himself; he would help Pharaoh carry out the plan that Pharaoh had bought from his importuning. So far, so simple. But did Joseph owe it to Pharaoh to do better for Pharaoh than Pharaoh could have done for himself? The situation reminds me of Colonel Nicholson in the movie *The Bridge On the River Kwai*, who, in order to demonstrate British superiority over the Japanese, builds a far better bridge for them than they could have done themselves.

By dint of repetition, the narrator makes sure we know that Joseph is working overtime on Pharaoh's behalf. Thus we learn not only that Joseph collected lots of money for the produce but that he "brought the money into Pharaoh's palace" (Gen. 47:14). If it is not enough that Egyptians became "serfs to Pharaoh" (Gen. 47:19), the narrator reminds us that "the land passed over to Pharaoh" (Gen. 47:20). Immediately Joseph is quoted as telling the Egyptians that he has "acquired you and your land for Pharaoh" (Gen. 47:23). And of the produce that the Egyptians gave as payment for the land, Joseph tells the farmers to give "one fifth to Pharaoh" (Gen. 47:24). On the one hand, Joseph is the loyal steward; on the other, the merit of his stewardship clearly depends on the Pharaoh whom, readers are informed over and over, all this is for.

Pharaoh was an idolator and a dictator. His self-worship and harsh rule were not worthy of support. One might well have qualms about working for such a ruler. To be sure, Joseph was not in a position to bargain; without Pharaoh he would be left to languish his life away in a dungeon. His almost instant transformation from darkness to light undoubtedly was impressive. A moral man might justify this decision in view of the circumstances. In my opinion, however, acting so as to make Pharaoh's rule more autocratic, even less dependent on the people than before, is way above what an administrator owes his chief.

Since this is first, last, and always an account about the Hebrews, however, there is no reason for going into detail about Joseph's administration in Egypt unless there are things to be learned about Jacob's family from the story. The last sentence describing the settlement of Jacob's clan in Goshen in Egypt reads, "Joseph sustained his father, and his brothers, and all his father's household with bread, down to the little ones" (Gen. 47:12). This was Joseph's great accomplishment; he saved his family from starvation and reconciled them to himself, emerging as the leader among the sons, while keeping them alive by the resources put at his disposal by Pharaoh. By moving the Egyptians off the land, Joseph created a parallel between them and the Israelites as a nation: if they were strangers in a strange land, so too did Joseph make Egyptians strangers in their own land. The parallel continues, as Joseph made Egyptians serfs to Pharaoh, so a later Pharaoh made serfs of the Hebrew people.

How do other commentators refer to Joseph's extraordinary actions in making Egyptian farmers landless? Sarna claims that the section on Joseph's administration has no connection with the family saga but is included to show what a wonderful leader Joseph was. A supplementary explanation he offers is that the Egyptian practice of collective ownership of land through Pharaoh stands in contrast to the Israelite ideal of private property ownership. Perhaps, Sarna continues, the narrator of the biblical story also wished to draw a contrast between the ingratitude of the later Pharaoh who had forgotten Joseph, much as had the cupbearer earlier in Joseph's life, thus linking this story to the Exodus of the Israelites from Egypt.[8]

The contrast with private ownership of land works exactly the wrong way, I think, because it suggests that Joseph should not have done to the Egyptians what Israelites ought not to do to one another. Why would an administrator whose own people valued residing on the same land as a God-given commandment make it impossible for another people to do so? The administrative measures Joseph employed have every connection with the saga of the Israelites, partly because they suffered from the concentrated power a later Pharaoh used against them, but mostly because implemented, perhaps formulated, by a Hebrew, these measures raise the question of whether the moral law may be violated in the name of survival.

Does the Pharaoh Run a Hierarchical Regime?

From the outside, the regime Pharaoh runs appears to be hierarchical. Certainly, Pharaoh is at the apex; his butler, his baker, and his highly placed administrators, of whom Joseph is just one, are part of a system of ranks connoting superiority and inferiority. There are mentions of the military (the guard to honor Jacob and to guard Jacob's sons) and the priesthood (Joseph marries the daughter of the high priest of On). Undoubtedly, there is specialization and division of labor; the ideal is for orders to come down from the top and obedience to rise up through the ranks. When this ideal is not realized, or Pharaoh is put out for some reason, his subordinates, as we see in the case of the baker, may have more to lose than their positions. True, Pharaoh's investiture of Joseph, though he has not risen through the ranks, is a violation of hierarchical procedure. This exception may be excused on grounds of either Joseph's special merit or the special circumstances surrounding a perceived threat, possibly to Pharaoh's kingdom, surely to Pharaoh's position. Yet there is something missing.

Pharaoh's kingdom lacks heart. One of the defining characteristics of a hierarchy is that the parts are taught to sacrifice for the whole. A collectivist form of organization, a hierarchy is supposed to inculcate in its members, including the most elevated, the overriding importance of the whole.[9] In systems language, the parts are allowed to vary so that the whole may remain stable. But when Joseph, at his own discretion but undoubtedly with Pharaoh's approval, made serfs out of the Egyptian peasantry, the whole of Egypt was being made to sacrifice for the benefit of a single part, the Pharaoh and his entourage. We cannot even be sure that Egyptian farmers were henceforth considered part of Pharaoh's people rather than a fatalistic mass outside the dominant hierarchy.

From an inclusive hierarchy in which landowning peasants were part of a system of reciprocal obligations, Egyptian society became an exclusive hierarchy in which only a few were deemed worthy and the rest were subjugated. Observe that the Pharaoh who knew not Joseph, but who did know Moses, also disregarded the welfare of his subjects by bringing plagues down upon them. It was only when he was forced by the Almighty to share his people's misery, by losing his first-born son, that Pharaoh gave up his personal pride in favor of releasing his people from multiple harm.

Insofar as we see Joseph's behavior within a context whose broad outlines are determined by Pharaoh, Joseph's moral stature rises. Instead of thinking that Joseph is the one who made private landowners into serfs, we may then think of him as one who not only saved Egyptians from starvation but whose terms for enabling Egyptian farmers to continue working the land were far less onerous than was customary, at least so far as I have been able to discover. In the end, however, the forced deportations ordered by Joseph would still be unconscionable.

Another view is to consider Pharaoh's regime to be state capitalism, a combination of oligarchic individualism and fatalism. Under such a regime, strong leaders form networks whose members are so dependent that they cannot withdraw to join other networks or to form their own. No one is suggesting that Pharaoh or Joseph wanted to kill off the people who produced their food, but making his subjects more malleable might seem desirable to a Pharaoh. Whether one thinks of the regime as an exclusive hierarchy or a personal network, however, the behavior the Torah records is inexcusable. For it prefigures the position of Jacob's children, literally the sons of Israel, under a new Pharaoh.

In Defense of Joseph

There are better defenses for Joseph's behavior than have appeared so far, but before we can come to these we must first dispatch the self-protecting defenses that only make things worse. One such justification, initiated by Dahlberg, is to regard Joseph as the new Adam, the "ideal for Israel and for the human race."[10] Dahlberg asks a rhetorical question addressed by Pharaoh to his courtiers: "'Could we find another like him, a man in whom is the spirit of God?'" (Gen. 41:38). Why, I retort, would one want to take the word of a dictator and idolator on the ideal man in the Torah? This defense of Dahlberg's flies in the face of the fact that the ideal man is discarded and replaced by his virtual opposite, Moses.

Another defense is that it is all predestined. Every time the enemies of the dream—Joseph's brothers, Potiphar's wife, Joseph's jailers, nature itself in the form of a famine—resist its outcomes, Brueggemann argues, they fail, for "The boy is without guile. He presumes this 'great expectations' in his body. But dreams cause conflict. They endanger 'pecking order.' So the hatred mounts. The one called to dream is imperiled because of this disruptive dream."[11] I find no evidence that Joseph's dreams contained subliminal messages compelling him to tell evil tales about his brothers "without guile."

Writing in the same vein, Maududi tells us that "The Quran has used this story to bring forth another truth: Whatever Allah wills, He fulfills it anyhow, and man can never defeat His plan with his counter-plans nor prevent it from happening nor change it in any way whatever."[12] If the outcomes are preordained, I ask, what is the point of human characters going through their charades? Always the Torah allows for the individual to turn back. Egypt is where the Hebrew people went, but it is not the only place they could have gone. Indeed, it proved a long and indirect way of fulfilling God's promise.

Had Joseph not acted in the belief that his dreams were divinely ordained, Ramban contends, he could not have justified prolonging his aged father's worries or imprisoning his brother Simeon. I cannot express my views better than did Isaac Arama in *Akedat Yizhak*

> I am astonished at Ramban's explanation that Joseph did what he did in order to make his dreams come true. What did this benefit him? And even if it profited him he should not have sinned against his father. As for the dreams, leave it to Him Who sends them to make them come true. It seems infinitely foolish for a man to strive to fulfill his dreams which are matters beyond his control.[13]

Nehama Leibowitz, from whose famous Torah lessons this quotation is taken, counters that many others in the Bible did not wait for providence (cf. Gideon in Judg. 7:13–14) to fulfill God's purposes. Did Joseph do what he did, a more critical observer might wonder, because he had come to think of himself as the god who could bring about the outcomes of his own dreams?

It is but a short path from predestination to relativism. The morality of the Bible, it is said, cannot be used to judge behavior in "the ancient Near Eastern world, by whose norms Joseph emerges . . . as a highly admirable model of a shrewd and successful administrator." Nevertheless, the narrator introduces a line of exculpation by suggesting that Egyptian small landholders asked Joseph to take their land and make them serfs. Why, they even professed to be grateful for being enslaved![14] Nehama Leibowitz attributes this acceptance to the servile character of Egyptians themselves:

> Deeply rooted is man's instinct to shirk responsibility for himself and his livelihood and that of his family. He would much rather saddle his superior with the burden of providing for him, let him do all the thinking for him, give him orders, lead him and support him, "that we and our land will be bondsmen to Pharaoh."[15]

A distinguished scholar of his time, S.R. Driver, had the same view: "Moreover . . . the Egyptian Fellah [small farmer] lacks inherently the spirit of independence, and, even to the present day, is content to enrich others by his labor rather than himself."[16] Yet if Israelites were so different from Egyptians, why, after Joseph's time, did they descend beyond slavery to fatalistic acceptance of oppression?

The most sustained effort to defend Joseph's behavior as administrator comes from Benno Jacob, who argues that

> Joseph's activities . . . have often been used for attacks on the Old Testament and have been called "despotism without ethical considerations" or "financial specula-tion" and even worse than that by modern anti-Semites. The following points must be considered:
>
> 1) Incontestably Joseph saves the Egyptians from starvation according to this story. Ex. 1,8 could not have been written if this would not have been regarded as meritorious and obliging Egypt to eternal gratitude to Joseph.
>
> 2) It is just that the people pay for the food as long as they possess money. Actually, they only repay that which they had received when Joseph bought their surplus. The herds as movable property are merely another form of money.
>
> 3) Indignation because of the people and land of Egypt falling into dependency is misplaced. Joseph does not demand it, but the Egyptians offer it. This is the true intention of the whole story. The book of Genesis is intended . . . as an introduction to Exodus. There the main topic will be Israel leaving Egypt, "the house of bondage." How did this country become a house of bondage? Through the servile attitude of this people for whom bread is more important than liberty. They are not so much attached to their soil that they would rather die than surrender it. In servility they positively thrust their enslavement upon Pharaoh as thanks for the expected food. This Joseph, the former slave, will not accept! Instead he buys the soil, but the people are only relocated. He avoids even the word "slaves" in his reply. The tax of 20% on the produce is moderate compared with agrarian conditions in other countries of antiquity.[17]

That anti-Semites use certain arguments, I think, says nothing positive about the evidence. To credit Joseph with saving the people from starvation, then blame them for preferring serfdom to starvation, seems lacking in sense. That the people asked to be made serfs does not excuse Joseph for acquiescing; since he (and the Pharaoh whom he served) had the means to make it otherwise. "They asked for it" (why not polygamy or incest?) is not a moral defense, especially for a people to whom "this ought not be done" prohibitions are a staple.

Speaking of moving people off land they gave up only under extreme economic duress as being "only relocated" is to miss a great deal. Were the Egyptians truly servile, there would have been no need to move them off what used to be their land. Their servility is at least partly a product of the condition under which Joseph left them. Are we to attribute the undoubted servility of the Hebrew people in Moses' time to character flaws alone or do we also take into account Pharaoh's oppression?

The one-fifth tax may have been appropriate under the then-existing conditions, but that speaks only to the conditions of serfdom, not to whether rulers ought to identify with their people instead of using their distress to deprive them of self-ownership. Ancient commentaries mentioning Joseph's and Solomon's early death (in comparison with the patriarchs) refer to them "as further examples of the truth that dominion buries him that exercises it."[18]

In doubting that Joseph should be considered a "type of Christ," Driver states that

> only the measures adopted by Joseph for the relief of the famine might be thought to strike a discordant note in his character. To appropriate the surplus produce of the seven years of plenty, and then to compel the Egyptians to *buy* back, even to their own impoverishment, what they had themselves previously given up, does not seem consistent with our ideas of justice and equity.[19]

To this I would add that members of families owe each other more than justice. The best rationale Driver can find is that "Joseph did not do more than was consistent with the conditions of the country, with the age in which he lived, and with the position in which he found himself placed at the time." Though this point expresses a note of realism about human conduct, it ignores the basis of Hebrew morality.

I am more in sympathy with Gibson, who asks, "Why does the writer claim that this situation came about through Joseph taking advantage of the famine and, like the cruelest bailiff of medieval feudalism, squeezing the lifeblood of an exploited and cringing peasantry? He even has him granting exemption to a pagan priesthood." Is the Bible, Gibson wonders, trying to tell us that Joseph had to do this to protect his people or that we should admire him "for his punctilious devotion to duty, even though it furthered the rise of a tyrannous system of government? . . . Or worse, that, though recently humbled, he still had too much of the arrogant ruler in him?"[20]

Searching for an explanation, Gibson observes that in the passage where Joseph asks and receives permission to settle his family in Goshen, the text refers to the father and brothers settling not in Goshen but "in the region of Rameses, as Pharaoh had commanded" (Gen. 47:11). From this name Gibson deduces a reference to one of the two storage cities that later generations of Hebrews built under extreme duress for the Pharaoh of their time.[21] How appropriate, I would add, according to exact Hebrew justice, that the oppression of the Egyptians, which came from food Joseph stored, should be visited upon his descendants. Could there be more in common between the two peoples than is commonly recognized? Perhaps the injunction in Deuteronomy against persecuting Egyptians stems from this recognition of a common suffering due to a shared weakness.

The difficulties of justifying Joseph's behavior as Pharaoh's administrator become evident when reading Thomas Mann's *Joseph and His Brothers*. Mann simply omits mention of forced deportations. For the rest, he invents a species of middlemen who are opposed to Pharaoh and who of course exploit both their ruler and the poor. Now we know what really happened: Joseph is just Robin Hood in disguise, helping the people and their good king Pharaoh against the bad barons.

The award for the most charming defense must go to S. R. Hirsch, who praises Joseph for his community spirit. He defends the uprootings by saying it was arranged so that "the residents who had always lived together remained together and found themselves still together with their friends but only in a fresh environment."[22] Here is truly a new man, not Joseph the provider, but Joseph the social director.

A stronger start belongs to Rabbi Chayim ben Ater in his *Light of the Living*, where he argues that Joseph's intention was to impoverish the Egyptians in order that his brothers should not be as poor as they.[23] Joseph's actions make most sense both strategically and morally as efforts to protect his own people. By moving everyone except the priests off their land, Joseph places the Egyptian people on an equivalent plane to his own family. Henceforth, in a manner of speaking, all Egyptians would be immigrants. They would have no more claim to the land than did the Hebrews. If anti-foreignism or anti-shepherdism or anti-Semitism was ingrained in the population, arranging a political economy in which Pharaoh rather than the people made choices might have made sense to Joseph the strategist. As his behavior toward his brothers shows, he certainly had been doing a lot of thinking ahead.[24]

And For Us

The best defense of Joseph available to me comes in a letter from Professor Marc Galanter, who sees Joseph's flaws in biblical times as virtues in modern times. It deserves to be quoted in full:

> Overall, I would make the case that Joseph is *not* the "path not taken." Yes, he is the path not taken by rabbinic Judaism, but I think one could make the case that he represents the path taken by the mainstream of American Jewry—and perhaps by other favored diasporas. Putting it another way, American Jews are a collective Joseph, who have risen to a favored position in this favored land.
>
> I would qualify the notion of Joseph as representing the path of assimilation by distinguishing a strong assimilationism that seeks the effacement and displacement of Jewish identity and a weaker form that seeks a fused, dual identity. Joseph is never portrayed in the tradition as a proponent or practitioner of strong-form assimilation. Indeed his success in transmitting a robust Jewish identity to his children amid the most seductive surroundings has made him a model diaspora parent as registered in the sabbath blessing in which we enjoin our children to be "like Manassah and Ephraim."
>
> Thus Joseph is the model of the "modern" Jew who manages to have it both ways—to remain Jewish while participating fully in the world of his place and time without abandoning his Jewishness.
>
> His is "modern," further, in that he acts without direct contact with or guidance from God. He proceeds by discernment and calculation, not by prayer. You describe this as "quintessential secularism." This silence is the path chosen by God—not His Moses-path of companionship. So Joseph is also a model of how to act when God is silent—how not be debilitated and undone by God's silence.
>
> I disagree that Joseph is corrupted and that leads to his rejection, for God's disposition to silence precedes the supposed corruption. Also I think one can make the case for his moral virtuosity. He makes tough decisions in a world of grays, not blacks and whites. Rather than as an administrator, I see him as Weber's "ethics of consequences" politician.
>
> So in important ways Joseph is the road taken—or the road on which we find ourselves travelling. Does the location of the story suggest that it is only and always the path to be rejected? Even if in the original sequence, your conclusion is true that he is not fit to announce the moral law—it doesn't follow that he is unfit for the application of it to a world of hard choices, that is, once the core is defined and solidified, departures from it or forays from it are different than before—so that what was insufficient in the absence of a core may be just what is needed once it exists. Thus, the Joseph story takes on a different meaning in context of rabbinic Judaism than in an imagined pre-Mosaic world—what was a failed attempt *before* may be a valuable offset or antidote or counterbalance *after*.
>
> For there has to be a periphery as well as a center if Jews are not to be an isolated, inward-looking self-contained sect like the Amish, concerned with their own perfection. Nor is Judaism a world religion with a mission to envelop by conversion like Islam and Christianity. It looks outward to influence (and redeem?) the world. Hence persuasiveness of Franz Rosenzweig's image of the star and its rays. Joseph is about the rays, the interface with the larger world.

Joseph represents the centrifugal impulse as opposed to the Moses-centripetal impulse. It is movement away from the center, embrace of surroundings, incorporation of the outside, addressing the tensions of moral action in the big world rather than "building a fense." This is a very real part of Judaism, for it is only these departures (and fallings away) that make possible journeys of return and rediscovery (like my own? your own?).

So you can see that I do not take Joseph as the failed experiment or the path not taken. It is at least part of the path taken—and an attractive part. So attractive in fact that the question in America is how to temper it with the centripetal impulse, how to keep the core from being overwhelmed by the outward-looking part.[25]

No doubt the perspective of rabbinic Judaism or, earlier, in Ezra and Nehemiah's time, is different from ours. By timeless standards, I still think Joseph's implementation of administrative wisdom cannot be condoned. But the oral tradition of commentary agrees with Galanter that interpretation is for us now as well as for them in ancient times.

Joseph as a Good Landlord

An economic defense of Joseph's behavior in buying the land and its animals from Egyptian peasants depends on a more sophisticated understanding of common practice. Here I shall assume that the Joseph stories cover a considerable period of time. Joseph could not have gathered all the grain, because there would then have been none to eat. About one-fifth of a crop was customarily withheld as seed grain, and perhaps this was what Joseph collected. Had he managed to store as much as half a crop, that would have made immense demands on storage facilities and, given the technology of the times, was unlikely to last for seven years.[26] Furthermore, half the crop would have provided for only three-and-a-half years of famine, especially in view of foreigners' coming to buy food. If we go to a more reasonable assumption of a fifth or a third of the crop, then the grain would have lasted from approximately one and a half to two and a half years. Since governments are not likely to depress consumption greatly in good times, which our contemporary experience would certainly validate, Joseph probably managed the aforementioned fifth to a third as a superabundance from bumper crops.

But what about the price charged? Money saved in good years does not provide grain in years of famine. If there was no way of replenishing those supplies in the short term, Egyptians would have had to eat less. Chances are low that Joseph, however persuasive, could induce two million peasants to eat less for seven years. Joseph the provider could provide only the provisions he had already stored.

This economic analysis still does not explain why the peasants' money ran out so soon, and the biblical story makes it appear that there was grain enough but not money. Was Joseph guilty of overcharging those least able to pay? Not necessarily. If we were to suppose a free market, seven years of famine resulting from lack of rain would not add much to the value of land. Indeed, there may have been no takers. And storing a lot of food for seven years would cost a bundle. Interest rates in those times were exceptionally high, with loans from the state running about fifty percent a year, not to mention the other fifty percent due if you did not pay the first on time.[27] If there was only two percent a year loss due to rats and fungus and another two percent for storage, which are very low rates, peasants would have owed the state under customary practice some fifty-four percent of each year's crop. Over seven years compounded that comes to over ninety percent.[28]

Even if we assume that peasant farms were worthless in an open market, there might not have been such a market. Even if there was, the question remains why Pharaoh through his chief administrator would want to take all the market permitted. Why did he not allow, indeed encourage, peasants to begin again when the famine was over? If the argument is that a market solution is morally desirable or even morally acceptable, one would have to explain why a solution that does away with the market forever is to be preferred to a solution that would do away with the market for only a few years.

Joseph, Adam, and Noah

During a famine that the Torah tells us afflicted the whole world, is it too far-fetched to see Joseph as a counterpoint to Noah, who also rescued humanity, or what was left of it, from the threat of extinction by flood? In Dahlberg's view, Joseph accomplishes what Noah set out to do. He sees the "storehouses built by Joseph against famine . . . as antitypes to the ark built by Noah against flood."[29]

Even more suggestive is Dahlberg's pointed parallel between Adam and Joseph, with Joseph resolving the problems posed in the creation. In support of his thesis that "the Joseph story is intended as the climactic outworking of the problems of humanity posed in the first eleven chapters of Genesis," Dahlberg contends that

> a correspondence exists between the beginning and ending stories in Genesis. The serpent had declared, "You will be like God." Joseph exclaims, "Am I in the place of God?" The serpent had promised, "knowing good and evil." Joseph declares, "You meant evil against me, but God meant it for good." The serpent had said, "You will not die." Joseph perceives life saved from death: "God meant . . . to bring it about that many people should be kept alive as they are today." It seems that the use of these specific words in Joseph's conversation with his brothers, a conversation in which he in effect responds to the serpent's lines (3:4–5) point for point, serves and is intended to serve dramatically and theologically as a reversal of the scene portrayed earlier in Eden, and as a resolution of the problem exposed there.[30]

Even the word for the coat or tunic that figures so prominently in the Joseph stories in Genesis (*kuttoneth*) occurs only one other time to describe the "garments of skins" (*kothnoth 'or*) that "the Lord God made . . . for Adam and his wife" (Gen. 3:21). Insofar as Dahlberg is concerned, such parallels suggest that Joseph "does on a grand scale what Adam was created to do but did not, back in the beginning";[31] that is, to use human wits and ingenuity to preserve life and to reconcile the members of a divided family despite their many faults.

Why comparison to the serpent, the skeptical scientist, is counted as favorable to Joseph requires further explanation. Why demand faith if skepticism and empiricism are substitutes for God? In short, Dahlberg's creative justification cannot serve as a religious teaching.

Joseph's Rationale, or Does God Preempt Human Choice?

One might have thought that upon his father's death Joseph's reconciliation with his brothers would be completed in joint mourning. Did he not sob loudly on hearing Judah's appeal to let Benjamin return to their aging father? Had he not revealed himself to them as "your brother Joseph" (Gen. 45:4)? Had Joseph not reassured his brothers, saying, "Now, do not be distressed or reproach yourselves because you sold me hither; it was to save life that God sent me ahead of you . . . in an extraordinary deliverance. So, it was not you who sent me here, but God" (Gen. 45:5,7,8)?

Of course, Joseph told his brothers not to reproach themselves only after he learned by eavesdropping (while pretending to use an interpreter) that they were doing exactly that. For this reason, thinking it was not normal for a person to forgive those who had sold him into slavery, the brothers became fearful that the restraining influence exercised by their father had been removed. Might not the person who had deceived them in the guise of Pharaoh's vizier bide his time until they were utterly in his control? Thus,

> When Joseph's brothers saw that their father was dead, they said, "What if Joseph still bears a grudge against us and pays us back for all the wrong that we did him!" So they sent this message to Joseph, "Before his death your father left this instruction: So shall you say to Joseph, 'Forgive, I urge you, the offense and guilt of your brothers who treated you so harshly.' Therefore please forgive the offense of the servants of the God of your father." And Joseph was in tears as they spoke to him. (Gen. 50:15–17)

Akin to their failure to assume responsibility for their actions in earlier times, they now send a messenger to Joseph to relate the story of their father's supposed deathbed wish. Further, they invoke "the God of your father" as protection. More than one person can invoke the name of God in their own interest. The brothers, it is obvious, were caught between a rock and a hard place. They could not have gone to their father, asking him to make such a plea, a far more effective source than the messenger they sent, because they had never told their father the truth about why Joseph might be angry at them. "It is my opinion, in line with the plain meaning of the Scripture," the Ramban declares, "that it was never told to Jacob throughout his entire lifetime that the brothers had sold Joseph."[32] Had they told their father, the brothers would have had reason to fear his wrath.

Though Joseph had no reason to believe his brothers, he again broke into tears. Early in his life his lack of control had cost him and his family dearly. Later, he perhaps had been overly controlled. These tears, then, signal Joseph's true feelings of reconciliation with his brothers. While self-restraint is a desirable feature of human character, as proverbial wisdom will have it, it is not an ultimate value. In context, loss of control may be desirable if it expresses mercy.

"His brothers went to him themselves," the Torah relates, "flung themselves before him, and said, 'We are prepared to be your slaves'" (Gen. 50:18). How much better will the Hebrew people be if they, like the Egyptians, are so eager to offer themselves up to slavery? Here we see again that the slave mentality was not unique to Egyptians. Like Reuben's offer to allow his sons' grandfather to kill them, the brothers offer Joseph more than is permissible. Although they are guilty of harming their brother, expiation of that sin cannot justify making their family-cum-people into slaves. Whatever the practice of the times, Hebrews cannot voluntarily become slaves without offending their God. Not only would they lose their free will, which they must retain to serve God by remaining responsible for their actions, they would tempt their master Joseph into the worse sin of idolatry. Might not Joseph, given absolute power over his brothers, begin to believe he was the Absolute?

In any event, Joseph rejects the offer to make him formally the master of his brothers without necessarily rejecting the substance of mastery. "Have no fear!" (Gen. 50:19), Joseph tells his brothers. Once more there is a doubling of the relevant phrase: "And so, fear not. I will sustain you and your children" (Gen. 50:21). The formula "fear not" is the same phrase God used to reassure his patriarchs Jacob (Gen. 46:3), Abram ("Fear not, Abram, I am a shield to you" Gen. 15:1), and Isaac at Beersheba ("Fear not, for I am with you" Gen. 26:24). Why, then, does Joseph use these divine words in addressing his brothers? Whence comes his perfect confidence—"I will sustain you"? For a man who has experienced so many sudden reversals in a short life, Joseph appears remarkably self-assured. Only a god could be so certain. And if in losing control, his truest thoughts are revealed, his drive for power is as strong as ever.

Having saved the people of the earth as he knew it, Joseph might think he was able to go into the god business. Whereas it is said that "Noah found favor with the Lord" (Gen. 6:8), Joseph finds favor with Potiphar (Gen. 39:4). And those Egyptians who have just been made serfs to Pharaoh speak of Joseph as their lord, to whom they are grateful. In all these instances, despite the slightly different translations, the Hebrew word *hen*, for favor or gratitude, is used. When the peasants say "We are grateful to my lord" (Gen. 47:25), they are treating Joseph as if he were a god. That is understandable. As Ward says, "Almost every official of any standing in Egypt held both secular and religious offices. This is especially true of those of higher rank."[33] The question is whether Joseph himself merged the two positions in his own mind.

Without His ever appearing on the scene (one might say, in person, if that were not idolatrous), Joseph claims that God guides his steps. Letting the guilty brothers off the hook, Joseph ascribes his near murder, actual kidnaping, and selling into slavery to the divine presence. God has sent Joseph before his brothers "to save your lives in an extraordinary deliverance," Joseph avers; "So, it was not you who sent me here, but God" (Gen. 45:7-8). Joseph calmed his brothers in the words of those who understand the role of unanticipated consequences in life: "although you intended me harm, God intended it for good" (Gen. 50:20). God may convert good out of evil, but this is not to say that Joseph himself is excusing his brothers. He does not in fact forgive them; not a word is said about forgiveness. Rather he suspends judgment, telling his brothers that this role, if it is to be played at all, belongs to the Almighty.[34]

Joseph's reassurance to his brothers is conveyed in a line I have partially quoted before: "Fear not: for am I in the place of God?" (Gen. 50:19).[35] It turns out that these words of humility and comfort are in Hebrew the same as those that Jacob, vexed by Rachel's lament that she must have children or die, wounded her with: "Am I in God's stead, who hath withheld from thee the fruit of the womb?" (Gen. 30:2). "The same words—but here," Feldman interprets, "Joseph, son of the wounded Rachel, has transformed the words into healing, and has redeemed the hurtful gesture."[36] Invoking God's will, I think, may be a way of excusing evil.

The key phrase, reiterated from the time Joseph the administrator made himself known as Joseph the brother, coming right after his declaration about not taking God's place, is this: "Besides, although you intended me harm, God intended it for good, so as to bring about the present result—the survival of many people" (Gen. 50:20). Joseph may believe this, but the narrator does not say and God does not appear to affirm that it is so.[37] Let us look more deeply into this matter of the will of God.

A proverb has it that "a man's heart [or mind; the word refers to the seat of judgment, to Hebrews the heart, to modern people the mind] deviseth his way: but the Lord directeth his steps" (Prov. 16:9). In the vernacular, man acts as he thinks best, but the Lord's purpose is served. Or, man's intentions are one thing but his accomplishments are another. That the aims of individuals are confounded by a multitude of purposers and purposes that they cannot fully comprehend, bringing home the statement that mankind is intendedly but not effectively rational, is broadly understood. How, in Hebrew morality, can human beings carry out their plans as intended? Only God can do that.

Which is it: Did the Almighty stage these events, as if Joseph and the rest were merely wind-up toys, acting out prearranged scripts at the behest of a master controller? Or does God make the best He can of human strivings, deflecting them onto His long-range plans? What would be the point of testing Abraham at the binding of Isaac if his response were predetermined? Abraham's faith consists of his willingness not only to be tested but to test God's promise on the knife's edge (if Isaac dies, Abraham and hence the Hebrew people will have no heirs). Why offer Moses an opportunity to reject his people, even to found a Hebrew lineage based on his own family, as God does when revealing the reveling around the golden calf to Moses on Mount Sinai, if he could not have so chosen? Moses' moral stature, as with Abraham before him (the only Hebrews who get to argue with their God), grows from his willingess to identify his life with the people he leads, insisting he will share their fate, contending, in his dialogue with God on the mountain top, that if moral perfection is the criterion, all would deserve to die.

Joseph and his family remained in Egypt. He lived 110 years, shorter than the patriarchs but long enough to know three generations of grand-children. Ambivalent to the end, the last two events in Joseph's life move in contradictory directions: his body is embalmed and placed in a coffin in the Egyptian manner, but he also makes "the sons of Israel swear, saying, 'When God has taken notice of you, you shall carry up my bones from here!" (Gen. 50:25). Joseph has made his choice to live and die in Egypt.

It is possible to interpret Joseph's invocation of divine purpose in a more favorable way. The two principal instances in which Joseph invokes the will of God do not directly concern his own actions but rather those of his brothers. It could be argued that Joseph's purpose in making his assertions about divine providence is, first, to comfort his brothers without denying their guilt and, second, to express a sense of a larger meaning encompassing the events of their lives. That human beings are responsible for their actions, so that divine providence does not cancel out the guilt of Joseph's brothers, while God directs the larger outcomes of events, is fundamental to this God-centered religion, in which discern-ing God's will is the aim but never quite the achievement. Joseph need not be held responsible for this basic paradox in religious life.

Furthermore, Joseph's obvious self-assurance need not necessarily be a form of self-worship or blasphemy in the sense of claiming the attributes of God. True, he acts in some ways that can be confused with God's actions (for example, having money put in his brother's sacks).

Thus the ceremonial respect in which his brothers address Joseph as "my lord" may be one of awe at his stature or fear of his retribution but need not necessarily imply idolatry.

Pharaoh's praise of Joseph's sagacity is not necessarily ironic in the sense of being seen to serve his self-interest. It indeed does, but Pharaoh is grateful to have at his command the one kind of wisdom he can appreciate, a prudential wisdom that the Bible regards as the highest achievement of non-Israelites.

If Joseph does have a moral blind spot it is that from beginning to end he does not recognize the potential of abuse of power without limits. Joseph's Egyptianization reflects his identification with power.[38] Judaism says submit to God and not to man. Joseph comes close to saying that submission to Pharaoh reflects God's will.

That Joseph's will to power does not change over the years cannot be doubted. His service to Pharaoh is due partly to that will and partly to the necessity of his liberation from prison. Whereas Moses frees himself so as to free his people, Joseph is liberated by Pharaoh to serve Pharaoh's purposes. We hear nothing of the abuses of this Pharaoh comparable to those the Pharaoh in Moses' time perpetrated on the Hebrew people. Hints that Egyptians abominate Hebrew customs are only that—hints. In the end, we must believe either that the later Hebrews had bad luck in their ruler or that Joseph's actions on behalf of his Pharaoh set the stage for institutional developments that allowed the next vicious leader to come along. While the both/and approach has its merits, especially in regard to the ambivalence of human nature, I believe that the either/or approach is faithful to the text taken as a whole. If we are not told to follow Moses rather than Joseph, we are not told anything at all.

Notes

1. Claus Westermann, *Genesis 37–50*, trans. John J. Scullion (Minneapolis: Augsburg Publishing, 1986), 92.
2. George W. Coats, "The Joseph Story and Ancient Wisdom: A Reappraisal," *Catholic Biblical Quarterly* 35 (1973): 285–297; at 292–93.
3. Gerhard von Rad, *Genesis: A Commentary* (Philadelphia: Westminster, 1972), 410.
4. Ivan Caine, "Numbers In the Joseph Narrative," *Jewish Civilization: Essays and Studies* 1 (1979): 3–17; quote on 9–10.
5. Tsariy Bezer, "'Failed Money' and Its Consequence," *Beth Mikra* 93 (1982): 177–79.
6. Albert Edward Bailey, *Daily Life in Bible Times* (New York: Charles Scribner's Sons, 1943), 64, 66.

7. Caine, "Numbers In the Joseph Narrative," 3-17; quote on 11.
8. Nahum M. Sarna, *The JPS Torah Commentary: Genesis* (Philadelphia: Jewish Publication Society, 1989), 321.
9. See Louis Dumont, *Homo Hierarchicus* (Chicago University Press, 1980); Mary Douglas, "Cultural Bias," in Douglas, *In the Active Voice* (London: Routledge and Kegan Paul, 1982), 183-254; Mary Douglas and Aaron Wildavsky, *Risk and Culture* (Berkeley: University of California Press, 1982), chap. 5, 83-101.
10. Bruce T. Dahlberg, "On Recognizing the Unity of Genesis," *Theology Digest* 24 (1976): 360-67; quote on 365.
11. Walter Brueggemann, *Genesis: A Bible Commentary for Teaching and Preaching*, in the *Interpretation* series (Atlanta: John Knox Press, 1982), 301.
12. S. Abul Maududi, *The Meaning of the Quran*, vol. 5 (Lahore Pakistan: Islamic Publications, 1973), 121.
13. Quoted in Nehama Leibowitz, *Studies in the Book of Genesis* (Jerusalem: World Zionist Organization, 1972), 459.
14. Sarna, *Genesis*, 322-23.
15. Leibowitz, *Studies in the Book of Genesis*, 524.
16. S. R. Driver, *The Book of Genesis*, 6th ed. (New York: Edwin S. Gorham, 1907), 401.
17. Benno Jacob, *The First Book of the Bible: Genesis*, His commentary abridged, ed. and trans. by Ernest I. Jacob and Walter Jacob (New York: KTAV Publishing House, 1974), 318.
18. Louis Ginzberg, *The Legends of the Jews*, vol. 5, notes, 373.
19. Driver, *Book of Genesis*, 401.
20. John C. L. Gibson, *Genesis*, vol. 2 (Philadelphia: Westminster Press, 1982), 301.
21. Ibid.
22. Samson Raphael Hirsch, *The Pentateuch, Vol. 1, Genesis*, 2nd ed. (New York: Judaica Press, 1971), 624.
23. Discussed in Bezer, "'Failed Money' and Its Consequence," 177-79.
24. See *Soncino Chumash: The Five Books of Moses with Haphtaroth*, by The Rev. Dr. A. Cohen (London: Soncino Press, 1966), 292.
25. Letter, Marc Galanter to Aaron Wildavsky, 25 May 1992.
26. George Steindorff and Keith C. Seele, *When Egypt Ruled the East* (University of Chicago Press, 1957), 88.
27. Oxyrhyncus Papyri Vol. 3, 184-86; Hunt and Edgar, *Select Papyri* II:317.
28. I am indebted to Stanley Lebergott, professor of economics at Wesleyan University in Middletown, Connecticut, for this argument.
29. Bruce T. Dahlberg, "The Unity of Genesis," in Kenneth R. R. Gros Louis, ed., *Literary Interpretations of Biblical Narratives*, vol. 2 (Nashville: Abingdon Press, 1982), 130; and Dahlberg, "On Recognizing the Unity of Genesis," *Theology Digest* 24 (1976): 360-67, at 364.
30. Dahlberg, "The Unity of Genesis," 129.
31. Dahlberg, "On Recognizing the Unity of Genesis," 364.
32. Ramban (Nachmanides), *Commentary on the Torah: Genesis*, trans. and annotated by Rabbi Dr. Charles B. Chavel (New York: Shilo Publishing, 1971), 541.
33. William A. Ward, "Egyptian Titles in Genesis 39-50," *Bibliotheca Sacra* 114 (1957): 40-59.
34. Peter D. Miscall, "The Jacob and Joseph Stories As Analogies," *Journal for the Study of the Old Testament* 6 (1978): 28-40.

35. Here I prefer the King James Version; the New Translation I have been using reads "Have no fear. Am I a substitute for God?"

36. Emanuel Feldman, "Joseph and the Biblical Echo," *Dor le Dor* 13 (1985): 161–66; quote on 166.

37. Miscall, "Jacob and Joseph Stories As Analogies."

38. I am indebted to David Eneloe for his formulation of "either/or" versus "both/and," though ultimately I take a different position.

7

If These Are Jacob's Blessings, What Would His Curses Be Like?

Whether Joseph is or is not a blessing to his family, literally the children of Israel, restates the central theme of the stories about him. He did help his family survive the famine and, for a time, the hostility of the local people. Whether the aping of Egyptian customs this required and the forgetting of Israelite law (as the account in Exodus indicates) was worth it is the tension the Joseph stories are meant to illustrate and, in part, but only in part, to resolve.

"The chapter," Sarna writes about Genesis 49, known traditionally as the Blessings of Jacob, "is the most difficult segment of the book of Genesis."[1] He is right there. He is also right in commenting, "There is much uncertainty of meaning, extreme allusiveness, and considerable double entendre."[2] Speiser seconds this opinion by stating that the interpretation of the poem is "beset with great difficulties—replete with unfamiliar expressions and allusions."[3] Indeed, Rand characterizes this speech as follows:

> powerful in its symbolism and lyrical in style, the poem is so markedly different from Jacob's usual speech pattern that it represents a residual mystery. It reflects the outpouring of pent-up emotion, resentment against three of his sons, and the tension arising from his newly-acquired prophetic power to foretell the future of his sons as eponymous founders of the Twelve Tribes.[4]

This combination of farewell address, prophecy, tribal characterization, and testament, seemingly pasted together, as if from different times and places, has led Sarna, among many others, to conclude that "no inner thread of logic binds the diverse elements together."[5] I disagree.

Chapter 49 is anticipated by the blessing of Pharaoh by Jacob (Gen. 47:7, 10). Here we begin to find out what "blessings" Jacob bestows. The Jewish Publication Society's new translation I have been using says simply that Joseph introduced his father to Pharaoh and Jacob greeted him and then said farewell. This makes it appear that Pharaoh's immediate question about Jacob's age (Gen. 47:8) came out of nowhere. Yet the older literal translation stating that Jacob blessed Pharaoh coming and going, while more enigmatic, fits in nicely with a reply inquiring into how many years Jacob had lived.[6]

Whether or not Jacob blessed Pharaoh, Jacob takes this opportunity not merely to answer the question about his age, 130 years, but to make a complaint: "Few and hard [the King James says "evil"] have been the years of my life, nor do they come up to the life-spans of my fathers during their sojourns" (Gen. 47:9). Yet, by anyone's count, 130 years is not bad. Jacob shows repressed anger, a feeling of being hard-done-by that will express itself as he turns blessings into curses. Fearful that his father, Isaac, would curse instead of bless him because of his deception (Gen. 27:12), Jacob has now cursed instead of blessed his sons. Jacob's ingratitude was understood and remarked upon in older commentaries such as Bereshis Raba. Rashi translates "When pious men try to settle down in quietude the Almighty exclaims: Is not what is prepared for pious men in the future world enough for them that they should want to rest in quietude also in this world?"[7]

Evidence

Here I must reiterate the standard of evidence used in interpreting texts, including poems, whose meaning is contested. To begin with, of no line can it be said that it is subject to only one interpretation. It is possible that the same line can have different meanings for those with different frames of reference. If it is the Torah we are interpreting, however, an additional test must be passed, namely, that the meaning not be opposed to the religious sentiment the Torah tries to teach. If it is the Bible we are interpreting, there is no leaving God out.

The determination of meaning, if there is enough information to do that, depends on having an initial hypothesis of what the stories we are interpreting are about. Only if we know whether and to what extent the expectations generated by a particular theory of meaning are met or violated can we say that the meaning of a text is or is not in accord with the general conceptions set out. Since we cannot rely on divine inspiration or special knowledge, the criteria worked out for scientific theories, in which arguments with evidence for and against a position are what matter, are the appropriate ones.

These abstractions may come to life through an example developed by Kugel about a line from the story known as Potiphar's wife. The narrator relates that "One such day, he [Joseph] came into the house to do his work" (Gen. 39:11). Who could disagree about the plain meaning of such a seemingly simple statement? From the *Babylonian Talmud* (*Sotah* 36b):

> R. Yohanan said: this [verse] teaches that the two of them [Joseph and Potiphar's wife] had planned to sin together. "He entered his house to *do his work*": Rab and Samuel [had disagreed on this phrase]: one said it really means to do his work, the other said it [is a euphemism that] means "to satisfy his desires." He entered; [and then it says] "And not one of the members of the household was present in the house." Is it really possible that no one else was present in the large house of this wicked man [Potiphar]? It was taught in the School of R. Ishma'el: that particular day was their festival, and they had all gone to their idolatrous rites, but she told them that she was sick. She had said [to herself] that there was no day in which she might indulge herself with Joseph like this day! [The biblical text continues:] "And she seized him by his garment . . . ."[8]

Could it be true that the straightforward and seemingly innocent phrase, going in to do his work, Kugel asks, "is merely a euphemism for 'to satisfy his desires.'"?[9] On face value, it appears that Joseph is blameless, pounced upon by the all-too-eager Mrs. Potiphar. But the second interpretation, which is that if Joseph was not necessarily the instigator, he was at least a willing volunteer, comes from a hypothesis about Joseph's being subject to the temptations of the pagan world, a hypothesis grounded in his acceptance of, even relishing in, Egyptian ways. This second view is challenged by Joseph's statement that he would not violate the trust Potiphar placed in him or commit adultery, which was a sin against God. And that, too, may either be accepted at face value or rejected as a coverup for sinister motives. In the much more difficult poem, call it Jacob's testament, in which Jacob either tells his sons what is in store for them or tells them off (usually both), we shall need all the interpretative resources that can be brought to bear.

Hypotheses about Jacob's Testament

Jacob is the last of the patriarchs. He alone of his family hears the voice of God. His name has been changed to Israel to make closer his identification with God's promise to found a nation on this people. Abraham is a vivid personality but a distant ancestor; his son, Isaac, is largely passive. It is Jacob who exhibits all the contrary characteristics—doubt and belief, cowardice and bravery, passivity and forcefulness, acuity and vacuousness—who is the true ancestor of his children, the children of Israel. His predictions, therefore, must be made true if his God and his people are to be connected. The poetic stanzas about each son-cum-tribe refer back to the past and forward to the future.

An obvious clue is the division of the tribes according to which mother and mother's maid (and Jacob's concubine) gave birth to them (table 7.1). Are any set of these treated better or worse or differently by their father, Jacob?

Table 7.1. Who Gave Birth to Whom? Mothers of the Tribes of Israel[10]

Leah	Bilhah (Rachel's maid)	Zilpah (Leah's maid)	Rachel
1. Reuben	5. Dan	7. Gad	11. Joseph
2. Simeon	6. Naphtali	8. Asher	12. Benjamin
3. Levi		(from Gen. 35:16–18)	
4. Judah			
9. Issachar			
10. Zebulun			

Another potential clue may be provided by the losses and gains among the tribes as they approached the Promised Land, as tabulated by Sacks (table 7.2).[11] (Levi is not counted in the second census because its members are given the priesthood.)

Simeon, we see, suffers a sharp drop in population, Judah has the most members and increases them slightly, while Manasseh grows greatly and Ephraim declines, the others moving up or down near their origins. Does Jacob treat the sons who started these tribes differently?

Table 7.2. Tribal Census Change in the Book of Numbers

Tribe	Census in Num. Chap. 1	Census in Num. Chap. 26
Reuben	46,500	43,730
Simeon	59,300	22,200
Levi	22,000	–
Judah	74,600	76,500
Dan	62,700	64,400
Naphtali	53,400	45,400
Gad	45,650	40,500
Asher	41,500	53,400
Issachar	54,400	64,300
Zebulun	57,400	60,500
Benjamin	35,400	45,600
Manasseh	32,200	52,700
Ephraim	40,500	32,500

"Insofar as the poems on Reuben, Issachar, and Simeon and Levi embody negative evaluations," Stanley Gevirtz reasons, "they can scarcely be supposed to have emanated from the tribes themselves, but only from someone who disapproved of the tribes or of their actions."[12] Such an interpretation signifies that the lines about each tribe are connected and that the search should be on to find who liked some tribes and not others. Of course, if all the evaluations are negative, then the verses are indeed connected but not by a principle of like and dislike.

Jacob's blessings or predictions or settling of scores, as you like, are often taken as explanations for why the leadership of the family was taken from those first in line, Reuben, Simeon, and Levi, and given to Judah who ranked only fourth in order of birth.[13] But why are other brothers also pummeled with blatantly negative statements? What about Joseph's aspirations to be fratriarch? Does the biblical evidence support the findings of the chronicler that the birthright was given to Joseph, but "the genealogy is not to be reckoned after the birthright" (I Chron. 5:1)?

Why, the reader should ask, is the content of this poem so unrelievedly negative? Though Jacob's anger at Reuben for violating his trust is understandable, that violation appears to be everything and the rest of Reuben's life nothing. The behavior of Simeon and Levi at Shechem was indeed terrible, but Jacob does not find fault with his own passivity in allowing this or in failing to reprimand the perpetrators severely afterward. The sons that escape censure for their activities during Jacob's lifetime, about whom the Torah says virtually nothing, are held to account for their tribes' lack of courage during the period of the judges and the monarchy. And Joseph, the son who did most to bring Jacob's family safely into Egypt, and Judah, who carried his father's name into the future—indeed, who gave his name to his people's religion—are also put down. Those that are treated harshly on the surface are condemned while those to whom kind words are said are criticized obliquely. In Jacob's bestiary, Joseph is deemed a wild ass, Judah compared to a young lion, Issachar derogated as a donkey, Dan a viper, Benjamin a wolf, and Naphtali a hind, which may be translated variously as a deer or a compliant (or too compliant) female animal.

In trying to infer the authorship of the Book of Deuteronomy, Richard Elliott Friedman says that it "appears to be written in their [the Levites] interests."[14] Gevirtz ascribes the authorship of Jacob's blessings to a sympathizer with the northern kingdom who

> judges the tribes and their actions from the point of view of what he holds to be the norm of pre-Davidic Israel. He lauds or condemns the 'sons' on the basis of whether their actions—from his perspective—may be judged to have been faithful to and supportive of, or disloyal to and destructive of, the pre-Judean union and the then-new Northern Kingdom's attempt to reassert it.[15]

This union, as I have argued elsewhere,[16] might at different periods be described in two ways. One is a union of equal states or tribes in which no one can tell any other one what to do and decisions must be made by consensus. No unity, no action. Nowadays we would call this a confederation. Another possibility is that the pre-Judean union operated on a principle of self-regulation in which tribes or alliances of tribes bargained with other tribes or alliances, the majority coalition shifting from issue to issue. Kenneth Waltz calls this a political self-help system.[17] In both types of rule, the point is, there was no hierarchy, no superiority or subordination of one tribe to another. The difference was that on some occasions a confederation of tribes made collective decisions binding on members, essentially by acclamation; at other times, they supported each other when they wished and avoided doing so when not. However one describes the pre-Davidic union, both of the forms it took were opposed in principle and in practice to the monarchy of the southern kingdom and the occasional efforts of some of its kings to establish a more centralized system of government.

Since the assumption that at least part of Jacob's testament is favorable is problematic, however, one might imagine that the failure of the divided monarchy to come together in a single Judean state led to a condemnation of all concerned. If Israel did not survive as a nation, Jacob-cum-Israel may be apportioning blame to all. Who is to blame? For a God-loving people, there can be only one answer: failure to follow God's commandments. As the first five lines of Lamentations remind us: "How doth the city sit solitary, that was full of people! how is she become as a widow! she that was great among the nations, and princess among the provinces, how is she become tributary!" (Lam. 1:1). The author of these lines is not a supporter of Joseph the administrator in an establishment but might well empathize with Jacob's feelings about what his children-cum-tribes have wrought.

Shechem

A preliminary word should be said about the city of Shechem, because a number of the allusions in the poem are based on events that occurred there. Shechem was the first place Abraham stopped when he arrived in the land promised to his descendants. God communicated with Abraham there and so he built an altar. There Jacob buried idolatrous materials found among his retainers. There Dinah was raped and Simeon and Levi took deceitful revenge on the male inhabitants (Gen. 34:25–29). Shechem was the place to which Jacob sent Joseph to meet his brothers and his fate; it is also the place he was ultimately buried after Moses took his mummified remains with him out of Egypt.

After Joshua made Shechem into a city of refuge, where those who killed accidentally could escape retribution, Shechem became the assembly point at which all of what then constituted Israel renewed their covenant. The Josephite tribes of Manasseh and Ephraim later were located around there. In addition to all this, "Sh'chem has remained the symbol of revolt against any threat of dictatorship."[18] When Solomon's son, Rehoboam, not only made excessive demands for taxation, but spoke condescendingly to the elders of the tribes of Israel, they uttered the traditional cry of returning to their tents thereby signifying the division of Israel into northern and southern kingdoms. Perhaps that is why Shechem became the first capital of the northern kingdom after it seceded. The tradition associating Shechem with revolt against arbitrary rule persuades Munk that Joseph's brothers went to Shechem "to decide what measures to take against the dreaded appearance of a family tyrant,"[19] none other than their brother Joseph.

Were Jacob and his children-cum-tribes to be favored, however, the main candidate would be David and Solomon. Always we keep in mind the proposition that the Torah is written forward as well as backward; whether we say that the Joseph stories were written to shore up support for King Solomon or that the accounts of Solomon's reign were slanted to support Joseph's example of how Jews should relate to the civil society in the Diaspora, there is no telling which came first.

Reuben

When Jacob knew he was dying, he called his twelve sons together in order that they might hear what was in store for them. He addressed the brothers, with one exception, in the order of seniority.

> Reuben, you are my first-born,
> My might and first fruit of my vigor,
> Exceeding in rank
> And exceeding in honor.
> Unstable as water, you shall excel no longer;
> For when you mounted your father's bed,
> You brought disgrace—my couch he mounted! (Gen. 49:3–4)

Beginning kindly enough, by the third line Jacob's testament descends rapidly into an accusation of incest because Reuben had intercourse with his father's concubine. Reuben is being told that the authority due him because he was the eldest is being withdrawn because he sought to usurp his father's power, literally his right to exclusive intercourse.[20] Reuben will no longer "excel," that is, he will not become Jacob's successor because, like Absalom, David's son, who showed his determination to overthrow his father by having intercourse with the old man's concubines, Reuben usurped his father's place, even perhaps pretending to his father's authority.

Having Jacob call Reuben unstable as water suggests that the son is some combination of reckless and wanton, "casting off all moral restraint, even as a torrent of water rushes wildly headlong."[21] The doubling of the accusatory phrase, defiling Jacob's couch and mounting it, intensifies Jacob's anger at the transgression.

Simeon and Levi

Simeon and Levi are a pair;
Their weapons are tools of lawlessness.
Let not my person be included in their council,
Let not my being be counted in their assembly.
For when angry they slay men,
And when pleased they maim oxen.
Cursed by their anger so fierce,
And their wrath so relentless.
I will divide them in Jacob,
Scatter them in Israel. (Gen. 49:5-7)

The first two lines may be freely interpreted as saying that Levi and Simeon are brothers in violence.[22] Essentially, Jacob accuses these two of making him so odious in the eyes of the inhabitants of Shechem that he has to leave. Instead of thinking only of Dinah's outraged virtue, they presumably should have thought what their impetuous actions would do to the safety of their community, an ancient theme of the collective versus the individual interest.

In mitigating Jacob's malediction, Rashi and Samuel Raphael Hirsch argued that Jacob cursed his sons' anger and not them personally.[23] This, I believe, is a distinction without a difference. For Jacob tells them they will be scattered rather than united and, what is worse, he withdraws his protection and, by implication, his God's protection from them. Considering that under Moses the tribe of Levi gained a monopoly over the priesthood, the withdrawal of divine support suggests that Levi was at least partly responsible for splitting the nation.

An older translation of "maiming" as "hamstringing" an ox brings these images together. Just as a soldier might hamstring an enemy's horse, so "the ox is Jacob," Carmichael interprets, "who, as representative and head of his house, has been weakened or hamstrung before his enemies because of Simeon and Levi's action."[24]

By no means all of this translation and hence interpretation are certain. Important differences emerge from a new translation of the first six lines by Stanley Gevirtz.

> Simeon and Levi are spent owls,
> Cashiered hawks are they.
>
> Into their council I will not enter,
> In their assembly I do not rejoice.
>
> For in their anger they kill(ed) men,
> And in their caprice tore out a bull.[25]

In this version, Jacob's rejection of Simeon and Levi is even more forceful. These two brothers/tribes are like exhausted owls and tied hawks whose beaks can no longer bite because they have aided in undermining Israel by destroying its unity. The tearing of a bull, Gevirtz argues, is a reference back to "Levi's despoliation of the bull-calf image at Beth-el."[26] They worship their anger, not their God's law. In short, referring backward to the people's apostasy in worshiping a gold calf while Moses was on Mount Sinai, the accusation is one of idolatry.

Issachar, Asher, Dan, Gad, Naphtali, Benjamin, Zebulun

Postponing the most difficult cases of Judah and Joseph, I turn to the poetic prophecies for the sons of Jacob who figure least in the Joseph stories. These testaments fit into a general theme in which the tribes of Israel are accused by Jacob of failing to defend the unity and security of Israel. The account of Issachar is about subservience, the moral being that Hebrews should be subservient only to God.

> Issachar is a strong-boned ass,
> Crouching among the sheepfolds.
> When he saw how good was security,
> And how pleasant was the country,
> He bent his shoulder to the burden,
> And became a toiling serf. (Gen. 49:14–15)

The name Issachar itself is a play on the root *skr*, "to hire." It is the same root that Leah uses when she says that she has hired Jacob's conjugal services with her mandrakes. Comparing Issachar to an ass does not give us an immediate meaning because the animal was looked upon positively in biblical times, though then as now an ass was a burden-bearing animal. (No matter how tempting to an English-speaking person, the Hebrew does not permit word play on "half-assed.) Progress can be made by recognizing that the son of the chieftain in Shechem was named Hamor, which is a word for ass. Carmichael sums up the meaning as I understand it: "The Hivites [Hamor's tribe] were a group representative of the Canaanites, and the enslaved position of the Issachar tribe is a reversal of the relationship which should prevail between the sons of Jacob and the Canaanites."[27] Bennett observes that with a very slight alteration, the term called "strong ass" yields "'ass of foreigners,' an allusion to the tributory state of Issachar."[28]

The remaining lines compare the tribe to a well-fed, docile beast of burden, satisfied to live richly but in a dependent position.[29] The term "crouching among the sheepfolds" points to a people "content to enjoy its safety at the expense of its freedom."[30]

The tribe of Asher is either praised or criticized (I favor the latter interpretation) for being rich:

Asher's bread shall be rich,
And he shall yield royal dainties. (Gen. 49:20)

Whether one prefers to read royal dainties as signifying "delicacies fit for a king" or gaining lucre by serving Canaanite kings[31] depends on a larger interpretive scheme. Gevirtz considers the lines a sarcastic protest against the excessive impositions of Solomon's government. The translation Gevirtz suggests fits his theory: "Asher, who rations his bread, *he* gives delicacies to the king."[32] The name of the tribe signifies good fortune or happiness. Whether this was gained at the expense of the other Israelite tribes is the question.

Read literally, the opening lines about another son says that

Dan shall govern his people,
As one of the tribes of Israel. (Gen. 49:16)

Only when the meaning of these lines is established can one interpret the rest. This is the first time, many commentators observe, that the phrase "tribes of Israel" occurs in the Bible. So what is wrong? A clue may be found in the fact that the term used for governing or judging comes from the same root as being subservient by doing corvée, labor that rulers like King Solomon requisition without consent from the people under their command. Such usage would suggest that the tribe of Dan bought a quiet life in return for giving a certain amount of labor to the surrounding Canaanites, not a desirable practice from the vantage point of Israel as a separate nation in charge of its own destiny.[33] Here is the rest of the stanza:

> Dan shall be a serpent by the road,
> A viper by the path,
> That bites the horse's heels
> So that his rider is thrown backward. (Gen. 49:17)

Is it that Dan is a snare to Israel's enemies, or is he a creature of guile and cunning, like the serpent in the Garden of Eden, who fools his own people (the "rider . . . thrown backward") into believing he is fighting on their side?

Next there is interpolated a single line in which Jacob speaks for himself: "I wait for Your deliverance, O Lord!" (Gen. 49:18). Long-suffering to the last is our Jacob. The fact that the first person pronoun is generally used when Jacob speaks makes it likely that this single line is his pause for prayer. Perhaps this sentence refers to Jacob's hope that the tribe of Dan will finally find a secure home in the chosen land. Perhaps it reflects Jacob's characteristic impatience with his exasperating sons. Perhaps, amidst the flux and tribulations of his people's history, much of it bad, Jacob feels a little prayer is always in order.

"Leah said, 'What luck!' So she named him Gad" (Gen. 30:11), Jacob's son by her maid, Zilpah.

> Gad shall be raided by raiders,
> But he shall raid at their heels. (Gen. 49:19)

A trans-Jordan tribe, frequently subject to attack by marauders, Gad's tribe is quite capable of repelling them. Is Gad here being criticized because he waits for others to defend the collective? The root *gadad*, translated as "to raid," also suggests something like "stomp." To stomp on others or be stomped on is a different matter. Whether Gad is being indirectly praised for his warriorlike qualities or criticized for engaging in professional warfare has not yet been determined.

Jacob's describing Naphtali is easier on translators. Jacob says no more than

Naphtali is a hind let loose,
Which yields lovely fawns. (Gen. 49:21)

Once free-born, an animal let loose to run at its own speed, now it is merely decorative.

As Davidson comments in regard to Naphtali, "Very different translations of this verse are possible."[34] Contradictory interpretations abound. The reader needs to know that "hind" (in Hebrew *'ayyalah*) is not only fast-footed and female, Naphtali being the only tribe compared to a woman, but also signifies "lamb" in several Semitic languages.[35] Sarna speculates that "The reference could then be to Naphtali being quick to pay tribute of sheep to its Canaanite overlords or to the beauty, openness, and the fruitfulness of its tribal territory."[36] Quite a difference. I agree with Gevirtz that the structured oppositions employed by the poet—"mountain-ewe" (hind) versus "lambs of the foal," masculine versus feminine, active versus passive participles[37]—show the "tone of its content to be derisive rather than complimentary."[38]

Three lines tell us all Jacob wants us to know about his youngest:

Benjamin is a ravenous wolf;
In the morning he consumes the foe,
And in the evening he divides the spoil. (Gen. 49:27)

Benjamin appears tough enough; certainly this is not the meek fellow Jacob and Joseph fought over! The Bible is full of references to the tribe's martial valor (Judg. 5:14, 20:15-16, 21:1; I Chron. 8:40, 12:2, etc.). Yet the overall impression—"ravenous wolf," "consumes the foe," and "divides the spoil"—suggests the tribe may have extended its might beyond the law. Jacob's description fits well with the behavior of the Benjamites in allowing the concubine of a Levite to be gang-raped and in refusing to turn over the perpetrators who the other tribes called the "children of Belial" (Judg. 20:13). The result was a civil war, with large losses on both sides, in which the tribe of Benjamin was defeated (Judg. 20-21). The phrase about dividing the spoil in the evening may well be an allusion to the time when the remaining tribes saved the tribe of Benjamin by capturing, and allowing it to capture, wives for its men (Judg. 21).[39]

The lines for Zebulun are either as plain or as mysterious as can be:

Zebulun shall dwell by the seashore;
He shall be a haven for ships,
and his flank shall rest on Sidon. (Gen. 49:13)

No one knows why Zebulun is portrayed as living along the seashore when his tribe was evidently located inland.[40] Was the tribe seafaring? Or, at least, did it provide provisions for ships?

Since Issachar is older than Zebulun, it may be expected that the latter would precede the former in Jacob's testaments. Instead, the usual order is reversed. And the same switch is true for Moses' blessings (Deut. 33:18). Either the records of their birth (Gen. 30:17-20) are wrong or a point is being made by deliberately subordinating the passive Issachar to the fighting Zebulun, as is stated in the song of Deborah (Judg. 5:14-18; see also 6:35) for contributing to Israel's defense.

Taking the testaments about these seven brothers together, we find the predominant tenor is critical. There is no instance where we are sure the tone is positive and several where it is negative. How do the heroes-anti-heroes of the Joseph saga, Judah and Joseph, fare in Israel's dispensation?

Judah

A fratriarch, as the reader has surmised by now, is the brother who has special authority over his other brothers. In Isaac's blessing to Jacob, for instance, the fratriarch is awarded the right to "Be master over your brothers, and let your mother's sons bow to you" (Gen. 27:29). And Jacob's brother Esau is told specifically that he shall serve his brother, although he will eventually be able to "break his yoke from your neck" (Gen. 27:40). Being the brother of an imperious fratriarch was not necessarily a blessing.

Similarly, the first three lines of Jacob's prophecy about Judah speak to his authority.

> You, O Judah, your brothers shall praise;
> Your hand shall be on the nape of your foes;
> Your father's sons shall bow low to you. (Gen. 49:8)

Note the reference to bowing low, which the brothers once did to Joseph but now must do to Judah. The emphasis on the father's relationship to his sons highlights what they have in common while omission of the fact that they have different mothers ignores what apparently drove them apart. The phrase "father's sons" is an unusual circumlocution, giving additional force to the statement about the brothers' submission to Judah who, for emphasis, holds his foes so tightly by the back of the neck they cannot escape.[41]

What about his brothers' praise? Judah has in fact been locked in a struggle for precedence with his three elder brothers, Reuben, Levi, and Simeon, and the young usurper, Joseph.[42] Did not Jacob make Joseph his main inheritor, a position difficult to deny him as a high-ranking official in Egypt? Yes and no. On the one hand, Joseph is given a double portion and his two sons inherit as if they were sons of Jacob, not as grandsons, so that each gets a full share. On the other hand, Judah is clearly made the future fratriarch. Judah is anointed for the future with Joseph left to rule in the present.

Does it not bode well for Judah to be compared to the lion, "the king of beasts" (Gen. 49:9), who presumably grows stronger by defeating and devouring his enemies? Not necessarily. If lions are unalloyedly good, why does the Ninety-first Psalm contain this injunction: "The young lion and the dragon shalt thou trample under feet" (Ps. 91:13)? Of the cub who became a young lion and learned to catch its prey, Ezekiel says twice, "It devoured men" (Ezek. 19:3, 6). The lion is an ambiguous symbol whose meaning alters with the context. Jacob says:

Judah is a lion's whelp;
On prey, my son, have you grown.
He crouches, lies down like a lion,
Like the king of beasts—who dare rouse him? (Gen. 49:9)

Because the testaments to Reuben, Simeon, and Levi that precede the one for Judah are condemnations of past behavior, it is a fair bet that Jacob will also rake up Judah's past. What, we may ask, was the "prey" on which Judah grew? Why does he crouch down like a lion? And on whom would he pounce? In trying to save Joseph from being killed by his brothers, Judah has him sold and, together with the rest of his brothers, covers up this deception by sprinkling Joseph's coat with goat's blood. Whether the line in question reads that Judah has grown on prey in general or, as Edwin Good translates, "From the prey of my son," there is a difference in intention.[43] Judah could well be portrayed here as a deceiver who attributes Joseph's death to a wild beast when it is really him in disguise.

Jacob continues by foreseeing that

The scepter shall not depart from Judah,
Nor the ruler's staff from between his feet;
So that tribute shall come to him
And the homage of peoples be his. (Gen. 49:10)

Although Jacob does not gainsay Judah's future as the leader of the other Israelite tribes—the scepter, the sign of authority, will remain with his tribe—the image of the just ruler holding the emblem of office between his feet is shattered by historical memory. Commentators agree that the ruler's staff is an allusion to Judah's intercourse with Tamar. There are also references to Judah's sons as the ensuing commentary will reveal.

The Jewish Publication Society's new translation contains a footnote to the last line of Genesis 49:10 suggesting an alternative translation that deletes the initial "And," revealing further that the words for "tribute to him" (*shai loh*) are obscure and may literally be read as "until he comes to Shiloh." The word has sometimes been translated as meaning that tribute shall come to Judah when a member of his tribe becomes king. Shiloh might also be a reference to the division of Israel between the northern ten tribes and Judah and Benjamin in the south as announced by the northern prophet, Ahijah of Shiloh.[44] These lines are carefully crafted to give Judah the appearance of power; the question is whether his tribe will use that wisely in view of the fateful division within Israel.

So sensitive are the matters referred to that the poetry describing Judah becomes more allegorical as it goes on. Let us take each of the images in turn.

He tethers his ass to a vine,
His ass's foal to a choice vine. (Gen. 49:11)

Here I begin with the obvious: tying an ass to a vine is not a brilliant idea. The second line is an intensification of the first, suggesting that two animals are being tied to the same vine. What kind of person would want to have one, let alone two, donkeys tearing down vines and trampling the grapes? The poet could be conjuring up an image of abundance so vast that the owner did not have to consider what happened to his vines.[45]

These lines also evoke the names of Judah's dead sons, Er, related to "his ass" and his second son, Onan, called "his ass's foal" or, as Rendsburg renders a more direct translation, "son of his she-ass" (in Hebrew, *benei atono*).[46] Carmichael, following upon Good, brings out the allusions to the first two sons of Judah. The Hebraic roots for the name Er and "ass" are similar, as is "she-ass" and Onan, at least by sound. Thus, in the poet's hands, Er and Onan become sons of the she-ass, the Canaanite woman who married their father, Judah.[47]

The poet is warning his people not to follow the path of their ancestor by mixing the two peoples. The principle, as Carmichael has it, is that "the Israelites' vineyard should not be sown with hybrid seed."[48] Thus Carmichael associates several of the commandments against mixing— not ploughing with an Israelite ox and a Canaanite ass together, and not putting the woolen Judah and the linen prostitute Tamar together.[49] The Hebrew for "choice vine," *sorekah*, refers to a location in the Timnah region in which Judah and Tamar act out their story.[50]

Now we understand that the death of Judah's first two sons is not accidential but part of the penalty for marrying outside his people. The penalty cannot be complete, however, because then the tribe of Judah would have no successors. And what would happen to God's promise? So Judah's son Shelah is saved, as is Tamar, whose sons become the ancestors of the line of King David, but only after Judah acknowledges that he was wrong, making Tamar right. Tamar is honored for her contribution to the continuity of the people; but Judah, we recall, has no further intercourse with her, and through him all Israelites are warned not to follow his path. He and his posterity are preserved while he and his behavior are condemned. To go further, we must now turn to Judah's washing his robe in blood.

Quite remarkably, Jacob says of Judah:

He washes his garment in wine,
His robe in blood of grapes.
His eyes are darker than wine;
His teeth are whiter than milk. (Gen. 49:11–12)

Immediately, we are reminded of Joseph's coat, which Judah and his brothers violently took from him and then smeared with blood to deceive their father. There is no mistaking, as Alter calls it, the "paradoxical intimation of violence embedded in the pastoral image."[51] Raised to a more general level, the destruction of Israel, or at least its gene pool, is portrayed as a consequence of thrashing about in foreign vineyards so that its people take on the characteristic hue of their surroundings. The reference to the redness or darkness of Judah's eyes (*e-naim*), Good advises, "recalls the name of the town where the encounter between

Judah and Tamar took place: Enaim."[52] The contrast between dark eyes and white teeth is that between two people's moralities and rival gods, which should be kept separate. The admixture will indeed make blood run in the streets as if it were wine.

Many times in the Torah we are told that the life is in the blood, hence the penalties for bloodletting, hence the prohibition against drinking blood, which is inserted into the provisions for kosher slaughtering of animals. For Hebrews, therefore, the blood metaphor runs to separation of the clean from the unclean and of this people dedicated to their vision of God from others. In Christianity, by contrast, the blood of the grapes is taken into the body by the priest in the sacrifice of the Mass to indicate that Jesus has mediated between God and man. "Blood," Soler argues, "which acted as an isolater between two poles, now becomes a conductor."[53]

Edwin Good relates the blood of the grapes to dipping a kid's skin in blood so father Jacob would think his son Joseph had been devoured by wild animals. Good argues,

> If, then, . . . allusions are as I have suggested, the whole "blessing" on Judah turns out to be an ironic reflection on Judah's misdeeds in two earlier incidents, and that in its turn casts a certain irony over the laudatory wordplay . . . with the Joseph incident. "Your father's sons shall bow down to you." . . . Is the remark in 49:8, then, not the straightforward statement of praise that it looks like, but an ironic reflection on Judah's attempt to get rid of the pest who had such high and mighty ideas of himself?[54]

Good concludes that "actually the only tribe unambiguously lauded in the whole passage is Joseph. Is the 'Blessing of Jacob,' then, a piece of Ephraimite nationalism?"[55] But if the passage about Joseph is also double-edged, more critical than complimentary, something else is being said.

Ultimately, it is Judaism's determination to raise an impenetrable barrier against the encroachment of man upon God's realm that has reinforced the decision to remain religiously a separate people. This is the grand theme of the interaction between God and man and Israelite and foreigner, a theme in which the survival of this peculiar people is intimately connected to the daily practices that effectively separate them from others, so that they are endangered both by impractical isolation and destructive spiritual union. This is the theme that provides the leitmotif of the Joseph stories.

Joseph

Jacob's words about Joseph are spoken on but their second encounter since the father came to live in the same land as the son. Their first lengthy exchange occurs when Jacob, sensing his death is near, calls Joseph to him. What Jacob asks is rather unusual: "Do me this favor, place your hand under my thigh as a pledge of your steadfast loyalty: please do not bury me in Egypt" (Gen. 47:29). Why did Jacob have to back up his request to be buried in the same place as his father and grandfather by asking Joseph to provide evidence of his "steadfast loyalty"? Indeed, after Joseph said he would do as his father asked, Jacob replied, as if uncertain, "Swear to me" (Gen. 47:31). Is this swearing a second time necessary in order to give Joseph the strength needed to get Pharaoh to comply with such an unusual request? To make sure no one will miss its significance, Joseph tells Pharaoh, "My father made me swear" (Gen. 50:5), and Pharaoh replies that Joseph should bury his father "as he made you promise on oath" (Gen. 50:6). Is Joseph saying too much in alluding to the element of compulsion, and is Pharaoh going along with this charade by repeating Joseph's words back to him so that neither need concern themselves with the truth?

Interpreters agree that the thigh refers to the seat of procreation. This ceremony, Sarna suggests, "may invoke the presence and power of God as the guarantor of the earth."[56] It may be that Jacob, fearing that Joseph has become too much an Egyptian, wants to make sure his son will not renege on the promise. By pledging Joseph on the site of his virility, Jacob may have wished to make his powerful son aware that the future of his people, encapsulated in God's promise to occupy the land He gave them, depends on their meeting their part of the bargain. Wedded to Egypt, unable to leave until his bones were long cold, Joseph may not have seemed to his father the ideal person to carry out an exodus. Too old to stand, Jacob "bowed at the head of the bed" (Gen. 47:31), to fate, to God, to Joseph, I cannot say.

There follows the previously analyzed story of Jacob's blessing of Joseph's sons, Manasseh and Ephraim. Without going into detail, it is evident that Jacob is his own man, for he reverses the usual age-graded precedence between the two sons and refuses to change it back when Joseph remonstrates with him. The irony of Joseph, who spent much of his life seeking to overturn the rule of primogeniture, insisting on it for his own sons should not be lost on the reader.

After assuring Joseph, who does not necessarily want that kind of reassurance, that God will bring him back to the land of his fathers, Jacob gives Joseph "one portion more than to your brothers, which I wrested from the Amorites with my sword and bow" (Gen. 48:22). There are many difficulties with the phrase "one portion." This JPS translation of the Hebrew *shekham* is the one that has largely been accepted, though it lacks a justification in the Hebrew language. Others translate *shekham* as an allusion to the city, others as "mountain slope."

Joseph is getting something, whether it is a side of a mountain or a city, because Jacob adds that he conquered it. Although we have learned that Jacob's sons led the massacre in Shechem, there is no hint that either they or Jacob retained possession of the city. It would be in character for the wily old man to send Joseph back to Shechem. This passage is close to one in the Book of Joshua in which God says that he helped his people drive out the kings of the Amorites (generally Canaanites), "but not with thy sword, nor with thy bow" (Josh. 24:12). In short, it is not the Israelites but their God who is to take the credit. How different is Jacob's claim that he did it "with my sword and bow"?

What Jacob says directly is this:

Joseph is a wild ass,
A wild ass by a spring
—Wild colts on a hillside [or: "Joseph is a fruitful bough, A fruitful bough by a spring,
Its branches run over a wall"].
Archers bitterly assailed him;
They shot at him and harried him.
Yet his bow stayed taut,
And his arms were made firm
By the hands of the Mighty One of Jacob—
There, the Shepherd, the Rock of Israel—
The God of your father who helps you,
And Shaddai who blesses you
With blessings of heaven above,
Blessings of the deep that couches below,
Blessings of the breast and womb
The blessings of your father
Surpass the blessings of my ancestors,
To the utmost bounds of the eternal hills.
May they rest on the head of Joseph,
On the brow of the elect of his brothers. (Gen. 49:22–26)

What are we to make of this Joseph, a wild ass, a colt cavorting on a hillside? There is always the possibility that the meaning is lost and so the various translations do not do it justice. Some interpreters follow "the fruitful bough approach," the references, they think, being to Manasseh and Ephraim, who have climbed high obstacles in order to gain equal status with their uncles.[57] But why would branches run over a wall? Possibly, if branches were women, they would want to behold the beauteous Joseph. The Targum Pseudo-Jonathan has it that in Egypt "the daughters of the rulers would walk along the walls and cast down in front of you [Joseph] bracelets and golden ornaments so that you might look at them."[58]

A more promising lead comes from Sarna, who believes that the words "spring" and "hillside" (*anayin, sur*) "may well be word play concealing the reference to the Ishmaelites who sold Joseph to Egypt" (Gen. 37:25,28).[59] The angel of the Lord, who always stands for God, upon urging Hagar to return to her harsh mistress, Sarah, said that she would bear a son called Ishmael, who "shall be a wild ass of a man; His hand against everyone, and everyone's hand against him" (Gen. 16:11). It is one thing to be rather wild as a youth, another to compare Joseph to someone who opposes everyone and is opposed by everyone, though, as far as Joseph's brothers are concerned, that was the truth. The surface praise of Jacob's testament about Joseph is beginning to dissipate.

Next we are told that archers harrassed and assailed Joseph. There is no recorded incident of Joseph's being shot at with arrows. But it is said of Ishmael that he "became a bowman" (Gen. 21:20). Sarna suggests that the arrows may be a figurative allusion to the accusations made by Mrs. Potiphar and the anger of Joseph's brothers.[60] In the Bible the metaphor of arrows is used to describe words of deceit (see Jer. 9:8). Similar metaphors are used to describe the slander against Joseph by Potiphar's wife as if he, not she, were the aggressor. It may be, therefore, that comments about Joseph's being harried and assailed by archers—that is, slanderers—but keeping his strong arms firm, is praise.[61] If Joseph is indeed the son of a fruitful tree, these verses are testimony to the fact that he defended himself and retained his manhood.[62]

Whether "The Mighty One of Jacob" who stiffened Joseph's resolve (that is, made his arms firm) was Jacob or God, "the Shepherd, the Rock of Israel—The God of your father who helps you," has been much debated. A possibility is that the Mighty One, sometimes translated as "the Bull of Jacob," is "connected with the calf at Beth-el, the great sanctuary of the Northern kingdom." Yet the Hebrew word for "Mighty One" may but does not have to mean bull.[63] Sarna probably has it right when he concludes: "The ambiguity as to whether the patriarch or the people of Israel is intended is probably deliberate."[64] Contending that in Assyrian literature the word "bow" is used as a term for "sexual vigor," E. F. Weidner speculates that the word implies turning warriors into women unable to fight by taking away their bow.[65]

The last verses about Joseph appear to be the most enigmatic; he is blessed by his God and by the natural order. One of the few things we know for sure is that the usual order, which would be womb and breast, "is here reversed for reasons of sound harmony (Hebrew *shamaim-shadayim*)."[66] Is Jacob really trying to say that his blessings on Joseph surpass the blessings that Jacob's ancestors gave him? This is not so, as we have seen, not to mention the fact that Jacob deceived his father to get those blessings. Is Jacob damning with faint praise as if to say that at least Joseph was getting more (however little that was) than Jacob's father willingly gave him? It would be like Jacob to think Joseph had it better. Whether calling Joseph "the elect of his brothers" (Gen. 49:26) is sarcasm (Joseph was certainly not elected by his brothers) or praise (Jacob loved Joseph more than all his other sons together), we cannot tell. But we can, I believe, get some perspective on the meaning of Jacob's words about Joseph by considering them in parallel with Moses' farewell address to his people.

As the Lord tells Moses that he will not enter the Promised Land and that he is about to die, He reveals that the people will fall away from the true faith, embrace alien gods, and break their covenant with Him, after which He will desert them and they will become prey to numerous evils. The sin of the people apparently is infidelity, "turning to other gods" (Deut. 31:18). As a sort of prophylactic to ward off these evils, the Lord commands Moses to "write down this poem and teach it to the people of Israel; put it in their mouths, in order that this poem may be My witness against the people of Israel" (Deut. 31:19). The poem reads in small part:

> The Rock!—His deeds are perfect,
> Yea, all His ways are just;
> A faithful God, never false,
> True and upright is He.
> Children unworthy of Him,
> That crooked and twisted generation . . . .

O dull and witless people?
Is not He the Father who created you. (Deut. 32:4-6)

Among the many things He did for His people was to enable them to drink "foaming grape-blood" (Deut. 32:14). This refers to one of the striking phrases of Jacob's testament to Judah.

Hear now the words of a vengeful God, incensed at His people's apostasy:

Use up My arrows on them:
Wasting famine, ravaging plague,
Deadly pestilence, and fanged beasts
Will I let loose against them,
With venomous creepers in dust. (Deut. 32:23-24)

Here we have the arrows and the creepers; more than that, we see that these are not exactly praises but rather arrows (like the arrows shot at Joseph?), words the Lord uses when condemning His people. "For," as the Lord says, "they are a folk void of sense, Lacking in all discernment" (Deut. 32:28).

This people could never have conquered others, the Lord continues, unless a greater power was on their side. His judgment is not that their vines are superabundant; rather

Ah! The vine for them is from Sodom,
From the vineyards of Gomorrah;
The grapes for them are poison,
A bitter growth their clusters. (Deut. 32:32)

Now we see why wine is called the blood of the grape. "I deal death," the Lord says (Deut 32:39). Those who reject Me "I will make drunk My arrows with blood," and thus "cleanse the land of His people" (Deut. 32:42-43). Judah and Joseph are shot with the same bloody arrow.

At one point the blessings of Jacob and of Moses for Joseph are in almost exact accord. Jacob ends his with the couplet "May they [the blessings] rest on the head of Joseph, On the brow of the elect of his brothers" (Gen. 49:26). Moses says the same except that the JPS new translation substitutes "crown" for "brow" in the second line (Deut. 33:16). The Hebrew word for "crown" is *nazir*, whose first meaning is "consecrated," secondarily "noble" or chief. I prefer the translation of the New Revised Standard version that reads "On the brow of him who was set apart from his brothers," though I disagree in part with its explanation of "set apart by prestige and position."[67] The word *nazir* is used to indicate doubt about the object of Joseph's affections, Israel or Egypt. Joseph indeed consecrated himself. But to whom?

The coffin in which Joseph is buried (Gen. 50:26) and in which Moses carries his bones out of Egypt is called by a name, *shekhina*, used only for one other object in the Bible, the Ark of the Covenant (Exod. 25:10-16).[68] What are we to make of this double image of the Egyptian mummy case/coffin and the Ark of the Covenant, the symbols of Egypt and of Israel? Is it that what (or who) was once Egyptian has become Hebrew? Is it an effort to paper over the fact that Joseph had become Egyptian by superimposing a Hebrew designation on an identifiably Egyptian object? Is it to symbolize Joseph's ambivalence to the very end, his bones buried in Israel but within an enduring Egyptian casket?

Moses describes Joseph in phrases similar to those Jacob uttered:

On the crown of the elect of his brothers.
Like a firstling bull in his majesty,
He has horns like the horns of the wild-ox;
With them he gores the peoples,
The ends of the earth one and all.
These [that is, the one horn] are the myriads of Ephraim,
Those [that is, the other horn] are the thousands of Manasseh (Deut. 33:16-17).

The horns refer to Joseph's sons, Ephraim and Manasseh. But who are the peoples he gores? Are they just the Canaanites or might they include the other Israelite tribes? And what explains the repeated references to bulls? Either the poet wishes to signify that Joseph was a fine fellow whose descendants unfortunately got on the wrong side of history or the poet is explaining why the Josephite tribes fell from favor. This is the Torah, God's teaching. And we know what God teaches: Thou shalt hold no other gods before me.

Why?

One way of treating Jacob's blessings is as prophecies that have to be correct anticipations of future history in order to justify his position as patriarch and thus the position of his God and His promises. Then we would take the words about Judah and Joseph at face value. They, the survivors, are truly blessed, whereas whose who disappeared into the population of other nations proved unworthy, as their father, Jacob, foresaw. While Jacob, as is his wont, may make fun of Judah's sexual proclivities, he does portray him as a lion whose brothers and enemies give him homage and who possesses such great abundance that he can afford to have his grapes trampled and his clothes washed in wine. As for Joseph, if his branches do go over a wall, that may merely indicate that one of the two tribes that sprang from him, Manasseh, moved away from the other, while Joseph, guided by God, overcame all adversity, the true "Mighty One of Jacob" (Gen. 49:24). I cannot entirely rule out this interpretation, but I have tried to show that the bulk of the evidence is against it.

Why might Jacob's blessings be negative? The rabbis and the writers had to account for the destruction of the temple and the ten tribes. They had to explain the subjugation of all of Israel, north and south, and the death and enslavement and exile of the rest of its peoples, leaving only scattered remnants in the Holy Land. And all this had to be reconciled with a just God. In this light, the only proper prophecies for Jacob to make would be a plague on all your houses, all being deemed unworthy of their God's protection.

Approaching death, Jacob does what a Jewish father is supposed to but what he did not do during his lifetime—chastise his children to lessen their faults. Unlike Moses, Jacob remembers his sons' faults but glosses over their virtues. He becomes a repository for the accusations his sons level against each other. This negative collective portrait helps explain why Israel's God seeks to make a new beginning with Moses.

Notes

1. Nahum M. Sarna, *The JPS Torah Commentary: Genesis* (Philadelphia: Jewish Publication Society, 1989), 331.
2. Ibid.
3. E.A. Speiser, *Genesis, The Anchor Bible* (Garden City, NY: Doubleday, 1964), 371.
4. Herbert Rand, "The Testament of Jacob, An Analysis of Gen. 49:18," *Dor le Dor* 18 (1989): 101.
5. Sarna, *Genesis.*
6. See Eric I. Lowenthal, *The Joseph Narrative in Genesis* (New York: KTAV Publishing House, 1973), 123.
7. *"Rashi" On the Pentateuch: Genesis*, trans. and annotated by James H. Lowe (London: Hebrew Compendium Publishing, 1928), 392–93.
8. James L. Kugel, *In Potiphar's House* (San Francisco: Harper, 1990), 94–95.
9. Ibid.
10. Sarna, *Genesis*, 401.

11. Robert D. Sacks, *A Commentary on the Book of Genesis*, Ancient Near Eastern Texts and Studies, vol. 6 (Lewiston, NY: Edwin Mellen Press, 1990), 409.
12. Stanley Gevirtz, "Siemon and Levi in 'The Blessing of Jacob'" (Gen. 49:5-7)," *Hebrew Union College Annual* 52 (1981): 93-128; quote on 113-14.
13. See Yair Zakovitch, "Assimilation in Biblical Narratives," in *Empirical Models for Biblical Criticism*, ed. Jeffrey H. Tigay (Philadelphia: University of Pennsylvania Press, 1985), 191.
14. Richard Elliot Friedman, *Who Wrote the Bible?* (New York: Summit Books, 1987), 120.
15. Gevirtz, "Simeon and Levi in 'The Blessing of Jacob,'" 117.
16. Aaron Wildavsky, *The Nursing Father: Moses As a Political Leader* (University of Alabama Press, 1985).
17. Kenneth Waltz, *Theory of International Politics* (Reading, Mass.: Addison Wesley, 1979).
18. Elie Munk, *The Call of the Torah, Volume II, Genesis, Part 2* (Jerusalem: Feldheim Publishers, 1969), 815.
19. Ibid.
20. See Stanley Gevirtz, "The Reprimand of Reuben," *Journal of Near Eastern Studies* 30 (1971): 87-98, at 98; K. Luke, "Two Birth Narratives in Genesis (Gen. 25:19-26; 38:27-30)," *Indian Theological Studies* 17 (1980): 155-180, at 177.
21. Sarna, *JPS Torah Commentary, Genesis*, 333. To show that mortar can be made to stand for character, Sarna quotes Isaiah 57:20: "But the wicked are like the troubled sea/Which cannot rest/Whose waters toss up mire and mud."
22. This malediction, as Vawter correctly calls it, has no echo in the vast praise heaped on Levi by Moses. (B. Vawter, "The Canaanite Background of Genesis 49," *Catholic Biblical Quarterly* 17 (1955): 1-10, at 3.
23. Thomas Blass, "The Tenacity of Impressions and Jacob's Rebuke of Simeon and Levi," *Journal of Psychology and Judaism* 7, no. 1 (1982): 55-61, at 57.
24. Calum M. Carmichael, "Some Sayings in Genesis 49," *Journal of Biblical Literature* 88 (1979): 435-444, quote on 435-36.
25. Gevirtz, "Simeon and Levi in 'The Blessing off Jacob,'" 93.
26. Ibid., 128.
27. Carmichael, "Some Sayings in Genesis 49," 437.
28. *The New Century Bible: Genesis*, ed. W. H. Bennett (Edinburgh: T. C. & E. C. Jack, n.d.), 398.
29. Robert Davidson, *Genesis 12-50* (Cambridge: Cambridge University Press, 1979), 306.
30. Sarna, *Genesis*, 339.
31. Ibid., 342; and Davidson, *Genesis*, 307.
32. Stanley Gevirtz, "Asher in the Blessing of Jacob (Genesis XLIX 20," *Vetus Testamentum* 37, no. 2 (1987): 154-163, quote on 161.
33. See Sarna, *Genesis*, 340.
34. Davidson, *Genesis*, 307.
35. Sarna, *Genesis*, 342.
36. Ibid.
37. Stanley Gevirtz, "Naphtali in the Blessing of Jacob," *Journal of Biblical Literature* 103/4 (1984): 513-521, quote on 520.
38. Ibid., 513.
39. *Soncino Chumash: The Five Books of Moses with Haphtaroth*, ed. the Rev. Dr. A. Cohen (London: Soncino Press, 1966), 309.

40. Sarna, *Genesis*, 337–38.
41. In stylistic terms, this is also a form of "elegant variation," that is, avoiding repeating "brothers."
42. For further discussion, see Edwin M. Good, "The 'Blessing' on Judah, Gen. 49:8–12," *Journal of Biblical Literature* 82 (1963): 427–432.
43. Ibid., 429–30. See also *Genesis Rabba* 98:12 and 99:9.
44. Sarna, *Genesis*, 336–37.
45. S. R. Driver, *The Book of Genesis* (London: Methuen, 1904), 386.
46. Gary A. Rendsburg, *The Redaction of Genesis* (Winona Lake, Indiana: Eisenbrauns, 1986), 84.
47. Carmichael, "Some Sayings in Genesis 49," 441.
48. Calum M. Carmichael, "Forbidden Mixtures," *Vetus Testamentum* 32 (1982): 394–415, quote on 401.
49. Ibid., 409–10.
50. Sarna, *Genesis*, 337.
51. Robert Alter, *The Art of Biblical Poetry* (New York: Basic Books, 1985), 16.
52. Edwin M. Good, *Irony in the Old Testament* (Sheffield: Almond Press, 1981), 111.
53. Jean Soler, "The Dietary Prohibitions of the Hebrews," trans. by Elbort Forster, *New York Review of Books* 26/10 (June 14, 1979), 30.
54. Good, "The 'Blessing' on Judah, Gen. 48:8–12," 432.
55. Ibid.
56. Sarna, *Genesis*, 162.
57. James Kugel, "The Case Against Joseph," in *Lingering Over Words: Studies in Ancient Near Eastern Literature in Honor of William L. Moran*, Tzvi Abusch, John Huehnergard, and Piotr Steinkeller, eds. (Atlanta: Scholar's Press, 1990), 271–287, at 280–81.
58. Cited in Kugel, "The Case Against Joseph." See also Stanley Gevirtz, "Of Patriarchs and Puns: Joseph at the Fountain, Jacob at the Ford," *Hebrew Union College Annual* 46 (1975): 33–54, quote on 35.
59. Sarna, *Genesis*, 343.
60. Ibid.
61. Martin I. Lockshin, *Rabbi Samuel Ben Mahir's Commentary on Genesis: An Annotated Translation*, Jewish Studies, vol. 5 (Lewiston, NY: Edwin Mellon Press, 1989).
62. For all we know, Bennett may be right: "Possibly Joseph here is the northern kingdom, and the enemy the Syrians of Damascus with whom the kings of Israel waged almost constant wars from about B.C.900. Or Joseph may be the separate tribe, and the reference may be to the period of the Judges, and to events which can no longer be identified." Bennett, *Genesis*, 401.
63. Ibid. See also Kugel, "The Case Against Joseph," 285–86.
64. Sarna, *Genesis*, 343.
65. E. F. Wiedner, "Der Staatsvertrag Assurniraris VI von Assyrien mit Mati'ilu von Bit-Agusi," *AFO* 8 (1932–33): 12–13.
66. Sarna, *Genesis*, 344.
67. *The New Oxford Annotated Bible*, New Revised Standard Version (New York: Oxford University Press, 1991), 67.
68. See Martin Buber, *Moses: The Revelation and the Covenant* (New York: Harper & Brothers, 1958), 20.

8

Why Joseph-the-Assimilator Is Superseded by Moses-the-Lawgiver

The Joseph stories, I have argued, reflect a conflict between different forms of Judaism, one urging assimilation, except in religion, the other demanding social separation as a support for religion. The Joseph stories foresee the future not in Joseph but in Judah. Moses is the lawgiver, which shows that the law comes from Judah.

Why did the Hebrew people go to Egypt? Because Joseph-the-assimilator, father to Pharaoh, by his own word (Gen. 45:8), took them there. Why did they stay so long? Because Joseph (meaning him and all those who followed his example) would not leave Egypt. Why were the Israelites so miserable in Egypt? Because Joseph helped make the pharaonic system more monopolistic and hence more arbitrary. How were the Hebrew people able, at long last, to throw off Pharaoh's yoke and leave Egypt for the land promised to them? Because Moses rescued them by reinventing the old-time religion, writing down its laws, and enforcing its practices.

When does Joseph come off well? When he demonstrates how Hebrews can be of use to foreign potentates. Joseph also appears heroic when he resists the advances of foreigners and their corrupt practices (Potiphar's wife). When does Joseph look bad? When he lords it over his own family and others, bringing his father evil reports about his brothers, manipulating his brothers and father, making serfs out of Egyptian landowners, claiming that he knew what God had in mind. Joseph's genius is amply demonstrated, while his flaws cause him to be superseded by a new hero, Moses, with the same brilliance but without Joseph's faulty history.

There is no need to overdo it. In the end, Moses is put down for a more subtle version of Joseph's overweening desire for power. The separation

191

between God and man is maintained, thus strengthening the Hebrew religion. Moses is denied entrance to the Promised Land where Joseph does not even try to go. But Moses' written laws go ahead. No one can say that Joseph's descendants are left out of the Israelite nation; his two sons found tribes. But the future belongs to Judah.

The historical evidence in and out of the Bible makes the thesis I have just expounded possible, perhaps plausible, but by no means certain. Other hypotheses may fit the data equally well. But there is a body of material, alluded to but not yet presented, that can make the case much stronger. So far as I know, no one has mentioned it—a sign either of discovery or idiocy on my part. The data consist of contrasts between Joseph and Moses so vivid and consistent that it can be said with confidence that Moses is explicitly, no doubt deliberately, crafted to be the anti-Joseph or vice versa. Moses is not so much to succeed Joseph as to reject everything he stood for.

Moses as the Anti-Joseph

Is it possible to design a figure who would be more the exact opposite of Joseph than Moses? I doubt it. There are a few similarities. Both men are born Hebrews; the difference is that Joseph becomes steadily less Hebrew while Moses becomes steadily more. Contrast Moses' involvement in ritual as well as law with their total absence in the Joseph stories. Moses is the epitome of the religious man, Joseph the quintessential secularist. One may say that Moses is wise but never that he follows in the Egyptian wisdom tradition to better himself materially the way that Joseph does.

Both Moses and Joseph marry daughters of priests, Joseph the daughter of the most Egyptian of all Egyptians, the daughter of the high priest of On, and Moses the daughter of a desert priest in a place where the God of the Hebrews first called out to him. Observe that Moses' wife, Zipporah, identifies completely with his mission to bring the Israelites out of Egypt. She circumcises her sons (Exod. 4:24–26), the supreme sign of the covenant (Exod. 4:24–26).[1] Thus Zipporah joins a long line of feisty foreign women who take big chances to keep their men on a God-given path. Of Asenath, Joseph's wife, nothing more is heard other than that she dutifully delivers two sons to her husband.

When a son is born to Moses in the desert, Moses names him Gershon (*ger sham*, "a stranger there"), "for he said, 'I have been a stranger in a foreign land'" (Exod. 2:22). Compare this to the meaning of the name Joseph gives his first born, Manasseh—"God has made me forget completely my hardship and my parental home" (Gen. 41:51). Whereas, outside of Canaan, Moses accounts himself a stranger, Joseph in Egypt claims to have forgotten his parental home, while abandoning the way to God's Promised Land.

An administrator as well as a politician, Moses distributes provisions, metes out justice, settles disputes, organizes marches across the desert, and otherwise implements the laws that defined the relationships among the Hebrew people and separated them from outsiders. A material provider, Joseph is not a spiritual leader, or spiritual at all. The results of their interventions also differ: the Hebrew people fare well under Joseph only to be enslaved by a future Pharaoh. Joseph essentially binds Egyptian farmers to dependence on Pharaoh, whereas Moses destroys that dependence for Hebrews. In short, Moses' administration tries to take Egyptian servility out of the Hebrews, while Joseph's stay in Egypt manages to put it in. This is as good a time as any, moreover, to recall that Joseph charged high prices for Pharaoh's food, while Moses (through God's intervention) provided manna for free.

The contrary theme—Joseph as a predecessor of Moses not only in historical but in moral time—has often been suggested by commentators. In the same way as Joseph's activities enable the Hebrews to survive by coming to Egypt, so is Moses considered an indispensable agent in preparing the Hebrew people for the Exodus from Egypt. No entry, no exit. In this view, it is said that Moses builds on a platform erected by Joseph. Nothing could be further from the truth. Growing up amidst Egyptian nobility, Moses decisively rejects Pharaoh's court and its customs in favor of identification with his Hebrew people. Joseph is part of his Pharaoh's administration; Moses opposes Pharaoh's authority. Joseph seeks and welcomes Egyptianization. If his bones are carried into the Promised Land, that may be because his body belongs to Egypt. When God asks Moses directly to lead the Hebrew people out of Egypt, Moses is reticent, saying, in effect, send someone else. Without warrant, Joseph assumes he is a divine instrument to lead his people into Egypt. It comes down to this: Joseph works for the dictator, idolator, self-worshiper

Pharaoh, while Moses works against him. High-ranking individuals are dangerous because it is so easy for them to believe they are divine.

Compare the relation of Joseph and Moses to their siblings. Joseph (unwittingly? half-wittingly?) goads his brothers into hostility by assuming and proclaiming his superiority; as a result, they attempt to kill him and are always wary of him. Aaron and Miriam, Moses' brother and sister, help him lead the people to the land promised to them, Aaron as the head priest and Miriam as the leader of the women. What happens when Aaron and Miriam, feeling that Moses has become too great, and they perhaps have diminished in comparison, level accusations against him? Moses intercedes for them directly with God. When Joseph's brothers sell him into slavery, Joseph bides his time until he is in a position to exert power over them. Then he plays a cat-and-mouse game with them, partly to be sure they have not gotten the same idea again, partly to demonstrate his powers.

Joseph does not tolerate rivals among his brothers. When the young men surrounding Moses, Joshua and Caleb among others, seek to protect his authority by urging him to deny the right of prophecy to Eldad and Medad, Moses replies that he wishes that all men were prophets. Joseph does not share authority, the point is, but Moses does. The one thing Moses and Joseph have in common is that they both end up outside the Promised Land, and for the same reason, a will to power denied by divine ordinance. The difference is that Joseph remains in Egypt voluntarily.

After his father dies, Joseph tells Pharaoh that Jacob made him swear to bury him in Canaan and asks for leave, promising he will return. Feature for feature, this is a preview of what Moses will ask of his Pharaoh, so that the people of Israel might worship their God on His mountain, Moses also promising to return. The results are quite the opposite: Moses takes his people out of Egypt; Joseph brings them back in. The parallels are constructed to highlight the differences between Moses, who serves God, and Joseph, who serves Pharaoh. As if producing a photographic blowup of a small scene, I shall develop the contrast between the two requests to the Pharaohs of their respective times.

At first blush it appears that Joseph's appeal to bury his father in the ancestral crypt meets with a more positive response than does Moses' request to the Pharaoh of his time to worship God outside of Egypt. Note, however, the conditions attached to Joseph's performance. The narrator reveals that

> Joseph went up to bury his father; and with him went up all the officials of Pharaoh, the senior members of his court, and all of Egypt's dignitaries, together with all of Joseph's household, his brothers, and his father's household; only their children, their flocks, and their herds were left in the region of Goshen. Chariots, too, and horsemen went up with him; it was a very large troop. (Gen. 50:7-9)

A splendid show, to be sure, but also a carefully controlled display of affection. We are specifically informed that "their children, their flocks, and their herds" remained behind in Goshen. The military honor guard was large. Was it so large the better to honor Joseph's family or the better to make sure they honored Joseph's commitment to return to Egypt?

Initially, Moses has a harder time. After several devastating plagues materialize in support of Moses' demand that Pharaoh let the Israelites leave Egypt, Pharaoh finally issues a qualified approval they can go, but only "within the land" (Exod. 8:21). More plagues. Then there is unsatisfactory dialogue over the conditions under which the Hebrews would go:

> So Moses and Aaron were brought back to Pharaoh and he said to them, "Go, worship the Lord your God! Who are the ones to go?" Moses replied, "We will all go, young and old: we will go with our sons and daughters, our flocks and herds; for we must observe the Lord's festival." But he said to them, "The Lord be with you the same as I mean to let your children go with you! Clearly, you are bent on mischief." (Exod. 10:8-10)

Finally, after further plagues,

> Pharaoh then summoned Moses and said, "Go, worship the Lord! Only your flocks and your herds shall be left behind; even your children may go with you." But Moses said, "You yourself must provide us with sacrifices and burnt offerings to offer up to the Lord our God; our own livestock, too, shall go along with us—not a hoof shall remain behind: for we must select from it for the worship of the Lord our God; and we shall not know with what we are to worship the Lord until we arrive there." (Exod. 10:24-26)

Every time the Pharaoh tries to impose limiting conditions in order to bring the Hebrews back to Egypt, Moses refuses. This time Moses raises the ante by imposing a new (and galling) condition of his own on Pharaoh to provide burnt offerings. Ultimately, after the tenth plague causes the death of Egypt's first-born sons (a quid pro quo, Egypt's first-born for the first-born of God),

> he [Pharaoh] summoned Moses and Aaron in the night and said, "Up, depart from among my people, you and the Israelites with you! Go, worship the Lord as you said! Take also your flocks and your herds, as you said, and begone!" (Exod. 12:31-32)

All Joseph got from his Pharaoh was agreement to let the adults bury Jacob, surrounded by an armed guard, while leaving their children, herds and flocks, and goods in Goshen as hostages against their return.

It is not possible, in my opinion, for Joseph and Moses to leave Egypt to go to the land promised to their people under diometrically different conditions, point-counterpoint, without this being done deliberately. These oppositions are staged so that listeners and readers can envisage a larger-than-life rendition of Israel's great dilemma.

Now we know why the patriarchs stop with Jacob, why the line of succession goes from Abraham to Isaac to Jacob and then stops before Joseph. The Torah peers over the precipice, sees the consequences of combining power with assimilation—Joseph's abandonment of God's moral law—and begins again with Moses. It is as if to say that things were going along a well-worn groove until observation of Joseph's behavior and its consequences for the Hebrew people caused the author to reverse tracks and begin again on sounder footing. Joseph is tried and found interesting, even admirable in some respects, but is ultimately found wanting. He is not the one through whom the moral law will be brought to the people of Israel. How can they follow Pharaoh's helper? Instead, they will follow his opposite, Moses, who proclaims God's law. Before we take up the essential concept of binary opposition, however, we must pause momentarily to consider the religious implications of the divide that has been demonstrated between Joseph and Moses.

Moses and Joseph as Leaders

In *The Nursing Father: Moses as a Political Leader* I sought to show that Moses' leadership varied with the political culture of his people. Always his leadership depends not only on him but on his followers. At the outset, he acts without authority. Brought up in the Egyptian court yet aware that he is Hebrew by birth (the son of a Jewish mother), Moses, upon spying an Egyptian taskmaster beating a Hebrew, kills the Egyptian and hides his body. The next day, upon observing two Hebrews fighting, he interferes, demanding of one to be told why he had struck the other. The retort, "Who made you chief and ruler over us? Do you mean to kill me as you killed the Egyptian?" (Exod. 2:14), informs all concerned not only that Moses has been found out but that the people with whom he chooses to identify distrust unauthorized violence, even if ostensibly carried out on their behalf. Why, they might be next.

Compare the accusatory question of the Israelite with the virtually identical question Joseph's brothers flung at him: "Do you mean to reign over us? Do you mean to rule over us?" (Gen. 37:8). Is it not Joseph who tells Pharaoh that having the same dream twice (just substitute asking a question for dreaming) "means that the matter has been determined by God" (Gen. 41:32)? Both Moses and Joseph, then, are asked the same question by their own people. This contrived occurrence indicates that we should compare the answers their lives give.

As long as the Hebrew people are passive, which means until the exodus from Egypt, so is their would-be leader. Moses' fatalism is evident from his imploring cries to the Almighty to save his people when he and they should be acting to save themselves. No abuse of authority over Israelites, to be sure, but still abuse of another kind: asking God to do what humans should attempt for themselves—their own liberation.

Both Moses and Joseph do things that place them in harm's way. But their deeds are quite different. Moses angers Pharaoh by striking one of his officers in order to defend an Israelite; Joseph appeals to Pharaoh's self-interest by interpreting his dreams so as to increase his power. Joseph places himself in danger by resisting the importunings of Potiphar's wife. And Joseph gets his reward by rising to a high position and ultimately marrying and therefore obtaining a legitimate right to mate with a high-ranking Egyptian woman.

The difference between these imposing leaders lies in the kind of morality that is encapsulated in their objectives, a difference well illustrated by the episode of the golden calf. Leaving aside its allusions to much later conflicts between the northern and southern kingdoms, the episode itself speaks to the people's rejection of the law to be instituted by the Ten Commandments. When the bonds of slavery were broken, the political culture of the Israelites changed from fatalistic to individualistic. Competition among tribes for leadership was then paralleled by competition among deities—different gods for different purposes. As the people cry when cavorting before the golden calf, "This is your God, O Israel, who brought you out of the land of Egypt" (Exod. 32:8). By acting on these terrible words—"Each of you [the Levites] put sword on thigh . . . and slay brother, neighbor and kin" (Exod. 32:27)—Moses took responsibility for enforcing the moral law. Joseph, by contrast, sheds none of his family's blood, but neither does he act according to the law Moses will bring. How could he? The law came long after Joseph departed this world. The same question could be asked about how Joseph claimed to know God's will. Whatever Joseph might have been expected to know, his leadership is insufficient without subjecting it to a higher law. If the question is, How save a people dedicated to which values?, Joseph saves only the body, Moses saves both body and spirit.

In pursuit of which ways of life do they act? My understanding of political cultures is that values are never just suspended out there, disembodied, but exist in permanent tension with the patterns of social relations they are intended to support. Let us begin with Moses.

"In the desert," as the Book of Numbers is called in Hebrew, Moses moves his people and himself from an individualistic to an egalitarian culture. Tribes are bound by group decisions. There appears to be relative equality among the tribes, with the Levites taking the priesthood and Moses adjudicating disputes. His sons do not inherit nor does he go to the land promised to the Israelites, nonevents that guard against a cult of leadership.

At this point in tribal history, the difference between Moses-the-egalitarian and Joseph-the-hierarch, assistant to Pharaoh among many ranks and stations, is at its greatest. As the Israelites came upon hard times, the people sought (and Moses became) a charismatic leader to replace the customary rules regulating social behavior, whatever they were, with God's law. His glory is reflected; the light of the Lord shines in his face. Then the outer appearances of Joseph and Moses begin to converge, though not the inner essence of their character. They look and they are autocratic—but with quite a difference. Charismatic leaders are subject to continuous charges of having violated their trust by inegalitarian, self-seeking actions, putting themselves above the law. These include profiting materially, abusing authority, and having illicit sexual relations. No such charges are leveled against Joseph. He says, without evidence and without prayer, that the events granting him eminence come from God. Moses does differently.

Now Korah . . . betook . . . Dathan and Abiram . . . to rise up against Moses . . . . They combined against Moses and Aaron and said to them, "You have gone too far! For all the community are holy, all of them, and the Lord is in their midst. Why then do you raise yourselves above the Lord's congregation?" . . . (Num. 16:1–3)

Then the Presence of the Lord appeared to the whole community, and the Lord spoke to Moses and Aaron, saying, "Stand back from this community that I may annihilate them in an instant!" But they [Moses and Aaron] fell on their faces and said, "God, Source of the breath of all flesh! When one man sins, will You be wrathful with the whole community?" (Num. 16:19–22)

Moses intercedes for his people.

In my earlier account, *The Nursing Father*, the fanaticism of the time of equality in the desert led Moses and his people to seek moderation by reintroducing hierarchical elements—captains of tens and hundreds, councils of elders, and a more structured priesthood. By comparison, Joseph moves within hierarchical-cum-patriarchal cultures from first to last. Either he is his father's favorite, on or near the top of the heap, or he is the object of his brothers' enmity. Later on he is in prison, the favorite of his master, or out of prison and in favor with Pharaoh, while lording it over his brothers. Even after they have ostensibly reconciled, Joseph keeps throwing his weight around in minor ways to show he is still pining after the patriarchal role. Only father Jacob keeps putting son Joseph down, for he, with all his faults, is the true patriarch to whom the words of God come directly. In sum, Joseph is always hierarchical, whether on top or on bottom, while Moses alternates between the various ways of life, equality and hierarchy mixed in him as in his people.

There is not much equality in Joseph. At times there is a lot of entrepreneurship; always, however, Joseph is part of (or tries to make others part of) his hierarchy. So what is the problem? Hebrews may be hierarchical at home (David and Solomon) but Hebrews may not be part of another people's hierarchy any more than they may worship foreign gods. This is the message of the wife-sister stories and of the massacre at Shechem. When Joseph is about to die and tells his family that "God will surely take notice of you and bring you up from this land to the land which He promised on oath to Abraham, to Isaac, and to Jacob" (Gen. 50:24), it is apparent that he lacks the strength to lead his people toward their destiny. That will take a leader less enamored of the Pharaohs of the earth.

Joseph is forever identified with the administrative power in a foreign hierarchy (I do not say "patriarchy" because his Pharaoh does not show sufficient concern for his people) while Moses is memorable for the laws he brought. The text of the Torah contrasts the commandments that come through Moses with the commands by which Joseph rules on Pharaoh's behalf. Where Moses fits the people for the land, Joseph takes the land from the Egyptians. The contrast remains. Joseph is respected but rejected. The apostle of pure administrative power, Joseph-the-assimilator, gives way to Moses-the-lawbringer.

It is time to look more closely at a social science concept—binary opposition. For this I have chosen the interpretation by the late Edmund Leach, a distinguished anthropologist who combined the two relevant subjects: translation of the work of Claude Lévi-Strauss and interpretation of the Bible.

Binary Oppositions and Biblical Interpretation

According to Leach, following Lévi-Strauss, who enunciated the concept:

> Binary oppositions are intrinsic to the process of human thought. Any description of the world must discriminate categories in the form 'p is what not-p is not.' An object is alive or not alive and one could not formulate the concept 'alive' except as the converse of its partner 'dead.'[2]

Leach goes on to say:

> Religion everywhere is preoccupied with the first, the antinomy of life and death. Religion seeks to deny the binary link between the two worlds; it does this by creating the mystical idea of 'another world', a land of the dead where life is perpetual. The attributes of this other world are necessarily those which are not of this world; imperfection here is balanced by perfection there. But this logical ordering of ideas has a disconcerting consequence—God comes to belong to the other world. The central 'problem' of religion is then to re-establish some kind of bridge between Man and God.[3]

The innumerable contrasts between Joseph and Moses are clear examples of binary oppositions. The contradiction in the case of the Israelites is that, on one side, they want to live by a formula of one God, one people, one way of life. Hence the importance their religion gives to appearances and outward forms as reflecting the inner meaning; hence the stress placed on fair weights and measures. Things and people must be what they appear to be. On the other side, unfortunately, history shows that Israel cannot always be whole. Instead of national unity, there are two kingdoms; instead of a united family there are factions within factions based largely on having different mothers. The Hebrew people should be able to combine separation with participation in foreign societies. But they have a hard time: either the community rejects them on the grounds that their strange ways are subversive or their people are tempted to assimilate. Either way, through ghettoization or assimilation, Jews and Judaism are harmed.

Think of how Joseph became absorbed by Egyptian culture—food, clothing, and soon enough even arbitrary rule. The contrast between Joseph as a member of his family and as part of Pharaoh's entourage has been explored by commentators over the centuries. Strangers are much better to Joseph than are his own relatives. Though his brothers hate him, the Egyptian court loves him. The very phenomena that enrage his brothers against him—namely, dreams—encourage Pharaoh to honor him. Whereas Pharaoh gives Joseph fine new clothes, his brothers disrobe him. His brothers cast him into a pit, and Pharaoh takes him out of a dungeon. In the light of these contrasts, it is no wonder that Joseph became attached to the people and the place where his fortunes rose.[4]

In cultural terms,[5] the Hebrew people under father Jacob were patri-archal and hierarchical, with substantial status differences ranging from sons of more-favored wives down to sons of the wives' maids. Socially speaking, the boundaries of the family-tribe were hardened and their roles and rules of conduct (men versus women, parents versus children, older versus younger sons) were strongly prescribed. After Joseph died, the boundaries separating this people from the surrounding Egyptian community greatly weakened. By the time of Moses, we know that the people had forgotten the name of their God: "When I come to the Israelites and say to them 'The God of your fathers has sent me to you,' and they ask me, 'What is His name?' what shall I say to them?" (Exod. 3:13). The response of the officers of the Israelites when Pharaoh increased their burden of brick-making but gave them no straw ("Why do you deal thus with your servants?" Exod. 5:15) indicates that they identified with Pharaoh, the demigod of the Egyptians, and not with the God of their fathers.

At the same time, the behavioral prescriptions binding the Israelites to Egyptian commands were maintained and even strengthened. As the Scripture says, "The Egyptians ruthlessly imposed upon the Israelites the various labors that they made them perform" (Exod. 1:13–14). "And the taskmasters pressed them, saying, 'You must complete the same work assignment each day as when you had straw" (Exod. 5:13). When individuals lack group support but are subject to prescriptions from outside forces, they believe that there is nothing they can do to improve their lot in life or affect their fate. Then they become self-persuaded fatalists who believe, as fatalists do, that there is nothing positive they can do to improve their position.

Individualism is rejected by force during the golden calf episode and again during the period of the Judges when the populace demands and gets a king to rule them so they can compete with other nations. As a religion that is embedded in a people, Judaism is a form of common observance. But what kind? Egalitarian or hierarchical? And if hierarchical, is it steep and narrow, as under the Pharaoh and the older Solomon, or broad and inclusive, as under Moses and the younger Solomon?

The Triumph of the Torah

The genius of the Joseph stories lies in their simultaneous rejection and wary appreciation of worldly wisdom. The writer knows that human beings are capable of rare moments of exaltation but that these will be followed by a continuation of life as usual. Observe the brothers' reconciliation followed by the usual deceit and family bickering. Joseph's elevation to one of Egypt's highest offices, full of belief in his own capabilities, including resistance to evil inclinations as demonstrated by the affair of Potiphar's wife, is soon followed by his making Egyptian farmers into state employees who have been removed from their own land. Had the writer merely dismissed Joseph's assimilation of Egyptian customs and mores as opportunistic, the reader would lack appreciation of how large a part worldly wisdom plays in life, even for noble purposes, such as rescuing one's family from starvation. The narrator makes us aware that with power comes a temptation to confuse evil with benevolence by persuading oneself that heinous acts, like forced deportations, are part of God's plan for man. Joseph saves lives but, by saving, is able to lord it over his family. Though Joseph the administrator is immensely more discerning about human motivation than he was as a youth, he never recognizes his own lust for power whether as an unthinking boy or as a scheming servant of Pharaoh.

Talented writers reveal the complexity of human motives. Jacob, in placing Joseph's sons in the line of succession, shows his old irascible self in giving the younger preference over Joseph's objections. And who is Joseph to insist that the elder come first! Soon after the crafty Joseph gives way to the compassionate Joseph in weeping over his brothers, he becomes Joseph the schemer who suggests that his brothers lie to Pharaoh

about their occupation. The brothers, who finally accept joint responsibility for Benjamin, lie to Joseph in suggesting that their father asked
them to tell their eminent brother not to take vengeance on them. In short,
the narrator shows us, after momentary heroics and self-revelation,
everything is back to normal.

Often in exile, the Hebrew people long to return to the land they
believe God promised to them. At one and the same time, they need
connections in high places for physical survival and connections to God
through His commandments to survive as Jews. Yet the worldly and
religious requisites of survival may well contradict each other. One is
gained by Joseph's worldly wisdom; the other by Moses' teaching of
God's laws. These contradictions are dramatized by embedding them in
attractive leaders, one of whom is not so much rejected as left behind.

Eventually, the Israelite community, as W. D. Davies expressed it,
came to be understood "as a corollary of the covenant" under which "the
laws were not related primarily to the political organization of a state,
but rather to a community of people in which the common allegiance to
Yahweh was the constitutive element."[6] Religious autonomy might yet
be combined with political dependence to make Judaism viable, whether
in the Diaspora or under foreign rule in the land of promises.

Within these firm boundaries, questions arose of what might and might
not be done, as Joseph said, to "save this people alive." The leading
answer was to maintain faith in God. But faith was not the only answer.
The wisdom of how to get along in this world was allowed to play its
part, providing that it did not violate God's law. Conversely, even the
strictest commands, such as those against marrying foreigners while in
their own country, could be breached if the women involved showed
extraordinary fidelity, as did Ruth and Tamar, to the promise.

"There is a sense," Davies tells us, referring to Abraham's originating
outside the Promised Land, "in which Israel was born in exile."[7] The
stories about Joseph the administrator for Pharaoh remain as eloquent
testimony to what an accomplished Hebrew could achieve for himself
and his people in a foreign court and what perils he was exposed to
through identification with a foreign god or a leader who fancied himself
a god. The Torah was placed above and beside the political power,
restraining it, even abandoning it when necessary (as the Pharisees
advised), if religious practice was not permitted. The Jewish view of
Hebrew history as potent with the possibilities of redemption explains

why its leading figures are portrayed with obvious faults. If there is hope for them, there is hope for us, the Josephs of this world. In the portrait of Joseph that has passed before us, a portrait crafted so as to reveal his extraordinary qualities while contrasting them to Moses, the Torah gives its readers a choice between two heroes representing different ways of life while indicating that Moses' God-centered way is the preferred way.

A Failed Theological Experiment

Is Joseph, as Philo thought, the perfect statesman, the one who can show us all by example how to lead people and administer government? Or is Joseph the antihero who exemplifies the way not to rule? Put another way, if the wisdom of Joseph is akin to the wisdom of Egypt, as Gerhard von Rad claimed in his influential work,[8] is that also the wisdom that ought to be applied to those perennial pupils, the children of Israel?

Throughout the ages, certain episodes of the story have led a few scholars to doubt the model of Joseph as paragon. In our time, for instance, George Coats has written that "his acts are governed not by wisdom and discretion, not by justice for his brothers under the authority of his office, but by capricious use of power, by deception, by false accusation . . . ."[9] The most thoroughgoing criticism of Joseph's behavior I have come across is Berel Dov Lerner's "Joseph the Unrighteous," in which he seeks "to demonstrate that the Torah does not condone Joseph's obviously inexcusable behavior."[10] As an indication, Lerner refers to the pathos evident in the pleadings of the Egyptian peasants. His comment— "These are not the words of a people benefitting from the care of a thoughtful ruler"—is well taken. Which reading, Joseph the scoundrel or Joseph the savior of his (and, perhaps all) people, is truest to the text?

A reminder of the accusations against Joseph's brothers comes from a medieval tale about Ten Martyrs whose murder was justified by a Roman tyrant on the grounds of their ancestors' maltreatment of Joseph: "Where are your fathers who sold their brother to a caravan of Ishmaelites and bartered him for shoes? . . . If they were alive, I would convict them in your presence, but it is you who must atone for the iniquity of your fathers."[11] Anti-Semites also made use of Joseph in the pit to condemn Israel's children.

Is it the presence of God as manifested in how far Joseph eventually rises on the Egyptian hierarchical ladder, or is it the absence of God as manifested by the essentially secular nature of the stories, that is most impressive? All we know is that the God of Abraham, Isaac, and Jacob does not speak to Joseph, whereas He speaks to Moses face to face (Deut. 34:10). All we know about the Lord's intentions is what Joseph tells us. To determine which interpretation is more nearly correct we cannot look to historical evidence outside the Torah, for there is none. Because I ask why Joseph is left out of the Bible beyond Genesis, the relation of the Joseph parts to the whole of the Bible is what matters.

The Joseph stories, as Eugene Bardach put it, represent

> a kind of *failed theological experiment,* but a failure from which we are intended to learn a great deal. God has withdrawn Himself from direct contact with Jacob's sons. It is as though He has assembled all the elements required for the continued realization of His presence in human society . . . and stepped back, like the God whom deists think of as a *watchmaker,* winding up the mechanism and then letting it run. . . . The withdrawal of God means that a heavier burden must fall on "nature," that is "human nature" and "natural social institutions" like the tribe and the clan. The withdrawal of God means that "nature" is left to "take its course"—or at least, "nature" as improved by knowledge of God's will, which is to eschew wickedness and embrace righteousness. Yet these *substitutes* for direct inspiration from God show themselves, in Chs. 37–50, to *be essentially and fundamentally inadequate.* . . . In place of the clan structure under a patriarch we have the nation with ritual sacrifices and a caste of priests and a political leadership based on *monarchical* principles. In place of . . . the Divinely inspired personal covenant the remaining four books of the five books of Moses propose the covenant of the *Law, the Torah, the mitzvoth.*[12]

It is not just the individuals named Joseph and Moses who are opposites but the institutions and the religions for which they stand that are opposed.

We cannot know whether Joseph considered from the beginning that he was part of a divine plan of community rescue, thought it up as events progressed—especially after his success with Pharaoh—or found it a convenient rationale after he decided to reconcile with his family. Von Rad put it nicely: "the way in which God's will is related to human purposes remains a mystery."[13] Joseph does not assume the passive posture of one who leaves things to fate, even if he believes they are foreordained.

What should Joseph have done? He should not have contributed to Pharaoh's despotism; he should have tried to take his family/people out of Egypt into the Promised Land. Waiting for a more propitious moment, if that is what it was, ended by making his people into fatalists. In any event, it is hard to imagine Joseph leading a revolt.

Joseph is a Jew, but if he is to continue being a Jew he cannot be a father to Pharaoh. The development of what became the 613 commandments (*mitzvot*) regulating the daily life of Jews makes it clear that the Joseph stories in Exodus 37–50 cannot be what both the tradition and modern scholarship see them as being, namely, "the bridge between the Patriarchs and Moses,"[14] between God's promises to the patriarchs and the liberation from Egypt.[15] This bridge is not a link between the same things but rather a radical disjunction. Joseph's path becomes the path not taken because it is unsuitable for a God-centered people, why, then, has Joseph been called a model for Christians as well as Jews to follow?

Notes

1. See Aaron Wildavsky, *The Nursing Father: Moses As a Political Leader* (University of Alabama Press, 1985), 42–43.
2. Edmund Leach, "Genesis as Myth," in *Genesis as Myth and Other Essays* (London: Jonathan Cape, 1969), 9.
3. Leach, "Genesis As Myth," 10–11. Thus a myth refers to a basic contradiction in a given society that is covered over or mediated (made tolerable) by a familiar story. Though I disagree with Leach and Lévi-Strauss on certain aspects of their conception of binary oppositions, my agreement with their general position is more important for understanding the Joseph stories. But the reader should have my qualifications: I do not doubt that it is possible to divide any body of thought or action into two opposite parts if one so desires. But why do it? One could (and, in my opinion, should) explain why other possibilities are left out. In my opinion, Leach confuses universal characteristics of human beings with Judaism's concern for maintaining the purity of its social relations. Only a strongly bounded social structure, either hierarchical or egalitarian, could try to maximize distinctiveness so as to reinforce the difference between the good inner group and the hostile outside. No boundaries, no need to maintain them against outsiders, no Judaism. Life is full of contradictions; narratives are full of ambiguities, both deliberate and unperceived by the author(s) and the actors. So what? We need to know when and for whom these contradictions matter and why. A theory spells out conditions of applicability; all we hear about binary oppositions is that the stories (Lévi-Strauss and Leach call them myths not so much to say they are false as to indicate that it doesn't matter whether they represent true history) perform the function of mediating (enabling the people concerned to live with) these contradictions. Aside from being vague, this formulation does not tell us what sort of contradictions matter to which sort of people. Besides, who says people cannot live with contradictions? Where would Tamar and Ruth and Esther be if they followed convention and the law? There is still the matter of divine origins to separate the scholar from the believer. In the past, both had faith in the authority of the text; both believed they had to justify their interpretations to their respective communities by how well they tied them to the text. Maybe that did not seem like much in those less combative times, but in the light of current modes of interpretation, which deny the authority of texts and glory in misreadings that show how almost any pattern can be imposed on any text, it

seems like bedrock. My own view is that interpretism is self-stultifying. The first few forays into such innovative forms of literary analysis as structuralism, poststructuralism, and deconstruction may have liberated the imagination of more hidebound scholars. Even going this far, however, requires a community of inter-preters who value the text, for only if the text is used as a measure of better or worse interpretations may departures be valued. After a while it will become clear that interpretive communities cannot be built on nihilistic grounds. Without the study that brings familiarity with the text and its times, no discourse is possible. With everyone speaking from his own idiosyncratic position, there can be no communi-cation. The Tower of Babel was designed to confuse; there is no need deliberately to recreate it. Mary Douglas concludes her review of Leach on the Bible thus:

> Here is the crux of the problem for myth analysis. The narrative form is always full of play; it rejoices in twists of meaning, double puns and structural jokes. As these constitute the form of the genre, they cannot be the clue to special, sacred meanings of religious texts. The narrative provides a commentary on life (as Leach teaches). But different sectors of a population make different uses of myths about their past, each for their own purposes (as Leach teaches). There is absolutely no method of analyzing myths that corresponds to a correct meaning or even a correct structure (as Leach teaches). The only method that is worth a clever scholar's time is that which requires him to be soaked for decades in the languages and literatures and historical circumstances in which the myths are told and to assume the humanist task of identifying the intentions of authors and the expectations of audiences. (Mary Douglas, "Betwixt, Bothered and Bewil-dered," review of Edmund R. Leach and D. Alan Aycock, *Structural Interpre-tation of Biblical Myth, New York Review of Books* (December 20, 1984): 43–46.

4. See the discussion in Lowenthal's *The Joseph Narrative in Genesis*, 78ff.
5. See Mary Douglas, "Cultural Bias," in Douglas, *In the Active Voice* (London: Routledge & Kegan Paul, 1982), 183–254; Mary Douglas, *Natural Symbols* (Lon-don: Barrie & Rockliff, 1970); Michael Thompson, Richard Ellis, and Aaron Wildavsky, *Cultural Theory* (Westview Press, 1990).
6. W. D. Davies, *The Territorial Dimension of Judaism* (Berkeley: University of California Press, 1982), 72.
7. Ibid., 93.
8. Gerhard von Rad, "The Joseph Narrative and Ancient Wisdom," in von Rad, *The Problem of the Hexateuch and Other Essays*, trans. by E. W. Trueman Dicken (New York: McGraw Hill, 1966), 292–300.
9. G. W. Coats, "The Joseph Story and Ancient Wisdom: A Reappraisal," *Catholic Biblical Quarterly* 35 (1973): 285–297.
10. Berel Dov Lerner, "Joseph the Unrighteous," *Judaism* 38 (1987): 278–281; quote on 278.
11. Sol Schimmel, "Joseph and His Brothers: A Paradigm for Repentance," *Judaism* 37 (1988): 60–65; quote on 65.
12. Eugene Bardach, "Notes on 'Vayyeshev,'" typescript, December 1989.
13. Gerhard von Rad, "The Joseph Narrative and Ancient Wisdom," in von Rad, *The Problem of the Hexateuch and Other Essays*, trans. by Rev. E. W. Trueman Dicken (New York: McGraw Hill, 1966), 297.
14. Eric I. Lowenthal, *The Joseph Narrative in Genesis* (New York: KTAV Publishing House, 1973), 1.

15. "The Joseph account, then," Walter Brueggemann states by way of summarizing
    Coats' views, "has no independent life or function. It never existed on its own but
    was formed after the other materials were fixed to make a narrative linkage" (Walter
    Brueggemann, *Genesis: A Bible Commentary for Teaching and Preaching*, in the
    Interpretation series (Atlanta: John Knox Press, 1982), 291. For more on Joseph
    stories "as a sort of bridge," see Bruce T. Dahlberg, "On Recognizing the Unity of
    Genesis," *Theology Digest* 24 (1976): 362-63.

9

The Path Not Taken

In marked contrast to its Greek [Platonic] counterpart, the rule of the biblical philosopher king is doomed to failure if he does not abide by law. Whereas the Greek philosopher king must transcend laws or customs to get a better view of the whole, the Bible maintains the necessity of abiding by law or custom if the rule is to be efficacious. . . . If Athens, then, argues that wisdom must transcend particular laws for true justice to be established, Jerusalem argues that without law there can be no true wisdom.[1]

The Hebrew Bible is about the formation of a people, their right to a land of promise, and the moral basis of their life as a community covenanted to obey God's commandments. Inevitably these objectives conflict with as well as reinforce each other. Dedication to the land and to the commandments, for instance, may endanger the ability of the people to survive. Similarly, actions taken to ensure the community's survival may threaten its internal unity or contravene God's commandments. The Joseph stories, I have argued, are about the difficulty of reconciling the conflict between right action, following the moral law, and the survival of the family, eventually the nation, called literally the children of Israel. The question in the Joseph stories is whether assimilation into the fleshpots of Egypt is equivalent to breaking God's law; whether along with Egyptian customs there will come a substitution of worldly wisdom for the moral law that distinguishes between what is prohibited and what is allowed. In this concluding chapter I seek to illuminate different answers to this question by expanding the canvass so as to consider how Joseph's behavior was viewed in David's, Solomon's, and Ezra's and Nehemiah's times. To sharpen the contrast, I shall start with ancient and modern Christian perspectives.

Joseph as a Precurser of Jesus

That Joseph, the son of Jacob the scamp, bearer of evil tales about his brothers, could prefigure Jesus, the Son of God, takes some doing, but it was and is said.[2] After all, just as it was Judas who sold Jesus, it was Judah who sold Joseph. St. John Chrysostom thought that Joseph filled by anticipation Christ's commandment: "Love your enemies, pray for those who spitefully use you." Did Joseph not also meet evil with good, thereby overcoming it?[3]

The Joseph of the surface story certainly does exist. In Charles Fritsch's pithy words, "He is wise, handsome, favored by God, noble, tenderhearted, and forgiving."[4] If it is true that "he is a God-fearing lad who is morally upright and pure . . . generous and forgiving . . . of . . . unshakable faith," then it does truly follow, as Fritsch concludes, that "Joseph's conduct throughout his whole life is a model for all to follow."[5] For Christian commentators, the matter is simple and allegorical. As Pascal put it, "Jesus Christ is prefigured in Joseph, his father's favorite, sent by the father to his brothers, the guiltless one, sold by his brothers for 20 pieces of silver and so become their Lord . . . such is the Church's vital portrayal of the Joseph story from time immemorial."[6]

The comparison between Joseph and Jesus extends to the words they use. As Joseph claims to be part of a divine plan, John, albeit more positively, declares that God sent His son to save the world.[7] Think again of "Joseph the provider" and Jesus saying "I am the bread of life" (John 6:35). If, as Joseph says, God has sent him ahead of his family to save lives, does not Jesus say the same about the human family?[8] And does not Jesus reassure his followers in words similar to Joseph's reassurance to his brothers, "Be not afraid" (Matthew 28:10) and "Why are ye troubled?" (Luke 24:38)?[9]

The identification of the Joseph stories with Jesus continues to this day. By offering up himself in Benjamin's place, Réne Girard proposes, Judah shows that he "is not willing to accept the expulsion of the victim."[10] Judah ends the violence within the family by offering to sacrifice himself. "In some respects," James Williams concludes, "the act of Judah anticipates the Suffering Servant of the Second Isaiah and Jesus as the Crucified in the Gospels."[11]

There is no need to speculate. The opening of the Gospel according to St. Matthew tells us what we need to know. The parallels are unmistakable. When King Herod heard that the king of the Jews had been born, he sent out a search party. But the angel of the Lord, who stands in God's stead, appeared to the appropriately named Joseph, husband of Mary, mother of Jesus, and told him, also appropriately, to flee to Egypt "for Herod will seek the young child to destroy him" (Matt. 2:13). Nor do we need to ask why they fled to Egypt. Matthew informs us directly that Egypt was chosen "that it might be fulfilled which was spoken of the Lord by the prophet, saying, Out of Egypt have I called my son" (Matt. 2:15). The only difference is that Herod had all children under two killed (Matt. 2:16), whereas the Pharaoh of Moses' time ordered the death of newborn Hebrew male children. To qualify for leadership, the patriarchs of the Hebrew people, like Moses after them, must come out of Egypt. While the Hebrew patriarchs had to experience the Diaspora in Egypt, however, Jesus goes to show that he is their legitimate successor.

That Christians have reason to recognize in Joseph a predecessor to Jesus is evident; whether Jews should recognize Joseph as suffering for them is the basic question of the stories about him. A little history should serve to place the stories in context.

The Two Israels

Hebrew history in biblical times runs from Abraham through Ezra. The problem presented is to create a people worshiping their own God in their own land while obeying His commandments. But there is more to it. By Ezra's time, most Jews are exiles living under the protection of foreign rulers, whether under a foreign regime's tutelage or in their own land. Their solution is to create practices separating these exiles from surrounding societies. The cost of arriving at this solution is internal division over regulation of relations with foreigners and, by implication, with foreign gods. Separatism breeds anti-Semitism and reduces opportunities within the larger society; assimilation portends physical survival; it also prefigures moral annihilation as a people who promise themselves to the one God.

Among the congeries of small states in the areas generally called Syria and Palestine, there were two independent Jewish states, the northern kingdom of Judah, which existed approximately from the tenth century before the common era until 722, and the southern kingdom of Israel, which remained independent until 597. The northern kingdom was conquered by Assyria, which sent large numbers, though by no means all, of its people into exile. The same phenomena of conquest and exile was repeated when Babylonia conquered Judah.[12]

In Kings and Chronicles the divisions within Israel are substantiated in time and place. The literal, physical split between the southern kingdom of Judah and Benjamin and the northern kingdom of the other Israelite tribes institutionalizes their differences: one ruled by a single davidic dynasty for over four centuries, the other subject to episodic plots by usurpers who would destroy the previous monarch and his entourage only to be destroyed themselves.[13] It would be helpful to know whether the southern kingdom was more hierarchical, its kings imbued with theological status, whereas the northern kings were more consensual, depending on the support of the tribes that made up their kingdom. Then we might contemplate whether one or the other kingdoms preferred stronger hierarchy versus either stronger egalitarianism, if one considers the northern kingdom a confederacy of relative equals, or individualist, if one considers the various buccaneering kings as temporary network leaders. Unfortunately, the histories of the period resolutely refuse to give up this secret.[14]

As times worsened, hope grew that the two kingdoms would reunite. As Ezekiel embellished this hope:

> The word of the Lord came again unto me, saying, Moreover, thou son of man, take thee one stick, and write upon it, For Judah, and for the children of Israel his companions: then take another stick, and write upon it, For Joseph, the stick of Ephraim, and for all the house of Israel his companions: And join them one to another into one stick; and they shall become one in thine hand. . . . And say unto them, Thus saith the Lord God; Behold, I will take the children of Israel from among the heathen, whither they be gone, and will gather them on every side, and bring them into their own land: And I will make them one nation in the land upon the mountains of Israel; and one king shall be king to them all: and they shall be no more two nations, neither shall they be divided into two kingdoms any more at all: Neither shall they defile themselves any more with their idols, nor with their detestable things, nor with any of their transgressions: but I will save them out of all their dwellingplaces, wherein they have sinned, and will cleanse them: so shall they be my people, and I will be their God. (Ezekiel 37:15-17, 21-23)

But it was not to be. How would the Hebrew people explain to themselves why there were two kingdoms but one God? How would their scribes and prophets explain their defeat and exile?

The stories these Hebrews tell themselves root their differences in Jacob's family history, the sons of the same father but different mothers contending for succession, the question being whether one will impose hierarchical authority over the others or whether each will compete on an equal plane. The family history covered in Genesis alone depicts practically every human evil: murder, robbery, incest, rape, genocide, dishonoring parents, selling siblings into slavery, deceiving family members. Getting this family so full of human frailty to the land their God promised occupies virtually all the attention.

The experience of Ezra and Nehemiah's time runs a parallel course. Many if not most Israelites had been taken to Babylon as a conquered people. The task of this "saving remnant" was to restore the ancient practices of their people. They returned to Jerusalem (in Judea, as it was called) to impose their old-time religion on those who stayed behind, the natives who had grown lax in their observances mixing with local peoples and matching their pagan ways. While the religion of their forefathers could be practiced only in the Holy Land, for the faithful shuttling between Babylon and places still more remote, religious observance had to be portable.

The leaders of Israel, desiring that their people adopt neither foreign practices nor foreign gods, developed practices to socially separate themselves from other peoples. Yet survival suggested accommodation, not enmity, in dealing with their foreign rulers. In those days, a strong sociological view was taken of customs: food, clothing, housing, and much more were held to be part of group and hence religious cohesion, not merely neutral artifacts to be used with impunity by anyone who cared to make use of them. Refusing to share in these local customs must have suggested disloyalty.

Their rival objectives—disassociating themselves from while ingratiating themselves with foreigners—left the Israelites divided. Moreover, this conflict was complicated by the fact that at times different groups of Israelites might prefer friendly relations with one foreign power but hostile relations with another, for example, Egypt and Babylon. The eventual solution was to base their religion on practices so numerous and off-putting that it would be difficult for Israelites to mix with foreigners while at the same time allowing political allegiance to any government that would not interfere with religious observance. In sum: political allegiance, yes, religious allegiance, no; political assimilation, yes, social assimilation, because it leads to religious assimilation, no. So they courted trouble.

However divided Jews may be about other matters, therefore, their desire in the Diaspora to demonstrate that it is beneficial for foreigners to be decent to them is overwhelming. Among the promises God gives to Abram in return for his fidelity to God's law,[15] including making his progeny into a great nation, are three directly relevant to the host nations of the Israelites: God promises to bless those who bless Israel and curse those who curse it, and, for good measure, promises that "in you will be blessed all the families of the earth."[16] Whether we refer to Potiphar, Joseph's master, or the jailer, his prison keeper, or Pharaoh, his administrative superior, everyone Joseph works for does well in regard to the things of this world. A similar theme runs through the stories of Daniel and Esther: Hebrew advisers and administrators (Joseph, Daniel, Esther, Mordecai) prosper foreign kings. Whenever the civil rulers of the Israelites in the Diaspora behave badly toward the Hebrew people, however, as did the Pharaoh of Moses' time, or curse Israel, as the pagan prophet Balaam was asked to do, terrible things happen to them. The intended message to foreign potentates is loud and clear: penetrate Israel's boundaries, the moral and the physical being one, and you die.[17] This is also the moral of the wife-sister stories analyzed in the first chapter.

Marrying peoples among whom the Hebrews lived, and by whom they were therefore most tempted, is forbidden. The friendly embrace might be more dangerous to a people who wish to preserve their peculiar practices than out-and-out rejection would be. Both Abraham and Isaac make a point of sending their sons to marry women who are from their own ancestral line, not women of Canaan. Although intermarriage with Canaanites is strictly forbidden (Exod. 34:16 and Deut. 7:3), foreign wives from other places are allowed (Deut. 20:14-15; 21:10-13). As time goes on, the picture gets murky. The Israelites are not in a position to dictate their own destiny. So rules change. At one time, as reflected in Genesis 25:5-6, the elder son received virtually the entire inheritance; in Deuteronomy 21:15-17 the eldest son received a double share, which is substantial but by no means the whole. Similarly, what is forbidden later may have been practiced earlier, especially by the patriarchs. Jacob marries two sisters, Rachel and Leah (the Torah explains in an entertaining manner why Jacob did this), but the practice is forbidden in Leviticus 18:18. Abraham marries his half-sister, Sarah, though later there are numerous ordinances (Lev. 18:9-11, 20:17; Deut. 27:22) forbidding the practice.[18] The lesson is plain: act according to God's commandments, not necessarily according to the ways of the patriarchs.

Among the many reasons that might be given for avoiding foreign entanglements, the most frequent is that these would lead the people into apostasy by worshiping foreign gods, mere idols, rather than the one true God (see Exod. 34:16 and Deut. 7:4). When surrounded by foreigners, however, things happen and exceptions arise. Moses marries a non-Jewish woman, Zipporah, and their children are not considered Hebrew. When Joseph marries an Egyptian woman, his sons are specifically adopted by their grandfather, Jacob, so as to legitimize them as Jewish. (It is also possible that the children are adopted because Joseph, having been sold into slavery, is no longer legally in Jacob's family.) In need of armed help, David serves Achish, the king of Gath, and later employs a considerable number of Philistine as well as Jebusite mercenaries. Both David and Solomon hire foreign craftsmen.

Conditions also appear under which it is possible for foreigners who are more loyal to Yahweh or to Israelite law than the Israelites themselves—Tamar and Ruth, for instance—to bear Israelite children.[19] Since the purpose of prohibiting intermarriage is to maintain the faith, another principle to accomplish the same purpose—demonstrating God's power through the triumph of the weaker over the stronger—brings triumph to Tamar, Ruth, and Esther over more powerful men. Paganism is condemned, but not the exceptional foreigner if she is more zealous to follow Israelite law than those born into its obligations.[20]

If to be younger is to be weaker, it is remarkable how often the younger son prevails: David over his older and stronger brothers; Jacob over Esau; Joseph, the youngest but one of twelve brothers, has them bow down to him, while in the end Judah moves up three places to become head of the family. No doubt such breaking of precedents was useful to justify Solomon's kingship in the presence of his older brother Adonijah. Perhaps, in a nation always in danger of being invaded by much larger forces, whether from Babylon or Egypt, the replacement of primogeniture with ultimogeniture was a source of hope. Remembering that the Torah is above all a religious text, I prefer the encompassing interpretation that would root the reversal of ordinary precedents in a display of God's greatness. If that interpretation has merit, the praise of Tamar and Ruth because they followed God's will despite their violation of the prohibitions against prostitution and enticement, not to say intermarriage, becomes understandable.[21]

Foreigners are acceptable if they do not interfere with the many practices of Judaism (Joseph's but not Moses' Pharaoh). Thus the "court Jew," as this role was called in later times, is in an equivocal position, neither Jewish nor goyish, that is, of the host nations. Situated to provide utmost help toward his people's survival, the Jewish adviser to a foreign king is also in a position to do maximal harm by exposing himself and his people to the worship of strange gods. There is further temptation to idolatry in associating with a foreign ruler who thinks himself a god. If Mordecai and Esther and Daniel show how Hebrews loyal to their jealous God should behave, by refusing to bow down to would-be deities, what is to be said about Joseph, who does differently?

There is a fine line between an anti-foreignism that would lead Jews to violate their own norms of just dealings and a pro-foreignism that would threaten obedience to their God's commandments. As might be expected, instead of choosing one or the other, the Hebrew people are commanded to do both: honor the stranger and abominate his practices. Wariness dominates friendliness, but both are ever present, their activation depending on circumstances that, as lawyers say, alter cases.[22]

In biblical times, Israelites were both strangers (in other countries) and natives (in their own). They ruled other peoples in their own land while being ruled by others abroad. They were also masters who held slaves (usually but not always foreigners) and slaves of foreigners who took them into captivity. The Joseph stories are set in Egypt where, in Moses' time, the Hebrew people became slaves to Pharaoh. It would not be so easy, therefore, for Israelites to write unequivocal rules about how natives and strangers, slaves and masters, should be treated. While the Torah forbids Israelites to make slaves of their own people (Lev. 25:39–40), it does permit them to own foreigners as slaves and, under conditions of dire poverty, to sell themselves into slavery to their own people. Perhaps using as a model the time Jacob labored for his wives, a Hebrew man was allowed to sell himself for seven years only; after that time his master was obliged to let him go unless he chose lifetime slavery.

In the Exodus, David Daube observes, the Egyptians are made to let their former slaves go in a manner prescribed by Israelite social arrangements.[23] When a master sets a slave free, the Lord orders, "Do not let him go empty-handed: Furnish him out of the flock, threshing floor, and vat, with which the Lord your God has blessed you. Bear in mind that you were slaves in the land of Egypt and the Lord your God redeemed you; therefore I enjoin this commandment upon you today" (Deut. 15:13-15). Anticipating the usual reaction of men who look after themselves first, the Lord provides a positive incentive by telling the master not to feel aggrieved upon release of a slave because "the Lord your God will bless you in all you do" (Deut. 15:18).[24]

The position of the stranger during Israelite rule is described by Jacob Milgrom:

> In return for being loyal to his protectors (Gen. 24:23) and bound by their laws (e.g. Lev. 24:22), the *ger*, as indicated by its Arabic cognate *jar*, was a "protected stranger" (WRS, 75-79). Israel regarded itself as a *ger* both in its land (during the time of the forefathers, Gen. 14:13; 23:4), and in Egypt (Exod. 2:22; Lev. 19:34). Moreover, since the land belonged to God, Israel's status upon it was theologically and legally that of a *ger*. (Lev. 25:23)[25]

The situation of the protected stranger is analogous to that set out by Jeremiah in regard to Jewish communities in exile who could hold no reasonable hope of return: "Build ye houses and dwell *in them*: and plant gardens, and eat the fruit of them that ye may be increased there . . . and seek the peace of the city whither I have caused you to be carried away captives, and pray unto the Lord for it" (Jer. 29:5-7).[26] Nevertheless, there is a clear differentiation between the stranger and the Israelite in that the former, the resident alien, may be treated as property and passed on to one's children, whereas the latter may not. The reason given in the Torah illuminates a God-centered religion: "For they are My servants," the Lord explains His relationship to the Israelites, "whom I freed from the land of Egypt; they may not give themselves over into servitude" (Lev. 25:42).

At least three views of relations with foreigners may be discerned in the Bible: utterly prohibited, all right if essential, and entirely welcome. Table 9.1, giving contrasting quotations from the main books of laws, Leviticus and Deuteronomy, "On the Treatment of Foreigners," demonstrates the point. It also reveals that the predominant position advocates separation.

Table 9.1. On the Treatment of Foreigners

Friendly	Hostile
"When a stranger resides with you in your land, you shall not wrong him. The stranger who resides with you shall be to you as one of your citizens; you shall love him as yourself, for you were strangers in the land of Egypt; I the Lord am your God" (Lev. 19: 33-34). "You shall have one standard for stranger and citizen alike: for I the Lord am your God" (Lev. 24:22). "You too must befriend the stranger, for you were strangers in the land of Egypt" (Deut. 10:19). "You shall not abuse a needy and destitute laborer, whether a fellow countryman or a stranger in one of the communities of your land" (Deut. 24:14).	"You shall not copy the practices of the land of Egypt where you dwelt, or of the land of Canaan to which I am taking you; nor shall you follow their laws" (Lev. 18:3). "When the Lord your God brings you to the land that you are about to invade and occupy . . . You will not intermarry with them: do not give your daughters to their sons or take their daughters for your sons. For they will turn your children away from Me to worship other gods, and the Lord's anger will blaze forth against you and He will promptly wipe you out. Instead, this is what you shall do to them: you shall tear down their altars, smash their pillars, cut down their sacred posts, and consign their images to the fire. For you are a people consecrated to the Lord your God: of all the peoples on earth the Lord your God chose you to be His treasured people" (Deut. 7:1-6). "No Ammonite or Moabite shall be admitted into the congregation of the Lord; none of their descendants, even in the tenth generation. . . . because they did not meet you with food and water on your journey after you left Egypt, and because they hired Balaam son of Beor, from Pethor of Aram-naharaim, to curse you. But the Lord your God refused to heed Balaam; instead, the Lord your God turned the curse into a blessing for you, for the Lord your God loves you" (Deut. 23: 4-6). "Be sure to set as king over yourself one of your own people; you must not set a foreigner over you, one who is not your kinsman" (Deut. 17:15).

This is tough talk: "tear down," "smash," "cut down," "consign . . . to the fire." The prevailing voice of the Book of Deuteronomy is against mixing with foreigners. They are to be shown respect and treated generally according to the same laws that bind the Israelites; but they are not to be married nor their customs followed, let alone their gods worshiped. And some are to be rejected forever. Indeed, were the commandment against the mixing of foods and clothes and animals and wives followed to the letter, it would be hard for Hebrews to mix with any other people.[27] Later writers attributed the destruction of the first temple and Israel's captivity in Babylon to breaking the covenant with their God under which He promised to protect them if they followed His commandments. Instead, the theory went, Israel broke the covenant by following foreign ways of social injustice and, as a consequence, worshiping foreign gods.

Why had the kings and their people gone wrong? It was because the Israelites lived among Canaanites and other strangers, the reasoning went, that they imbibed their customs, including idolatry, child sacrifice, and other abominations. Since this evil was externalized, it was easy to argue that if these Canaanite-cum-foreigners were driven out of Israel, like the mixed multitude that followed Moses out of Egypt, the remaining remnant would follow the one God's commandments.[28] Whether this thesis is accepted depends in part on how Joseph's experience as a top aide to Pharaoh is evaluated.

The treatment of strangers has been two-sided from that day to this. It comes out nicely in a second-century colloquy between Reb Johanan bar Nappaha and his brother-in-law and colleague in the rabbinical academy, Reb Simon ben Lakish: "R. Johanan said that a Gentile who engaged in a study of the Torah is deserving of death as it is said, 'Moses commanded us Torah as an inheritance—an inheritance for us and not for them.'" The Gemara finds a contradictory statement by Reb Meir to the effect that "A Gentile who engages in the study of the Torah is like the high priest." Even here, however, the Gemara qualified this statement by saying that it refers only to the laws God gave to all mankind via Noah and not to the entire Torah of Moses.[29] It is said in truth that the God of the Israelites is possessive of His people. To this should be added the possessiveness of His people for their God-given Torah. By implication, all kingships, especially the most splendid of all, Solomon's, speak to the snares occasioned by intercourse with foreigners and their gods.

David, Solomon, Joseph

The story of Judah and Tamar, in Rendsburg's interpretation, may be understood "to refer more to David and his family than it does to Judah and his."[30] Judah's friend Hirah is made equivalent to David's friend Hiram, the king of Tyre; Judah's wife Shua, a Canaanite, is made equivalent to David's consort, Bathsheba. The mysterious death of Er, the first son of Judah and Shua, is then equated with the death of the unnamed son of David and Bathsheba as a punishment for David's calculated murder of Bathsheba's husband, Uriah, the Hittite. Judah's second son, Onan, who refused to act so as to enhance the survival of his people, is compared to David's son Amnon, who rebelled against him (a rather forced comparison). Judah's last son, Shelah, who helped carry on his line, is said (with how much conviction it is hard to say) to be comparable to Solomon, who carried on David's line. The numerous parallels between the David and the Joseph stories do suggest more than a passing resemblance.

As David's life comes to an end, the question of succession to his throne becomes urgent. This succession crisis may be equivalent to the question of who should receive the scepter of leadership from Jacob the patriarch. In King David's time, both Adonijah, the elder brother, and Solomon, the younger brother, contend for the throne. Solomon wins. It could be, as Ellis argues, that the emphasis in the Torah on God's choice of the younger son is "an antecedent of Apologia for Solomon who was God's choice over Adonijah."[31] To be sure, David was also the younger son in his family. God's selection of the younger, His freedom to elect whom He will, runs parallel, in this interpretation, to the legitimation of David and Solomon by grounding their regimes in God's will.[32]

A word should be said about the nature of Solomon's policies that led to the secession of the northern tribes. In addition to removing from office the high priest of the northern tribes, Abiathar, Solomon's high taxes and forced labor (the corvée) were disproportionately imposed on the north for the benefit of the south, or so these acts were perceived. The northern tribes felt they did not receive the kind of protection against possible invasion by Syria that Solomon provided his own tribe of Judah against invasion by Egypt. Solomon also ceded some northern territory involving about twenty cities to the Phoenician king, Hiram of Tyre, in return for building materials for the temple. Moreover, the twelve new administrative districts Solomon set up, partly to provide food for the temple, one district per month, not a small task in those times, did not correspond with traditional tribal boundaries.

In short, Solomon sought to establish a centralized system with governors essentially like the European prefects who administer a geographical area on behalf of the center. By contrast, Judah's tribal boundaries were kept intact. After Solomon died and his son intensified centralizing policies, claiming his little finger would be thicker than his "father's loins" (I Kings 12:10), the rebellious northerners began to kill his tax collectors.[33]

The most compelling case made for the relationship between the histories of Solomon and the stories of Joseph comes from Avraham Wolfensohn. Because it has not been published, I am (with permission) presenting his view in full.[34]

I have found seven similarities between the stories of Solomon and of Joseph:
(1) One is a king, the other is a vice-king.
(2) Both married an honored Egyptian wife.
(3) King Solomon prayed to God in his dream and asked (and received) wisdom; Joseph accepted wisdom from God and by this wisdom was saved from an Egyptian prison.
(4) Wisdom was given to King Solomon in his dream; wisdom enabled Joseph to explain dreams.
(5) "And Solomon became awake—and it is a dream" (1 Kings 3:15); "And Pharaoh became awake—and it is a dream" (Gen. 41:7).
(6) In the Solomon story, "I have given you a clever and wise heart that no one like you has been before you and no one (like you) will ever be" (I Kings 3:12); "And Pharaoh said . . . there is no one clever and wise like you" (Gen. 41:39).
(7) "And King Solomon reigned over all Israel"; "And Pharaoh said [to Joseph] 'you see, I have made you the ruler of all the land of Egypt." Each ruler came into power only after he had proven his wisdom (like Oedipus, after resolving the riddle of the Sphinx in the Greek mythology).
   There is, as we see, much similarity between King Solomon—the real king, according to our knowledge of him historically and archeologically—and Joseph—as the model of a statesman according to Philo.
   Joseph as a model; King Solomon as the fulfillment of that model. (I have to add that there is a warning of Professor Azriel Shochat that the stories about the Fathers, Abraham, Itzchak and Jacob, were written in support of the opposition to David and Solomon.)[35] Shochat finds many proofs to his interpretation. For example: Abraham (to Itzchak) and Itzchak (to Jacob) insist that their children would not marry foreign wives. But King Solomon did marry foreign wives, so the stories of the Fathers were used as a way to protest against King Solomon.
   If we accept his thesis, then the story of Joseph is the fable and King Solomon (in reality) is the moral lesson, because both models are so similar to each other. If Shochat is not right, then we have similarity between both stories and real life. It is important to note that in both stories the statesman appears as a man, with human

weaknesses, with limited human wisdom (which needs God's assistance), and with a lust for power.

As a result of the fact that Joseph, by his wisdom, had saved Egypt from hunger, two things occurred:

(1) In the economic field, there came into existence an Egyptian "Efendi," feudal landlord, Pharaoh, who had in his hands all the private lands of Egypt, i.e., feudalism.

(2) In the social field, there came into existence in Egypt the slavery of the whole people: the farmers in order to get food sell to Pharaoh their lands and themselves (as slaves) and since that time Egypt is called (in the Bible) the "House of Bondage."

Let us ask ourselves: What does happen in Egypt in the political field when the whole Egyptian people are slaves not citizens? Then only the subjects obey the law but the ruler is above the law and that is the reason behind the ancient Egyptian pictures showing the king standing on a chariot harnessed to horses and in his hands there is a long whip (symbolizing the law) that he aims against little people. This is the real situation in Egypt as it is described in Chapter 47 of Genesis.

But when Moses brings the tribes of Israel out of Egypt, he gives them a constitution that is an anti-model, opposite to the Egyptian model:

Subject	The Egyptian Model	The Anti-Model
Economics	Centralistic feudalism	"The Land shall not be sold for ever" (Lev. 25, 23). "To many thou shall give the more inheritance . . . and to few . . . the less" (Num. 25,54).
Society	Total slavery ("House of Slaves")	Liberating slaves (the only culture in the ancient world that ordered it!)
Politics	The king (Pharaoh) (above the law)	The king is obedient to law, a constitutional government, with democratic parliamentarian elements.

In the case of Moses' constitution, there could not be feudalism in the economic field because Moses' legislation says that "The land shall not be sold for ever." You can't sell your father's estate/inheritance, and that is why Navot of Izre-el disobeyed King Ahab's order to give/sell to him the vineyard that he had inherited from his fathers (I Kings 21). The land is also justly divided—a greater family gets more land, as is needed for its economic existence and this law is essentially anti-feudalistic.

In Egypt the whole population was enslaved; every human being became a slave of Pharaoh, while Moses' book is the only constitution in history that demands the liberation of slaves. More than that, a slave that refuses to become free gets a sign in his ear, that he could be free but chose serfdom—what a shame!

As against Egyptian political inequality (the citizens must obey the law while the ruler is above the law) came Moses' "The law of the King" (Deut. 17:14-20), which is the anti-model of a constitutional king, who is obedient to the law and the constitution. "He shall not multiply horses . . . nor cause the people to return to Egypt" (i.e., the Israeli king should not behave like the Egyptian Pharaoh, whose chariot and horses symbolize that he is above the law). "That his heart be not lifted up above his brethren" warns Moses at the end of this passage, i.e., equality of both king and citizens in obedience to the law of the constitution.

Genesis 41–44 is the introduction to the beginning of the serfdom of the Egyptian people to Pharaoh and later of Israel to the Egyptian ruler. Joseph had been the temptation to Jacob's family to immigrate into Egypt. This serfdom of the tribes of Israel in Egypt produced the opposite model, that of Moses:

(1) Anti-feudalistic economics

(2) A society that orders liberation of slaves

(3) Government and ruler obedient to the laws.

All these are nowadays elements of modern democracy (the freedom of man that there will be no slavery, and the freedom of the citizen, that the ruler would be obedient to the law). These modern democratic elements were initiated by Moses as a product of the rebellion against serfdom in Egypt. The beginning of that serfdom lies in the stories of Joseph; the end of that serfdom is described in the stories of Moses.

The parallels between Solomon and Joseph can be taken further. Kennick notices efforts are made to present Solomon as the "new Moses" or at least the one through whom the prophecies of Moses will be fulfilled. Like Moses, Solomon judges Israel, establishes a bureaucracy, publicizes the law, builds a throne for God, and promises good things for those who obey the law and bad things for those who disobey.[36] "But," Parker summarizes in his important paper, "whereas Moses leads the people out of Egypt, Solomon adopts Egyptian customs and practices."[37] In this way, as well, Solomon and Joseph are built upon each other's templates.

Though the young Solomon is gifted with both knowledge and worldly wisdom, God places on the king the usual proviso about keeping His commandments and walking in His ways (I Kings 3:14), that is, keeping both to the letter and the spirit of His law. Solomon's fault, as Kennick demonstrates, is failure to recognize that his kingship is dependent on following the law, especially not (see I Kings: 9:6) following after other gods. As the Bible says, "So Solomon did what was evil in the sight of the Lord" (I Kings 11:6). The infidelities in which Solomon engages, from marrying foreign wives and making gold and silver common in Jerusalem to trading horses with Egypt,[38] I would add, have their echoes in Joseph, down to his use of a chariot, his silver goblet used for dining, and his gold necklace.

What is more, not only King Solomon but his father, King David, are related to Joseph. Van Seters shows that the language of the stories about them are often similar (table 9.2).

Table 9.2. The David and Joseph Stories Compared

David -	I Samuel	Joseph -	Genesis
16:12 (cf. 17:42 LXX.)	Now he (David) was ruddy, and had beautiful eyes, and was handsome	39:6	Joseph was handsome and good looking
16:13	the Spirit of the Lord came mightily upon David	41:38	Can we (Pharaoh and his servants) find such a man as this (Joseph), in whom is the Spirit of God.
16:18	(David) who is skilful in playing, a man of war, prudent in speech, a man of good presence, and the Lord is with him.	41:39	there is none so discreet and wise as you (Joseph)
		39:3 (cf.v. 21)	the Lord was with him.
16:21	And David came to Saul and entered his service.	41:46	Joseph was thirty years old when he entered the service of Pharaoh.
16:22	he (David) has found favour in my (Saul's) sight.	39:4 (cf. v.21)	Joseph found favour in his (Potiphar's) sight.
17:18	David is sent by his father to see how his brothers fare.	37:14	Joseph is sent by his father to see how his brothers fare.[39]

Not only is Joseph connected to Solomon; Van Seters demonstrates that the Joseph and David stories are modeled on each other.

What, then, in light of the similarities between Joseph the administrator for Pharaoh and the most famous Hebrew kings, David and Solomon, can be said about the authorship of the Joseph stories?

Who Wrote It?

It is apparent that the Joseph stories are meant to refer forward to future Hebrew history as well as back to Joseph's family origins. These references have led to speculations, sometimes buttressed by evidence from the Bible, about the authorship of all or part of the Joseph stories. The underlying academic theory is that the content of the stories reflects the interests of its writers. *Interests*, though one of the most frequently used words in political analysis, covers up as much as it reveals. Generally, interests are synonymous with preferences, desires, motives, reasons, in sum, with the causes of the behavior in question. Although it may appear that "interests" explains why something is done, the term actually assumes a given motive or cause. Unless we know why people perceive their interests as they do, we are no wiser than before.[40]

The assumptions most often made about the Joseph stories, in this respect, are that they were written to suit David and Solomon, on one theory, or Ezra and Nehemiah, on another. One strand of thought professes to find pro-monarchical sentiments in the stories. No doubt; but this would not distinguish between the two suggested sources of authorship, because David and Solomon were domestic kings and Ezra and Nehemiah were in the service of foreign kings who granted them and their people domestic autonomy in regard to religion. The other major view sees opposition to foreign influences in the stories. This finding, if sustained, would advantage the Ezra-Nehemiah interpretation because of their fierce opposition to foreign influences, whereas David and Solomon welcomed them. David was aided crucially by his band of foreign mercenaries, and Solomon must have had relations through marriage with almost all the surrounding kingdoms.

The level of generality in the attribution of authorship of the books of the Bible makes choice difficult. It is possible to say that demanding separation from foreigners is anti-Solomonaic. The trouble is that the generations that came after were all part of kingdoms, whether the contesting northern and southern kingdoms within Israel or the kingdoms of the Diaspora. No chance here of subversion in the form of an anti-monarchical attack. The question of whether the monarchy should be foreign or domestic is answered. The people prefer a homegrown monarchy, though that is not what they end up getting.

Reviewing the evidence, there is no doubt that interspersed in the Solomon and Joseph accounts are objections to indulging in foreign practices. But there is also admiration of them. These accounts are studies in ambivalence, fascination with Egyptian life and revulsion against it. I Kings recounts how the Lord is dissatisfied with King Solomon, who "loved many strange women, together with the daughter of Pharaoh, women of the Moabites, Ammonites, Edomites, Zidonians, and Hittites" (I Kings 11:1), "for surely they will turn away your heart after their gods" (I Kings 11:2). Thus "Solomon did evil in the sight of the Lord" (I Kings 11:6). Then, the Bible continues, God stirred up insurrections against Solomon, insurrections led by men who had taken refuge in Egypt. An evident question arises: Does Egypt and hence Solomon and perhaps David represent a narrow hierarchical way of life to be emulated or to be rejected?

How can the Joseph stories be directed against domestic kings and foreign influences if they are written to justify if not to glorify David and Solomon? My interpretation is that the Joseph stories warn against the corrupting influence of power gained through assimilation into pagan ways. But painting the portrait bleakly, without romance or color or excitement, would remove the essential element of temptation. Listeners and readers have to be tempted in order to overcome this temptation. If there were no temptation to adopt Egyptian ways and follow Egyptian gods, there would be no Joseph stories.

Nehemiah embraces this ambivalence to suit his purposes. "Did not Solomon king of Israel sin by these things?" he asks rhetorically, "yet among many nations was there no king like him, who was beloved of his God, and God made him king over all Israel: nevertheless even him did outlandish women cause to sin" (Neh. 13:26). Where the moral may have been that foreign relations are essential to a great society, Nehemiah turns it into a statement that even the greatest can be corrupted. When assimilation threatens, the differences between Joseph and Moses and Moses and Solomon are magnified to the disadvantage of the assimilator.

Nehemiah's answer was to interpret Solomon's story as a solemn warning. Upon discovering that the children of mixed marriages spoke Hebrew poorly or not at all, he "contended with them, and cursed them, and smote certain of them, and plucked off their hair, and made them swear by God, saying, Ye shall not give your daughters unto their sons, nor take their daughters unto your sons, or for yourselves" (Neh. 13:25). And he tried as hard as he could to force Hebrew men who had already married foreign women to leave them.[41]

During the Babylonian exile, after the destruction of the first temple, the Jewish community was reconstituted during the reign of Artaxerxes I Longimanus who ruled from 465 before the common era to 424.

Roughly, this was also the time when Sophocles, Socrates, Pericles, and Aeschelus lived. A member of the Judean community, Nehemiah, was then a part of the king's court: indeed, going back to Joseph, he was the king's cupbearer (the one who survived). Asking and receiving permission to rebuild Jerusalem's fortifications—materially and symbolically building barriers against foreigners—Nehemiah was also named governor of the territory then called Judah.[42]

In the tradition of exiles who are often more nationalistic than those who remain at home, Nehemiah was part of an expatriate community that gloried in a strict interpretation of biblical law. This put him in conflict with the Judeans who remained in the land and whose observances, in his opinion at least, had grown lax. After ruling for approximately a dozen years, Nehemiah returned to Babylon only to discover that in his absence observance had rapidly fallen into disuse. In regard to his enemy, Tobiah, who was not a Levite (according to the law only Levites could be priests) yet had a room in the temple, we learn from Nehemiah that "it grieved me sore: therefore I cast forth all the household stuff of Tobiah out of the chamber" (Neh. 13:8). Arranging for tithes to be paid so that the Levites did not have to work outside the temple, Nehemiah had wood collected for sacrifices at the altar and stopped business-as-usual on the sabbath.[43] From this encounter we have the "saving remnant," the carriers of the creed, who bring the people back to their origins.

Ezra the priest, who is described as "a scribe of the law of the God of heaven" (Ezra 7:12), got a commission to come to Judah to do for the religious life of the people what Nehemiah had done for its government.[44] He carried with him some document—a copy of the Torah, possibly compiled by him or others in contemporary Babylon, or the code of priestly laws or Deuteronomy—and read them aloud to the assembled people.[45] When he heard that "The people of Israel and the priests and the Levites have not separated themselves from the people of the lands, doing according to their abomination . . . so that the holy seed have mingled themselves with the people of those lands," Ezra rebuked them for their pollution (that is, mixing with foreigners) and got them to agree to "separate yourselves from the people of the land, and from the strange wives" (Ezra 10:11). This harsh measure applied even to those who had children.[46]

Once again, who wrote it? In whose interest was it, to use the usual locution, to write the stories about Joseph in the way they were written?

That depends on our interpretation of them. Are they about an un-alloyedly good person? That brings Solomon forward. Are they about a bad person? That reverses the order of authorship. Because the stories of Solomon and Joseph have much in common, we cannot be sure which one was based on the other. Without direct evidence, we must rely on inference and surmise, which in turn depend on an interpretive frame-work. Perhaps a better question would be "Who would you like to have written it?" The tradition of biblical interpretation, the midrash, I invoked in acknowledging my obligations, holds that every interpretation reason-ably grounded in the text is part of the original revelation. If that is so, as I believe, then authorship and interpretation are different sides of the same coin.

John Bright observes that two things were happening at once: the prohibition against mixed marriages was accompanied by the creation of a Judaism based on the law rather than on residence. Thus Jews outside of the province of Judah could be Jews by observing the law and without going to the temple.[47] "The distinguishing mark of a Jew would not be political nationality, nor primarily ethnic background, nor even regular participation in the Temple cult (impossible for Jews of the Diaspora), but adherence to the law of Moses."[48] It is this principle that a Torah written for all times seeks by revelation, direction, story, and song to inculcate in its readers.

Notes

1. K. I. Parker, "Solomon as Philosopher King? The Nexus of Law and Wisdom in I Kings 1-11," *Journal for the Study of the Old Testament* 53 (1992): 75-91, quote on 89.
2. The Rev. A. W. Argyle, "Joseph the Patriarch in Patristic Teaching," *The Expository Times* 67 (Oct. 1955-Sept. 1956): 199-201.
3. Ibid., 200.
4. Charles T. Fritsch, "God Was With Him: A Theological Study of the Joseph Narrative," *Interpretation* 9 (1955): 21-23; quote on pp. 21-22.
5. Ibid., 23-24.
6. Cited in Claus Westermann, *Genesis 37-50*, trans. John J. Scullion (Minneapolis: Augsburg Publishing, 1986), 18.
7. David Daube, *Appeasement or Resistance and Other Essays on New Testament Judaism* (Berkeley: University of California Press, 1987), 91-92.
8. Ibid., 89.
9. See the Rev. A. W. Argyle, "Joseph the Patriarch in Patristic Teaching," *Expository Times* 67 (Oct. 1955-Sept. 1956): 200; G. R. H. Wright, "Joseph's Grave under the tree by the Omphalos at Shechem," *Vetus Testamentum* 22 (1972): 482-83.

10. Réne Girard, *Things Hidden Since the Foundation of the World*, trans. by Stephen Bann and Michael Metteer, (Stanford, Calif.: Stanford University Press, 1987), 152.

11. James G. Williams, *The Bible, Violence, and the Sacred: Liberation From the Myth of Sanctioned Violence* (San Francisco: Harper, 1991), 58.

12. Richard J. Coggins, "The origins of the Jewish diaspora," *The World of Ancient Israel: Sociological, Anthropological and Political Perspectives*, R. E. Clements, ed. (Cambridge: Cambridge University Press, 1989), 163-181.

13. Hayim Tadmor, "'The people' and the kingship in Israel: The Role of Political Institutions in the Biblical Period," *Journal of World History* 11, nos. 1-2 (1968): 46-68.

14. See, for instance, J. Alberto Soggin, *A History of Israel: From the Beginnings to the Bar Kochba Revolt, AD135* (SCM Press). See also Herbert Donner, "The Separate States of Israel and Judah," *Israelite and Judaism History*, John H. Hayes and J. Maxwell Miller, eds. (Philadelphia: Westminster, 1977), 381-434. It may be that "the transition from segmented egalitarian structures to a defined stratified society with the king at the centre . . . produced structural transformations which were bound to lead to opposition and conflict." But what these were is not known. (Keith W. Whitelam, "Israelite Kingship. The royal ideology and its opponents," *The World of Ancient Israel*, Clements, ed., 119-139.

15. I agree with Turner that "the plain meaning of the text is that the fulfillment of the promises *is contingent on obedience to the imperatives* (Laurence A. Turner, *Announcements of Plot in Genesis*, Journal for the Study of the Old Testament Supplement Series 96 (Sheffield: Sheffield Academic Press, 1990), 58.)

16. Umberto Cassuto, *A Commentary on the Book of Genesis*, Part II From Noah to Abraham, Genesis VI9–XI32 (Jerusalem: Magnes Press, 1974), 312.

17. Similarly, Laban, Jacob's father-in-law, tells him that "I have learned by divination that the Lord has blessed me on your account" (Gen. 30:27). See also Robert Davidson, *Genesis 12–50* (Cambridge: Cambridge University Press, 1979), 235. Note that Laban is not a nice fellow.

18. Martin J. Selman, "Comparative Methods and the Patriarchal Narratives," *Themelious* NS, 3 (1977): 11.

19. See Robert L. Hubbard, Jr., *The Book of Ruth* (Grand Rapids, Mich.: Eerdmans Publishing, 1990), 45.

20. See Isaac M. Kikawada and Arthur Quinn, *Before Abraham Was the Unity of Genesis* 1-11 (Nashville: Abingdon, 1985), 119.

21. Edmund Leach's analysis of the story of Tamar and Judah as justifying Solomon's kingship, no matter which line of descent or ascent is used, suffers from a fatal defect (Edmund Leach, "The Legitimacy of Solomon," in Leach, *Genesis as Myth and Other Essays* [London: Jonathan Cape, 1969], 25-83). "In a period when Leach takes it for granted that Tamar was believed to be an Israelite, the available evidence is agreed that she was not" (J. A. Emerton, "An Examination of a Recent Structuralist Interpretation of Genesis XXXVIII," *Vetus Testamentum* 26 [1976]: 797-98; quote on 93).

22. My father was simultaneously a landlord and a tenant, a worker and employer. I can testify that being cast in what are usually opposing roles does wonders for one's objectivity. See Aaron Wildavsky, "The Richest Boy in Poltava," *Society* 13/2 (Nov/Dec 1976); also in Wildavsky, *Craftways* (New Brunswick, NJ: Transaction Publishers, 1989), 121-37; and "Family Characters," 139-146 in *Craftways*.

23. David Daube, "Concerning Methods of Bible Criticism, Late Law in Early Narratives" *Archiv Orientlnt* 17 (1949): 89.

24. Similarly, in enjoining the Israelites to be kind to their "needy kinsman" (Deut. 15:7), the Lord reminds the people to "beware lest you harbor the base thought, 'The seventh year, the year of remission, is approaching,' so that you are mean to your needy kinsman and give him nothing. He will cry out to the Lord against you, and you will incur guilt. Give to him readily and have no regrets when you do so, for in return the Lord your God will bless you in all your efforts and in all your undertakings" (Deut. 15:9-10).

25. Jacob Milgrom, *Commentary on the Book of Numbers. The JPS Torah Commentary* (Philadelphia: Jewish Publication Society, 1989), Excursus #34, 398. Roland de Vaux wrote that "among the Arab nomads, the *jar* was the refugee or lone man who came seeking the protection of a tribe other than his own. In the same way the *ger* is essentially a foreigner who lives more or less permanently in the midst of another community, where he is accepted and enjoys certain rights." Quoted in David Novak, *The Image of the Non-Jew In Judaism*. Toronto Studies in Theology, vol. 14 (New York: Edwin Mellen Press, 1983), 18.

26. Outside of the Torah, I use the King James translation of the Bible.

27. For the locus classicus of this interpretation, see Mary Douglas, "The Abominations of Leviticus," in Douglas *Purity and Danger: An Analysis of Concepts of Pollution and Taboo* (London: Routledge and Kegan Paul, 1966), 41-57.

28. See Margaret Pamment, "The Succession of Solomon: A Reply to Edmund Leach's Essay 'The Legitimacy of Solomon,'" *Man* 7 (1972): 635-43, for more a more detailed discussion.

29. Novak, *Image of the Non-Jew in Judaism*, 27.

30. Gary A. Rendsburg, "David and his Circle In Genesis XXXVIII," *Vetus Testamentum* 36 (1986): 438-46; quote on 441.

31. Quoted in Rendsburg, "David and his Circle," 440.

32. J. A. Emerton, "Judah and Tamar," *Vetus Testamentum* 29 (1979): 403-15; quote on 407-408.

33. Richard Elliott Friedman, *Who Wrote the Bible?* (New York: Summit Books, 1987), 44-45.

34. Dr. Avraham Wolfensohn is the manager of the Zalman Arianne Workers' College and a lecturer in political science at Haifa University and Technion. The paragraphs that follow are his writing edited to conform to standard English usage.

35. Azriel Shochat, "Political Tendencies in the Stories of the Fathers," *Tarbaitz* 24 (1955): 252-267 (Hebrew).

36. H. A. Kennick, *Design for Kingship* (Missoula, Mont.: Scholars Press, 1983).

37. Parker, "Solomon as Philospher King?" 81.

38. Ibid., 82-86.

39. Arthur Van Seters, "The Use of the Story of Joseph in Scripture," dissertation, Union Theological Seminary, Richmond, Virginia, May 1965, 87-88.

40. See Aaron Wildavsky, "Why Self-Interest is an Empty Concept Outside of a Social Context: Cultural Constraints on the Construction of 'Self' and 'Interest,'" typescript, November 1991. See also Michiel Schwarz and Michael Thompson, *Divided We Stand* (London: Harvester Wheatsheaf, 1990).

41. See Michael Grant, *The History of Ancient Israel* (New York: Charles Schribner's, 1984), 191-192, for an account of the presumed authorship of the *Books of Nehemiah and Ezra*. The part ascribed to Nehemiah is regarded largely as an autobiography.

42. John Bright, *A History of Israel*, 3rd ed. (Philadelphia: Westminster, 1981), 380-381.

43. Ibid., 384–85.
44. Ibid., 385–86.
45. Ibid., 384-90; Herschel Shanks, *Ancient Israel* (Washington, D.C.: Biblical Archaeological Society, 1988), 169.
46. Bright, *History of Israel*, 387–88.
47. Ibid., 389-90; Grant, *History of Ancient Israel*, 190-91.
48. Bright, *History of Israel*, 390.

Index

Ackerman, James S., 99
Administrator, attributes of, 17
Alter, Robert, 11-12, 36-37, 94-95, 179
Andriolo, Karin R., 72
Anti-wisdom, in Joseph stories, 9
Arama, Isaac,147
Argyle, A. W., 111
Ark of the Covenant, 186
Assimilation: dilemmas in, 10; impermissible, 2, 15; versus separation, 2, 15, 26, 99, 116, 191, 211, 213. *See also* Separation
Ater, Rabbi Chayim ben, 50

Bardach, Eugene, 205
Bechtel, Lynn M., 119
Bennett, W. H., 173
Binary opposites, Joseph and Moses, 1, 146, 200-202, 206
Bird, Phyllis, 41
Bright, John 228
Brueggeman, Walter, 17, 43, 115, 125
Burrows, Millar, 51
Bush, George, 95-96

Caine, Ivan, 140-141
Carmichael, Calum M., 34, 48-49, 171, 173, 178-179
Cassuto, Umberto, 22
Chertok, Chaim, 47
Christensen, Duane, 74
Clothing: for concealment, 35, 37; as preferment, 75; role in deception, 57
Coats, George W., 139, 204
Cohen, Hermann, 3
Commentaries: B. R. Hayya bar Abba, 83; Babba Kamina, 22; Bereshis Raba, 164; Zohar, 22
Confederation of tribes, 169
Conflict: of Joseph's brothers, 93; between Jacob and Joseph, 114-116; between wisdom and fidelity, 7

Dahlberg, Bruce T., 93, 146, 153-154

Daniel, Book of: as satire on Joseph, 126-129
Daniel: compared to Joseph, 127-129; as interpreter of dreams, 127-128
Daube, David, 8, 37-39, 50, 133, 216
Davidson, Robert, 31, 120, 175
Davies, W. D., 203
Deception: in families, 74, 107; in Jacob's family, 81-82; of Jacob, 6; comparing Joseph and Jacob, 8; role of clothing, 35, 58; of Tamar, 35
Delitzesch, Franz, 115
Deportation of Egyptians, 141-142, 144-146, 148, 150
DeVine, C. F., 33
Discernment, of God's will, 158
Divination, practice of, 104, 107, 109
Doubling: of dreams, 87; as dual perspective, 10; in the Joseph stories, 9; Joseph with his brothers, 96, 99-101, 156; of promises, 5; in wife-sister stories, 18
Dreams: from God, 86; as inherent in dreamer's character, 69-71, 78, 83-84, 86, 125-126, 128; interpretation of, 69-70; kinds of, 70-71; Pharaoh's, 77; as predictions, 88; repetition of, 69, 77; as subversive, 78
Douglas, Mary, 4, 34
Driver, S. R. 147, 149

Egypt, as threat to Hebrews, 5-6
Esther and Mordecai, compared to Joseph, 129-132

Famine: in Egypt, 139-144; Joseph's provision against, 14, 94, 110, 122, 139-140, 142, 144, 152-153; survival during, 14, 149, 163
Feldman, Emanuel, 95
Fidelity: to customs and practices, 46; to God's law, 7, 45, 214; to God's purpose, 40